2019

CHARTERED FINANCIAL ANALYST

LEVEL 1

25TH HOUR NOTES

SECOND Edition

By Havels learning System®

Welcome to the 2019 Havels Learning System® 25ᵀᴴ Hour Notes

Thank you for trusting Havels learning System® to help you reach your goals. We are pleased to be able to help you prepare for the CFA level 1 exam.

To retain what you have learn, it is important that you quiz yourself often. This notes is an important tool for gaining the speed and skills you will need to pass the exam.

How to Succeed

There are no shortcuts for this exam. Expect CFA institute to test you in a way that will reveal how well you know the curriculum. You should begin studying early and stick to your study plan. You should first read the curriculum and complete the concepts checkers for each topic. At the end, you should practice the question bank to understand how concepts may be tested on the exam. Do refer Question Bank from Havels Learning System. Finally extract the juice from 25th Hour notes for total understanding of conceps.

Wishing you all the very best for each and every one of your future endeavors!

Follow our Facebook Page "Havels Learning System" for exciting coupons, Discounts and Free materials.

Best regards,

Havels Learning System®

25th Hour Notes®

CFA Level I - 2019

This document should be read in conjunction with the corresponding readings in the 2019 Level I CFA® Program curriculum. Some of the graphs, charts, tables, examples, and figures are copyright 2018, CFA Institute. Reproduced and republished with permission from CFA Institute. All rights reserved.

Required disclaimer: CFA Institute does not endorse, promote, or warrant the accuracy or quality of the products or services offered by Havel Learning System. CFA Institute, CFA®, and Chartered Financial Analyst® are trademarks owned by CFA Institute.

Table of Contents

1. Ethical and Professional Standards

R 1	Ethics and Trust in the Investment Profession	1
R 2	Code of Ethics and Standards of Professional Conduct	2
R 3	Guidance for Standards I-VII	4
R 4	Introduction to Global Investment Performance Standards	7
R 5	The GIPS Standards	9

2. Quantitative Methods

R 6	Time Value of Money	12
R 7	Discounted Cash Flow Applications	15
R 8	Statistical Concepts and Market Returns	20
R 9	Probability Concepts	27
R 10	Common Probability Distributions	33
R 11	Sampling and Estimation	41
R 12	Hypothesis Testing	45
R 13	Technical Analysis	53

3. Economics

R 14	Topics in Demand and Supply Analysis	60
R 15	The Firm and Market Structures	63
R 16	Aggregate Output, Prices and Economic Growth	69
R 17	Understanding Business Cycle	75
R 18	Monetary & Fiscal Policy	82
R 19	International Trade and Capital Flows	90
R 20	Currency Exchange Rates	96

25th Hour Notes®

Table of Contents

4. Financial Reporting and Analysis

R 21	Financial Statement Analysis: An Introduction	102
R 22	Financial Reporting Standards	104
R 23	Understanding Income Statements	108
R 24	Understanding Balance Sheets	119
R 25	Understanding Cash Flow Statements	123
R 26	Financial Analysis Techniques	132
R 27	Inventories	136
R 28	Long-Lived Assets	140
R 29	Income Taxes	146
R 30	Non-Current (Long-Term) Liabilities	149
R 31	Financial Reporting Quality	153
R 32	Financial Statement Analysis: Applications	156

5. Corporate Finance

R 33	Corporate Governance and ESG: An Introduction	158
R 34	Capital Budgeting	160
R 35	Cost of Capital	164
R 36	Measures of Leverage	168
R 37	Working Capital Management	170

6. Portfolio Management

R 38	Portfolio Management: An overview	175
R 39	Portfolio Risk and Return: Part I	178
R 40	Portfolio Risk and Return Part II	183
R 41	Basics of portfolio planning and construction	189
R 42	Risk Management - An Introduction	192
R 43	Fintech in Investment Management	194

7. Equity

R 44	Market Organization and Structure	197
R 45	Security Market Indexes	207
R 46	Market Efficiency	214
R 47	Overview of Equity Securities	216
R 48	Introduction to Industry and Company Analysis	221
R 49	Equity Valuation: Concepts and Basic Tools	226

25th Hour Notes®

Table of Contents

8. Fixed Income

R 50	Fixed-Income Securities - Defining Elements	232
R 51	Fixed Income Markets - Issuance, Trading and Funding	235
R 52	Introduction to Fixed-Income Valuation	238
R 53	Introduction to Asset-Backed Securities	242
R 54	Understanding Fixed-Income Risk and Return	246
R 55	Fundamentals of Credit Analysis	250

9. Derivatives

R 56	Derivative Markets and Instruments	255
R 57	Basics of Derivative Pricing and Valuation	256

10. Alternative Investments

R 58	Introduction to Alternative Investments	263

Ethics

R1 Ethics and Trust in the Investment Profession

Ethics definition

- The word ethics is derived from the Greek word 'ethos,' which means character.
- Ethics means making good choices.
- Ethics includes a set of moral principles and rules of conduct that help guide our behavior.

Role of a code of ethics in defining a profession

Profession is the final development of an occupation.
Profession is:
- based on specialized knowledge and skills.
- based on service to others.
- practiced by members, who share and agree to adhere to a common code of ethics.

In any given profession, the code of ethics openly communicates the established principles of the profession and how its members are expected to behave. It serves as a benchmark for the minimally acceptable behavior required of members of a group in service to others. It helps in building public confidence that members of the profession will use their skills and knowledge for the benefit of their clients.

Challenges to ethical behavior

- One challenge is that people tend to believe that their ethical standards are above average. This leads to overconfidence bias and therefore people place too much importance on internal traits.
- However, studies show that external factors (situational influences) are the main determinant of ethical behavior. They shift our focus to the immediate rather than long-term impacts of a decision. The three main types of situational influences are:
  o Money & prestige.
  o Loyalty to employer and/or colleagues.
  o Strong compliance culture.

Need for high ethical standards in the investment industry

- High ethical standards are always important. However, they are of particular importance in the investment industry, because this industry is based almost entirely on trust. Also the products and services of this industry are intangible in nature.
- Clients trust investment professionals to use their skills and knowledge to serve clients and protect client assets.
- If investment professionals adhere to high ethical standards, all stakeholders gain long-

term benefits.

Ethical v/s legal standards

- Legal and ethical conduct is not always the same.
- Law is not always the best mechanism to reduce unethical behavior because:
    - Legal standards are often created to address past ethical failings. They do not provide direction for an ever changing and increasingly complex world.
    - Laws are often rule based.
    - Laws will vary across countries.
- Ethical conduct goes beyond legal standards.

Framework for ethical decision making

A framework for ethical decision making can help people look at and assess a decision from different perspectives. This enables them to make good decisions, and to limit unplanned consequences.

A general ethical decision making framework has the following four steps:
1. **Identify**: Relevant facts, stakeholders and duties owed, ethical principles, conflicts of interest.
2. **Consider**: Situational influences, additional guidance, alternative actions.
3. **Decide and act.**
4. **Reflect**: Was the outcome as anticipated? Why or why not?

R2 Code of Ethics and Standards of Professional Conduct

CFA Institute Professional Conduct Program

Structure

All CFA Institute **members** and **candidates** must comply with the **Code** and **Standards**. The CFA Institute **Board of Governors** maintains oversight and responsibility for the PCP. The **Disciplinary Review Committee (DRC)** is responsible for enforcement of Code and Standards.

- DRC is a volunteer committee of CFA charterholders.
- DRC partners with Professional Conduct staff to establish and review professional conduct policies.
- DRC is also responsible for reviewing conduct when there is a potential violation.

The CFA Institute Bylaws and Rules of Procedure for Professional Conduct (Rules of Procedure) form the basic structure for enforcing the Code and Standards.

Process for Enforcement

Professional Conduct inquiries can come from:

Ethics

- Self-disclosures by members/candidates on their annual Professional Conduct Statements.
- Written complaints received by the Professional Conduct staff.
- Evidence of misconduct received through public sources such as media or regulatory notices.
- A report by a CFA exam proctor.
- Analyzing exam material and monitoring social media.

Once an inquiry is initiated, the Professional Conduct staff may:
- Request a written explanation from the member/candidate.
- Interview the member/candidate, the complainant or other third parties.
- Collect documents and records relevant to the investigation.

After investigating, the Professional Conduct staff may:
- Take no disciplinary action.
- Issue a cautionary letter.
- Propose a disciplinary sanction.

If a disciplinary sanction is proposed, the member/candidate can either accept or reject the sanction. If rejected, the matter is referred to a panel of Disciplinary Review Committee members for a hearing. The panel then determines if a violation occurred and if so, what sanction should be imposed.

Sanctions imposed may include:
- Public condemnation.
- Suspension of membership and revocation of CFA charter (for members).
- Prohibition from further participation in the CFA Program (for candidates).

Six Codes of Ethics and Seven Standards of Professional Conduct

Six Codes
Members/Candidates must:
- Act with integrity, competence, diligence, and respect and in an ethical manner with the public, clients, prospective clients, employers, employees, colleagues in the investment profession, and other participants in the global capital markets.
- Place the integrity of the investment profession and the interests of clients above their own personal interests.
- Use reasonable care and exercise independent professional judgment when conducting investment analysis, making investment recommendations, taking investment actions, and engaging in other professional activities.
- Practice and encourage others to practice in a professional and ethical manner that will reflect credit on themselves and the profession.

- Promote the integrity and viability of the global capital markets for the ultimate benefit of society.
- Maintain and improve their professional competence and strive to maintain and improve the competence of other investment professionals.

Seven Standards
I. Professionalism
II. Integrity of Capital Markets
III. Duties to Clients
IV. Duties to Employers
V. Investment Analysis, Recommendations, and Actions
VI. Conflict of Interest
VII. Responsibility as a CFA Institute Member or CFA Candidate

R3 Guidance for Standards I-VII

Ethical responsibilities required by the Code and Standards

I. **Professionalism**

A. **Knowledge of the law**
- Understand and comply with all applicable laws, rules and regulation.
- In a case of a conflict, comply with the stricter law.
- Do not knowingly participate in any violation. Disassociate from such activity.

B. **Independence and objectivity**
- Use reasonable care and judgment.
- Maintain independence and objectivity.
- Do not offer, solicit or accept gifts; however, small token gifts are ok.

C. **Misrepresentation**
- Do not guarantee investment performance.
- Avoid plagiarism (the practice of taking someone else's work or ideas and passing them off as one's own).
- Do not omit important facts.

D. **Misconduct**
- Do not lie, cheat, steal or behave in a manner that affects your professional reputation or integrity.

II. **Integrity of capital markets**

A. **Material nonpublic information**
- Do not act or help others to act on material nonpublic information. (Information

which would be likely to affect a stock's price once it becomes known to the public).
- However, mosaic theory (material public information + nonmaterial nonpublic information) is not a violation.

B. Market manipulation
- Do not manipulate prices/trading volumes to mislead other market participants.
- Do not spread false rumors.

III. Duties to clients

A. Loyalty, prudence, and care
- Act with reasonable care and exercise prudent judgment.
- Place client's interest before your employer or your interests.
- Soft dollars must be used for the benefit of the client.
- Seek best execution.
- Vote proxies in the best interest of clients.

B. Fair dealing
- Do not discriminate against any clients when disseminating recommendations and taking investment action.
- Different level of service is allowed, as long as it does not negatively affect any client.
- Different service levels should be disclosed to all clients and prospects.

C. Suitability
- In advisory relationships, develop and update an IPS periodically. Understand the client's risk profile.
- In fund/index management, ensure that investments are consistent with the stated mandate.

D. Performance presentation
- Do not misstate performance.
- Make detailed information available on request.

E. Preservation of confidentiality
- Maintain confidentiality of current, former and prospective clients.
- Unless (1) disclosure is required by law (2) information concerns illegal activities by a client (3) client permits the disclosure.

IV. Duties to employers

A. Loyalty
- Do not harm your employer.

Ethics

- Obtain written consent from the employer before starting an independent practice.
- Do not take confidential information, client lists, financial models etc. when leaving an employer.

B. **Additional compensation arrangements**
- Do not accept gifts, benefits or compensation that will create a conflict of interest with your employer.
- You may accept if you obtain written consent from all parties involved.

C. **Responsibilities of supervisors**
- Prevent employees under your supervision from violating applicable laws, rules, regulations and the Codes and Standards.

V. **Investment analysis, recommendations, and actions**

A. **Diligence and reasonable basis**
- Have a reasonable and adequate basis for any investment analysis, recommendation or action (even when using a third party research).

B. **Communication with clients and prospective clients**
- Tell clients about your investment process.
- Distinguish between fact and opinion.

C. **Record retention**
- Maintain records (Standards recommend storing records for at least 7 years).

VI. **Conflicts of interest**

A. **Disclosure of conflicts**
- Disclose conflict of interest in plain language.

B. **Priority of transactions**
- Client transactions come before employer transactions which come before personal transactions.
- Avoid front running.
- Fee-paying family member should be treated no different than any other client.

C. **Referral fees**
- Disclose referral arrangements to clients, prospective clients and employers.
- Disclosure of referral fees helps the clients evaluate any possible partiality shown in the recommendation of service.

VII. **Responsibilities as a CFA Institute member or CFA candidate**

A. **Conduct as participants in CFA Institute programs**

- Don't cheat on the exams.
- Keep questions and exam information confidential.

B. **Reference to CFA Institute, the CFA designation, and the CFA program**
- Fill professional conduct statement and pay membership dues annually.
- References to partial designation not allowed (wrong usage: I am a CFA Level I). However, you can say that you have passed Level I, II or III.
- Not to be used as a noun. Only use it as an adjective.
- Do not state that holders of CFA charter are better than others or that they produce better investment results.

R4 Introduction to Global Investment Performance Standards

Overview of GIPS

GIPS stands for 'Global Investment Performance Standards'.

Why were the GIPS standards created?

In the past, investment performance presentations were misleading. Questions about the accuracy and credibility of data made comparisons among different investment firms difficult. Common misleading practices included:

- <u>Representative accounts</u>: Using only the best performing portfolios to represent the firm's overall performance.
- <u>Survivorship bias</u>: Excluding accounts that performed poorly and were consequently terminated.
- <u>Varying time periods</u>: Selecting time periods during which the fund had exceptional performance.

The GIPS standards were created to prevent misrepresentation of performance. They establish an industry-wide, standard approach for calculation and presentation of investment performance.

What parties do the GIPS standards apply to?

GIPS apply to investment management firms. Compliance to GIPS is voluntary and not required by any legal or regulatory authorities.

Who is served by the standards?

- <u>Existing and prospective clients of investment management firms</u>: They get credible and standard data. This allows them to have more confidence in reported performance and makes comparisons among firms easy.
- <u>Investment management firms</u>: Compliance with GIPS helps firms with their marketing activities. It can also strengthen the firm's internal controls.

Construction and purpose of composites

GIPS standards require the use of composites.

- A composite is formed by grouping portfolios that represent a similar investment strategy, objective or mandate.

  For example, if you are managing 100 accounts and one of your strategies is to invest in large cap value stocks, and you use this strategy for 70 accounts. Then these 70 accounts will form one composite. Similarly, if you have another strategy to invest in small cap growth stocks; and you use this strategy for the remaining 30 accounts. Then these 30 accounts will form another composite. You will have to report performances of these two composites separately.

- A composite representing a particular strategy must include only fee-paying, discretionary portfolios that the firm has managed in accordance with this particular strategy.

  For example, if you are managing funds for a charity organization and not charging them any fees, then this account should not be included because it is a non-fee paying account. Similarly, if you are managing an account for a large client, where you cannot use your discretion and the client tells you what securities to buy and sell. Then you should exclude this account because it is a non-discretionary account.

- GIPS standards require that the criteria for classifying portfolios into composites are decided before the composite performance is known and not after the fact. This prevents firms from choosing only their best performing portfolios in the composite.

Requirements for verification

Firms that claim compliance with GIPS self-regulate themselves. To increase confidence in the firm's claim of compliance, a firm may voluntarily hire an independent third party to perform verification.

Verification tests:
- Whether the investment firm has complied with all the composite construction requirements on a firm-wide basis; and
- Whether the firm's policies and procedures are designed to calculate and present performance in compliance with the GIPS standards.

The requirements for verification are:
- Verification applies to the entire firm, not on selected composites.
- An independent third party must perform verification. It cannot be performed by the firm itself.

R5 The GIPS Standards

Key features of the GIPS standards & the fundamentals of compliance

Key Features of GIPS

The objectives of GIPS are:
- To establish best practices for calculating and presenting investment performance.
- To obtain global acceptance of a single standard.
- To promote the use of accurate and consistent data.
- To promote fair competition among investment firms.
- To promote self-regulation.

The key features of GIPS standards are:
- In order to claim compliance, firms must adhere to all the requirements of the GIPS standards. Partial compliance is not allowed.
- In addition to adhering to the minimum requirements, firms should also adhere to the recommendations to achieve best practice in the calculation and presentation of performance.
- All actual, discretionary, fee-paying portfolios should be included in at least one composite to prevent cherry-picking.
- The accuracy of performance presentation depends on the accuracy of input data. It is, therefore, essential that the inputs are accurate. Hence, GIPS standards require firms to adhere to certain calculation methodologies and to make specific disclosures.

Fundamentals of Compliance
- The GIPS standards must be applied on a firm-wide basis.
- Total firm assets must include the fair value of all accounts – fee-paying as well as non-fee-paying, discretionary as well as non-discretionary. Total firm assets must include assets assigned to a sub-advisor, provided that the firm has discretion over the selection of the sub-advisor.
- Changes in a firm's organization must not affect historical GIPS performance.
- When jointly marketing with other firms, the firm claiming compliance must ensure that it is clearly defined as separate from noncompliant firms.
- Firms must document in writing their policies and procedures used to comply with GIPS.
- Only allowed statement is *'ABC has prepared and presented this report in compliance with the Global Investment Performance Standards (GIPS)'*. Partial compliance is not allowed. Statements such as "in accordance with GIPS", "calculated as per GIPS methodology" are not allowed.
- Firms must provide compliant presentations to every prospective client. Firms must provide a complete list of composites along with their description to any prospective

clients that make such a request.

Investment firm's definition and historical performance record

Investment Firm's Definition
- Firms must be defined as an investment firm, subsidiary or a division that is held out to clients and prospects as a 'distinct business entity'.
A **distinct business entity** is a sub-division within a company that is completely autonomous from the rest of the company. It has a separate product line or different services from the rest of the company. Also, it has complete control over how it utilizes its assets and organizes its management.
- If a firm has different geographic locations, all doing business under the same name, then the definition of the firm must include branches from all locations.

Historical Performance Record
- Initially:
  - A firm must present a minimum of five years of compliant presentation.
  - If the firm or composite has been in existence for less than five years, the presentation should include performance since inception.
- After initial compliance:
  - The firm must add one year of compliant presentation each year,
  - So that the firm eventually presents a minimum performance history of ten years.

GIPS and local regulations

- In countries where there are no investment performance regulations, use and promote the GIPS standard.
- In countries where there are existing laws and regulations regarding performance presentation, adhere to GIPS in addition to the local laws.
- In case of a conflict with the local laws, follow the local law but disclose the conflict.

Nine major sections of the GIPS standards

The nine major sections of the GIPS standards are:

0. **Fundamentals of compliance**: This section discusses issues related to the definition of the firm, documentation of policies and procedures, complying with GIPS updates, a proper reference to claim compliance, a proper reference to verification done by a third party.
1. **Input data**: To get full, fair and comparable presentations, the input data must be consistent. This section provides details on how you need to handle input data.
2. **Calculation methodology**: If a firm wants to calculate the returns on its composites it has to follow a certain calculation methodology. This section will provide instructions

on what method should be used to calculate returns. The same method needs to be used across the firm.

3. **Composite construction**: To create a composite, you group together portfolios that are managed with the same investment mandate. Only discretionary and fee-paying accounts should be included in composites. This section tells us what additional criteria should be fulfilled while creating composites. The end objective is that we should create composites that are meaningful and asset-weighted.

4. **Disclosures:** While showing investment presentations, certain information must be disclosed. This section gives us details on what disclosures are required to stay in compliance.

5. **Presentation and reporting**: This is the most important section for an investment firm. To be compliant, an investment management firms prepares and reports investment performance data in accordance with the GIPS requirements. This section tells us what those requirements are.

Note: Sections 6, 7 and 8 are add-ons to the main sections only if you have these types of investments in your portfolio.

6. **Real estate**: Applicable if you have real estate in your portfolio. This section provides the details.

7. **Private equity**: Applicable if you have PE investments. They must be valued as per the GIPS Private Equity Valuation Principles. This section provides the details.

8. **Wrap Fee/ separately managed account (SMA) portfolios**: Performance record of all wrap fee / SMA portfolios must be included in appropriate composites.
A **separately managed account** is a portfolio where the securities are directly owned by the investor, and the investment manager only executes trades on the investor's behalf. Such accounts also usually have a comprehensive charge levied by the investment manager for providing a bundle of services such as investment advice, investment research, brokerage services etc. This charge is called a wrap fee.

Quantitative Methods

R6 Time Value of Money

Interpretation of interest rates

Interest rates can be interpreted as:
- **Required rate of return:** If you invest $100 today on the condition that you get $110 after a year, then your required rate of return is 10%.
- **Discount rate**: For the same example, if you discount the future cash flow of $110 using a discount rate of 10%, you get a present value of $100.
- **Opportunity cost:** If you spend the $100 today instead of investing, then you lose the opportunity of earning 10% interest. In this sense interest rates can also be thought of as opportunity costs.

Components of interest rates

Interest rates have the following components:
- **Real risk-free rate:** Return on an investment with zero risk, assuming no inflation.
- **Inflation premium:** Extra return required to compensate for inflation.
- **Default risk premium:** Extra return required to compensate for the risk that the borrower will not make the promised payments.
- **Liquidity premium:** Extra return required to compensate for the risk of receiving less than the fair value of an investment if it must be sold quickly for cash.
- **Maturity premium:** The prices for longer-term bonds are more volatile than shorter-term bonds i.e. they have more maturity risk. Extra return required to compensate for maturity risk is called maturity premium.

Interest rate = real risk-free rate + inflation premium + default risk premium + liquidity premium + maturity premium.
Nominal interest rate = real risk-free rate + inflation premium

In a country ABC, the real risk-free rate is 4% and the expected inflation is 3%. Company X domiciled in this country issues a 5-year bond with an estimated default risk premium of 2%, liquidity premium of 1% and maturity premium of 1%. Calculate the interest rate of this bond.
Solution:
The interest rate for this bond will be 4 + 3 + 2 + 1 + 1 = 11%.

Effective annual rate

The stated annual rate is a quoted interest rate that does not consider the effect of compounding. The effective annual rate (EAR) is the rate at which money invested will grow in a year when we do consider compounding.
The EAR when there are *m* compounding periods in a year is:

Quantitative Methods

$$\text{Effective annual rate} = \left(1 + \frac{\text{stated annual rate}}{m}\right)^m - 1$$

The EAR for continuous compounding is:

$$\text{Effective annual rate} = e^{\text{stated annual rate}} - 1$$

Calculate the EAR for:
1. A stated annual rate of 12% and semiannual compounding.
2. A stated annual rate of 12% and quarterly compounding.
3. A stated annual rate of 12% and monthly compounding.
4. A stated annual rate of 12% and continuous compounding.

Solution:
1. EAR = $1.06^2 - 1 = 12.36\%$
2. EAR = $1.03^4 - 1 = 12.55\%$
3. EAR = $1.01^{12} - 1 = 12.68\%$
4. EAR = $e^{0.12} - 1 = 12.75\%$

Note that for the same stated annual rate, the EAR increases as the frequency of compounding increases.

Non-annual compounding frequencies

Step 1: Divide the stated annual interest rate by the number of compounding periods per year (m).
Step 2: Multiply the number of years by the number of compounding periods per year (m).
Step 3: Use the following formula to calculate future value.

$$\text{Future value} = \text{present value}\left(1 + \frac{\text{stated interest rate}}{m}\right)^{mN}$$

You invest $10,000 in a 5-year bond. The bond offers a stated annual interest rate of 12% compounded semi-annually. What will be the value of the investment at the end of five years?

Solution:
Step 1: 12 / 2 = 6%
Step 2: 5 x 2 = 10 periods
Step 3: FV = $10,000 (1.06)^{10}$ = $17,908.47

Calculating PV and FV of different cash flows

Present value is the current value of a future cash flow.
- Longer the time period till the future amount is received, lower the present value.
- Higher the discount rate, lower the present value.

Future value is the value to which an investment will grow after one or more compounding periods.

Quantitative Methods

- Longer the time period till which the investment is allowed to grow, higher the future value.
- Higher the interest rate, the higher the future value.

The future value and the present value of a single sum of money can be calculated by using the formulae given below or by using the TVM keys on a financial calculator (recommended approach for the exams).

$FV = PV (1 + I/Y)^N$

$PV = FV / (1 + I/Y)^N$

You invest $100 today at an interest rate of 10% for 5 years. How much will you receive after five years?
Solution:
Plug the following values in the calculator.
N = 5; I/Y = 10; PV = 100, PMT = 0; CPT FV = $161.05

An **ordinary annuity** is series of finite but equal cash flows which occur at the end of each period.
How much should you invest today at an interest rate of 10% to receive $100 at the end of each year for 5 years?
Using the calculator: N = 5; I/Y = 10; PMT = 100; FV = 0; CPT PV = $379.08

An **annuity due** is a series of finite but equal cash flows which occur at the start of each period.
How much should you invest today at an interest rate of 10% to receive $100 at the beginning of each year for 5 years?
Solution:
Put the calculator in BGN mode and plug the following values. (Remember to exit the BGN mode once you are done with your calculations.)
N = 5; I/Y = 10; PMT = 100, FV = 0; CPT PV = $416.98

A **perpetuity** is a series of equal cash flows at regular intervals occurring forever. The present value of perpetuity can be calculated as:

$$\text{PV of a perpetuity} = \frac{PMT}{I/Y}$$

How much should you invest today at an interest rate of 10% to receive $100 at the end of each year forever?
Solution:
PV = 100/0.1 = $1,000

The present (future) value of any series of cash flows is equal to the sum of the present (future) values of the individual cash flows.

What is the future value of the following series of cash flows, given an interest rate of 10%?
$1,000 at the end of year 1, $2,000 at the end of year 2, $3,000 at the end of year 3, $4,000 at the end of year 4 and $5,000 at the end of year 5.
Solution:
The future value is 5000 + 4000 x 1.1 + 3000 x 1.1² + 2000 x 1.1³ + 1000 x 1.1⁴ = $17,156

Using time lines

A time-line is a diagram that shows the inflow and outflow of money at various time periods. Constructing a time-line will help you solve time value of money problems. Consider the following simple example.

Suppose you will receive $100 at the end of Year 3, Year 4 and Year 5. What is the PV at time 0 given a discount rate of 5%?

Time:	0	1	2	3	4	5
	5%					
Cash flows:	PV=?	$0	$0	$100	$100	$100

Solution:
To solve this problem you can draw the above time-line, depicting the cash flows. The three payments of $100 can be treated as an ordinary annuity and we can calculate its PV at the end of year 2.
Plug the following values in the calculator:
N = 3; I/Y = 5; PMT = $100, FV = 0; CPT PV = $272.32

The time line now simplifies to:

Time:	0	1	2	3	4	5
	5%					
Cash flows:	PV=?	0	$272.32	$0	$0	$0

To discount to time 0, plug the following values in the calculator:
N = 2; I/Y = 5; PMT = 0; FV = 272.32; CPT PV = $247.

R7 Discounted Cash Flow Applications

Net present value (NPV) & Internal rate of return (IRR)

The **NPV** of an investment is the present value of its cash inflows minus the present value of its cash outflows. The NPV of a project is calculated as:

$$NPV = CF0 + \left[\frac{CF1}{(1+r)^1}\right] + \left[\frac{CF2}{(1+r)^2}\right] + \left[\frac{CF3}{(1+r)^3}\right]$$

Consider a project which requires an initial investment of $10,000. It is expected to generate $5,000 in the first year, $6,000 in the second year and $7,000 in the third year.

Quantitative Methods

The cost of capital for this project is 10%. Calculate the NPV of this project.
Solution:
$$NPV = -10,000 + \frac{5,000}{(1.1)^1} + \frac{6,000}{(1.1)^2} + \frac{7,000}{(1.1)^3}$$
$$NPV = \$4,763.33$$

Using the financial calculator: CF0 = -10,000; CF1 = 5,000; CF2 = 6,000; CF3 = 7,000; I = 10. CPT NPV = 4,763.33

The **IRR** is the discount rate the makes the NPV equal to zero. i.e. it equates the PV of the cash inflows to the PV of the cash outflows. The IRR of a project is calculated as:
$$CF0 = \left[\frac{CF1}{(1+IRR)^1}\right] + \left[\frac{CF2}{(1+IRR)^2}\right] + \left[\frac{CF3}{(1+IRR)^3}\right]$$

Consider a project which requires an initial investment of $10,000. It is expected to generate $5,000 in the first year, $6,000 in the second year and $7,000 in the third year. Calculate the IRR of this project.
Solution:
$$10,000 = \left[\frac{5,000}{(1+IRR)^1}\right] + \left[\frac{6,000}{(1+IRR)^2}\right] + \left[\frac{7,000}{(1+IRR)^3}\right]$$
$$IRR = 33.87\%$$

Using the financial calculator: CF0 = -10,000; CF1 = 5,000; CF2 = 6,000; CF3 = 7,000; I = 10; CPT IRR = 33.87

Conflict between NPV & IRR

NPV Rule
- For independent projects, accept a project if NPV > 0.
- For mutually exclusive projects, select the project with the highest positive NPV.

An **independent project** is one where the decision to accept or reject the project has no effect on any other projects being considered by the company. Hence, if a company is evaluating two independent projects, it can invest in both projects.

A **mutually exclusive project** is one where the acceptance of such a project will have an effect on the acceptance of another project. Hence, if a company is evaluating two mutually exclusive projects, then it can invest in only one of the projects.

IRR Rule
- For independent projects, accept if IRR > required rate of return.
- For mutually exclusive projects, select the project with the highest IRR.

Problems associated with IRR
- IRR wrongly assumes that the interim cash flows are reinvested at the IRR rate and not at the cost of capital.
- A project may have multiple IRRs or no IRR.

Quantitative Methods

- For mutually exclusive projects, due to differences in project size or timing of cash flows, the IRR and NPV rankings may differ. If there is a conflict in ranking, go with the NPV rule.

Holding period return

The holding period return is the total return for holding an investment over a given time period. It is calculated as:

$$HPR = \frac{P_1 - P_0 + D_1}{P_0}$$

where:
P_0 = price at the start of the holding period
P_1 = price at the end of the holding period
D_1 = dividend/coupon paid by the investment at the end of the holding period

An investor bought a stock for $100. Five months later, he received a dividend of $4 and he sold the stock for $108. Compute the HPR.

Solution:

$$HPR = \frac{108 - 100 + 4}{100} = 0.12 = 12\%$$

Money-weighted & Time weighted rate of return

Money-weighted rate of return

- The money-weighted rate of return is simply the IRR of a portfolio taking into account all cash inflows and outflows.
- If a manager controls the cash inflows and outflows of a portfolio, then use money-weighted return to measure performance.

An investor buys a stock for $10 at time t=0. At the end of Year 1, he receives a dividend of $1 and purchases another stock for $12. At the end of Year 2, he receives a dividend of $0.5 per share and sells both shares for $13. Calculate the money-weighted return.

Solution:

Year	Outflow	Inflow	Net Cash Flow
0	$10 to purchase the first share		-10
1	$12 to purchase the second share	$1 dividend received on first share	-11
2		$1.00 dividend ($0.50 x 2 shares) received $26 received from selling 2 shares @ $13 per share	+27

Enter the following in a calculator: CF0 = -10; CF1 = -11; CF2 = 27; CPT IRR = 18.28%. The money weighted return is 18.28%.

Time-weighted rate of return

- Time-weighted rate of return is the compound growth rate at which $1 invested in a portfolio grows over a given measurement period.
- If a manager cannot control the cash inflows and outflows of a portfolio, then use time-weighted return to measure performance.

An investor buys a stock for $10 at time t=0. At the end of Year 1, he receives a dividend of $1 and purchases another stock for $12. At the end of Year 2, he receives a dividend of $0.5 per share and sells both shares for $13. Calculate the time-weighted rate of return.

Solution:

1. Break the measurement period into two sub-periods based on the timing of the cash flows.

Holding period 1	Beginning value = $10 Dividends paid = $1 Ending value = $12
Holding period 2	Beginning value = $24 (12 x 2) Dividends paid = $1 (0.5 x 2) Ending value = $26 (13 x 2)

2. Compute the HPY for each sub-period.
   $HPY_1 = (12 - 10 + 1)/10 = 30\%$
   $HPY_2 = (26 - 24 + 1)/24 = 12.5\%$

3. Calculate the compounded annual rate by taking the geometric mean of the two sub-periods.
   $(1 + TWRR)^2 = 1.30 \times 1.125$; TWRR = 20.93%

Yield measures for money market instruments

Bank discount yield (BDY) $= \left(\frac{D}{F}\right) \times \left(\frac{360}{t}\right)$

Holding period yield (HPY) $= \frac{P_1 - P_0 + D_1}{P_0}$

Effective annual yield (EAY) $= (1 + HPY)^{\frac{365}{t}} - 1$

Money market yield (MMY) $= HPY \times \frac{360}{t}$

Consider a T-Bill with a face value of $100 and 60 days to maturity. It is selling at a discount of $2 i.e. at a price of $98. Calculate BDY, HPY, EAY and MMY.

Solution:

Bank discount yield (BDY) $= \left(\frac{2}{100}\right) * \left(\frac{360}{60}\right) = 12\%$

Holding period yield (HPY) $= \frac{100 - 98 + 0}{98} = 2.04\%$

Effective annual yield (EAY) = $(1 + 0.0204)^{\frac{365}{60}} - 1 = 13.07\%$

Money market yield (MMY) = $2.04\% \times \frac{360}{60} = 12.24\%$

Conversion among yield measures

We can convert back and forth between holding period yields, money market yields, and effective annual yields by using the holding period yield, which is common to all the calculations. To calculate HPY use the following formulae. Then convert HPY to the required yield measure.

$HPY = MMY \times \frac{t}{360}$

$HPY = (1 + EAY)^{\frac{t}{365}} - 1$

From BDY → compute discount and initial price P_0 → compute HPY.

An investor purchased a $100 T-bill that will mature in 60 days. The money market yield on the T-bill was 12.24% at the time of purchase. Compute HPY and EAY.

Solution:

$HPY = 12.24 \times \frac{60}{360} = 2.04\%$

$EAY = (1 + 0.0204)^{\frac{365}{60}} - 1 = 13.07\%$

An investor purchased a $100 T-bill that will mature in 60 days. The bank discount yield on the T-bill was 12.00% at the time of purchase. Compute HPY and MMY.

Solution:

$BDY = \left(\frac{D}{F}\right) * \left(\frac{360}{t}\right); 0.12 = \left(\frac{D}{100}\right) * \left(\frac{360}{60}\right); D = 2, P_0 = 98$

$HPY = \frac{P_1 - P_0 + D_1}{P_0} = \frac{100 - 98 + 0}{98} = 2.04\%$

$MMY = HPY \times \frac{360}{t} = 2.04\% \times \frac{360}{60} = 12.24\%$

To calculate **bond-equivalent yield**, first convert to semiannual YTM, then use the following formula.

Bond-equivalent yield = 2 x semi-annual YTM

A 3-month investment has a holding period yield of 2%. What is the yield on a bond equivalent basis?

Solution:

First calculate the semiannual YTM = (1+ 3-month HPY)^2 – 1 = 1.02^2 – 1 = 4.04%

BEY = 2 x semiannual YTM = 2 x 4.04 = 8.08%

Quantitative Methods

R8 Statistical Concepts and Market Returns

Fundamental concepts

Descriptive statistics refer to how large data sets can be summarized effectively to describe their important characteristics.

Inferential statistics refers to making forecasts, estimates or judgments about a large data set based on a small representative set.

Population includes all members of a particular group.
Sample is a subset drawn from a population.

Measurement Scales: Data can be measured using the following scales:
- Nominal scales: put data in categories but do not rank them.
- Ordinal scales: nominal scale + data can be ranked with respect to some characteristic.
- Interval scales: ordinal scale + the differences in the data values are meaningful.
- Ratio scales: interval scale + the ratios of value, such as twice or half as much are meaningful.

The scale on which data is measured determines the type of analysis that can be performed on the data.

Parameter, sample statistic & frequency distributions

Parameter is a descriptive measure of a population.
Sample statistic is a descriptive measure of a sample.
Frequency distribution is a tabular display of data categorized into a relatively small number of intervals or classes. It allows us to evaluate how data is distributed.
Frequency distribution of the marks scored by 100 students.

Marks Interval	Absolute Frequency
0 - 25	10
26 - 50	30
51 - 75	40
76 - 100	20

Relative frequencies and cumulative relative frequencies

Relative frequency is calculated as the absolute frequency of an interval divided by the total number of observations.
Cumulative relative frequency for an interval, is calculated as the sum of the relative frequencies of all intervals lower than and including that interval.
Frequency distribution of the marks scored by 100 students.

Quantitative Methods

Marks Interval	Absolute Frequency	Relative Frequency	Cumulative Relative Frequency
0 - 25	10	10%	10%
26 - 50	30	30%	40%
51 - 75	40	40%	80%
76 - 100	20	20%	100%

Histograms & frequency polygon

Histogram is a bar chart of data that has been grouped together into a frequency distribution. The height of each bar is equal to the absolute frequency of each interval.

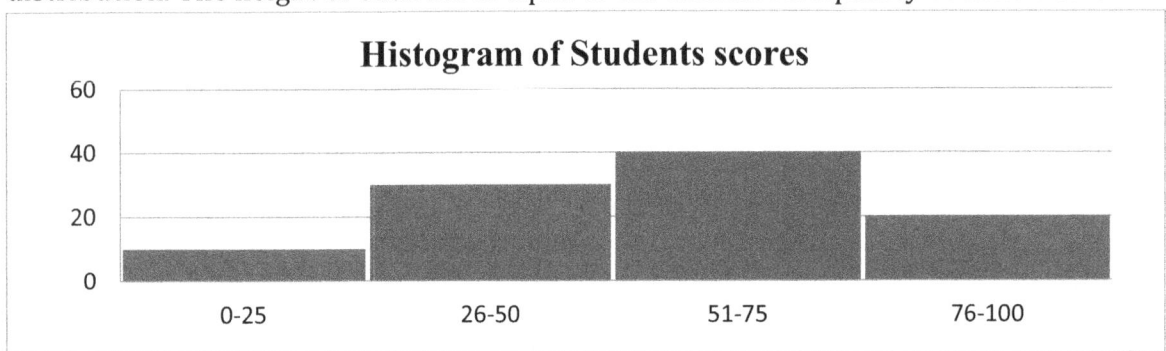

Frequency polygon plots the midpoints of each interval on the X-axis and the absolute frequency of that interval on the Y-axis, and connects these points with straight lines.

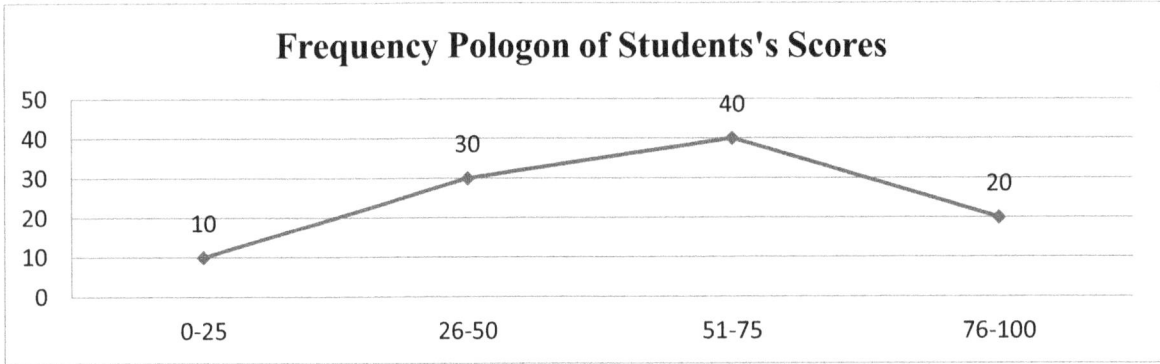

Measures of central tendency

Arithmetic mean is the sum of all the observations divided by the total number of observations. A population average is called population mean (μ). A sample average is called sample mean ($\bar{x}$). The sample mean is used as the 'best guess' approximation of the population mean.

$$\mu = \frac{\sum_{i=1}^{N} X_i}{N}$$

A stock had the following returns in the past three years: 10%, -5%, and 20%. Calculate the arithmetic mean.

Quantitative Methods

Solution:
Arithmetic mean = (10 − 5 + 20)/3 = 8.33%

Median is the midpoint of a data set that has been sorted from largest to smallest. If we have an even number of observations, then the median is the average of the two middle observations.

Calculate the medians for the following data sets:
A) 1, 2, 3, 4, 5
B) 1, 2, 3, 4, 5, 6

Solution:
A) Median = 3
B) Median = (3+4)/2 = 3.5

Mode is the value that occurs most frequently in a data set. A data set can have more than one mode, but only one mean and one median.

Calculate the mode for the following data set: 1, 2, 2, 3, 4, 4, 4, 5, 5

Solution:
Mode = 4

Geometric mean is used to calculate compound growth rate.

$$R_G = [(1 + R_1)(1 + R_2) \ldots (1 + R_n)]^{1/n} - 1$$

A stock had the following returns in the past three years: 5%, -5%, and 20%. Calculate the geometric mean.

Solution:
$R_G = [(1.05)(0.95)(1.20)]^{1/3} - 1 = 6.17\%$

In a **weighted mean** different observations are given different weights as per their proportional influence on the mean.

$$\bar{X}_w = \sum_{i=1}^{n} w_i X_i$$

An investor has 20% of his portfolio in Stock A, 30% in Stock B and 50% in Stock C. If the returns were 4% on Stock A, 7% on Stock B and 8% on Stock C. Calculate portfolio return.

Solution:
Portfolio return = 0.2 x 4 + 0.3 x 7 + 0.5 x 8 = 6.9%

Harmonic mean is used to find average purchase price for equal periodic investments.

$$X_H = n / \sum_{i=1}^{n} \left(\frac{1}{X_i}\right)$$

An investor purchased $1,000 worth of stock A each month for the past three months at prices of $5, $6 and $7. Calculate the average purchase price of the stock.

Solution:

Quantitative Methods

Average purchase price = 3 / (1/5 + 1/6 + 1/7) = 5.88

If returns are constant over time: AM = GM = HM
If returns are variable over time: AM > GM > HM

Quartiles, quintiles, deciles, & percentiles

A quantile is a value at or below which a stated fraction of the data lies. Some examples of quantiles include:
- **Quartiles:** distribution is divided into quarters
- **Quintiles:** distribution is divided into fifths.
- **Deciles:** distribution is divided into tenths.
- **Percentile:** distribution is divided into hundredths.

The formula for the position of a percentile in a data set with n observations sorted in ascending order is:

$L_y = (n+1) y /100$

Calculate the first quartile of a distribution that consists of the following portfolio returns: 3%, 4%, 6%, 9%, 11%, 12%, 14%

Solution:
The first quartile = (7+1) 25/100 = 2nd item in the data set (4%). i.e. 25% of the observations lie below the second observations from the left.

Measures of dispersion

Range is the difference between the maximum and minimum values in a data set.

Range = maximum value – minimum value

The annual returns of a portfolio manager for the past 4 years are 4%, 2%, 6%, 8%.
Calculate the range.

Solution:
Range = 8% - 2% = 6%

Mean absolute deviation (MAD) is the average of the absolute values of deviations from the mean.

$MAD = [\sum_{i=1}^{n}|X_i - \bar{X}|]/n$

The annual returns of a portfolio manager for the past 4 years are 4%, 2%, 6%, 8%.
Calculate MAD.

Solution:
X = (4 + 2 + 6 + 8)/4 = 5

Quantitative Methods

$$MAD = \frac{|4-5|+|2-5|+|6-5|+|8-5|}{4} = \frac{1+3+1+3}{4} = 2$$

Variance is defined as the mean of the squared deviations from the arithmetic mean.
Population variance $\sigma^2 = \sum_{i=0}^{N}(X_i - \mu)^2 / N$
Sample variance $s^2 = \sum_{i=0}^{n}(X_i - \bar{X})^2 / (n-1)$

Standard deviation is the positive square root of the variance. It is often used as a measure of risk.

The annual returns of a portfolio manager for the past 4 years are 4%, 2%, 6%, 8%. Calculate the population and sample standard deviations.

Solution:

It is advisable to use the financial calculator instead of the formula on the exams. The keystrokes for the above example are: [2nd] [DATA], [2nd] [CLR WRK], 4 [ENTER], [↓] [↓] 2 [ENTER], [↓] [↓] 6 [ENTER], [↓] [↓] 8 [ENTER], [2nd] [STAT] [ENTER], [2nd] [SET] press repeatedly till you see 1-V. Keep pressing [↓] to see the following values: N = 4, X = 5, Sx = 2.58, σx = 2.24.

Note: If you are asked to calculate the variances, simply square the standard deviations.

Chebyshev's inequality

According to Chebyshev's inequality, the proportion of the observations within k standard deviations of the arithmetic mean is at least:
$1 - 1/k^2$ for all k > 1.

Determine the minimum percentage of observations in a data set that lie within 2 standard deviations from the mean.

Solution:

% of population within 2 std deviations = $1-1/k^2 = 1 - 1/2^2 = 75\%$

Thus, Chebyshev's inequality permits us to make probabilistic statements about the proportion of observations within various intervals around the mean for any distribution with finite variance. As a result of Chebyshev's inequality, a two-standard deviation interval around the mean must contain at least 75 percent of the observations, no matter how the data is distributed.

Coefficient of variation & Sharpe ratio

Coefficient of variation measures the risk per unit of return. When evaluating investments, a lower value is better.

$CV = \frac{s}{\bar{X}}$

Calculate the coefficient of variation for the following portfolios and interpret the results.

	Mean return	Standard deviation

Portfolio A	10%	9%
Portfolio B	6%	4%
Portfolio C	9%	2%

Solution:
$CV_A = 9/10 = 0.9$
$CV_B = 4/6 = 0.66$
$CV_C = 2/9 = 0.22$
Portfolio C has the lowest risk per unit of return, so it is the most attractive investment.

Sharpe ratio measures excess return per unit of risk. When evaluating investments, a higher value is better.

$$S_p = \frac{\bar{R}_p - \bar{R}_F}{s_p}$$

A portfolio has a mean return of 8% and a standard deviation of 10%. Calculate the Sharpe ratio, given that the risk-free rate is 3%.
Solution:
Sharpe ratio = (8 – 3)/10 = 0.5

Symmetry and skewness in return distributions

A distribution is said to be **symmetrical** when the distribution on either side of the mean is a mirror image of the other. In a symmetrical distribution, mean = median = mode.

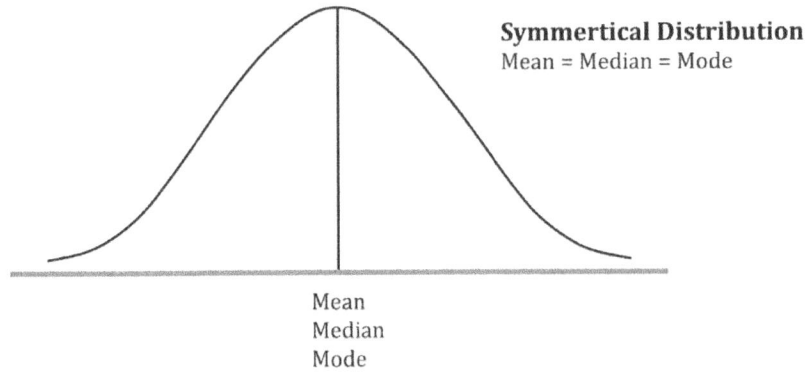

If a distribution is non-symmetrical, it is said to be skewed. Skewness can be negative or positive.

A **positively skewed distribution** has a long tail on the right side, which means that there will be frequent small losses and few large gains. Here the mean > median > mode. The extreme values affect the mean the most which is pulled to the right. They affect the mode the least.

Quantitative Methods

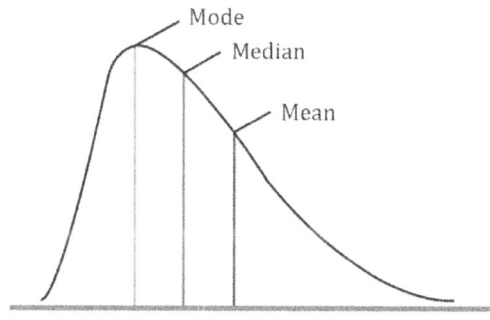

Right - Skewed (Positive Skewness)

A **negatively skewed distribution** has a long tail on the left side, which means that there will be frequent small gains and few large losses. Here the mean < median < mode. The extreme values affect the mean the most which is pulled to the left. They affect the mode the least.

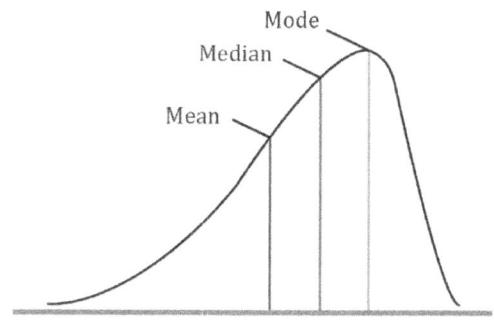

Left - Skewed (Negative Skewness)

Kurtosis

Kurtosis is a measure of the degree to which a distribution is more or less peaked than a normal distribution, which has a kurtosis of 3. Excess kurtosis = kurtosis - 3. An excess kurtosis with an absolute value greater than 1 is considered significant.
- A **leptokurtic** distribution is more peaked and has fatter tails than a normal distribution.
- A **platykurtic** distribution is less peaked and has thinner tails than a normal distribution.
- A **mesokurtic** distribution is identical to a normal distribution.

Using geometric and arithmetic means

The **geometric mean** is appropriate to measure past performance over multiple periods. The portfolio returns for the past two years were 100% in year 1 and -50% in year 2. What was the mean return?
Solution:

Quantitative Methods

Past return = geometric mean = $(2 \times 0.5)^{0.5} - 1 = 0\%$

The **arithmetic mean** is appropriate for forecasting single period returns.
Two possible returns for the next year are 100% and -50%. What is the expected return?
Solution:
Expected return = arithmetic mean = $(100 - 50)/2 = 25\%$

R9 Probability Concepts

Fundamental concepts

A **random variable** is an uncertain quantity/number.
An **outcome** is the observed value of a random variable.
An **event** can be a single outcome or a set of outcomes.
Mutually exclusive events are events that cannot happen at the same time.
Exhaustive events are those that include all possible outcomes.

- When you roll a die, the result is a random variable.
- If you roll a 2, it is an outcome.
- You can define an event as rolling a 2 or rolling an even number.
- Rolling a 2 and rolling a 3 are examples of mutually exclusive events. They cannot happen at the same time.
- Rolling an even number or Rolling an odd number are exhaustive events. They cover all possible outcomes.

Properties of probability

The two properties of probability are:
- The probability of any event has to be between 0 and 1.
- The sum of the probabilities of mutually exclusive and exhaustive events is equal to 1.

The methods of estimating probabilities are:
- <u>Empirical probability</u>: based on analyzing the frequency of an event's occurrence in the past.
- <u>A priori probability</u>: based on formal reasoning and inspection rather than personal judgment.
- <u>Subjective probability</u>: informed guess based on personal judgment.

Odds for and against the event

Odds for an event are defined as the probability of the event occurring to the probability of the event not occurring.
Odds against an event are defined as the probability of the event not occurring to the

Quantitative Methods

probability of the event occurring.

Odds for E = P (E) / [1 – P (E)]
Odds against E = [1 – P (E)]/P(E)

If the probability of the market rising tomorrow is 0.2. Calculate the odds for the market rising and against the market rising.

Solution:
Odds for the market rising = 0.2/0.8 = 1 to 4
Odds against the market rising = 0.8/0.2 = 4 to 1

Unconditional v/s conditional probabilities

Unconditional probability is the probability of an event occurring irrespective of the occurrence of other events. It is denoted as P(A).

Conditional probability is the probability of an event occurring given that another event has occurred. It is denoted as P(A|B), which is the probability of event A given that event B has occurred.

Multiplication, addition, and total probability rules

Multiplication rule is used to determine the joint probability of two events.

P (AB) = P (A|B) P (B)

For independent events, P (A|B) = P (A). Hence the formula simplifies to

P(AB) = P(A) P(B)

We are given the following information:
- Probability that the economy will improve P(E) = 0.6
- Probability that stock price will increase given that the economy has improved P(S|E) = 0.4

Compute the probability that the stock price will increase **and** the economy will improve.

Solution:
P(SE) = P(S|E) x P(E) = 0.4 x 0.6 = 0.24

Addition rule is used to determine the probability that at least one of the events will occur.

P (A or B) = P(A) + P(B) – P(AB)

For mutually exclusive events P (AB) = 0. Hence the formula simplifies to

P(A or B) = P(A) + P(B)

We are given the following information:
- Probability that price of Stock A increases = P(A) = 0.4
- Probability that price of Stock B increases = P(B) = 0.5
- Probability that price of Stock A and Stock B increases = P(AB) = 0.2

Compute the probability that the price of stock A **or** the price of stock B increases.
Solution:
P (A or B) = P(A) + P(B) − P(AB) = 0.4 + 0.5 − 0.2 = 0.7

Total probability rule is used to calculate the unconditional probability of an event, given conditional probabilities.

$P(A) = P(A|B_1)P(B_1) + P(A|B_2)P(B_2) + ... + P(A|B_n)P(B_n)$

We are given the following information:
- Probability of above average economic growth = $P(B_1) = 0.4$
- Probability of average economic growth = $P(B_2) = 0.5$
- Probability of below average economic growth = $P(B_3) = 0.1$
- Probability of stock price rising given above average economic growth = $P(A|B_1) = 0.9$
- Probability of stock price rising given average economic growth = $P(A|B_2) = 0.6$
- Probability of stock price rising given below average economic growth = $P(A|B_3) = 0.1$

Compute the probability that the stock price will increase.
Solution:
$P(A) = P(A|B_1)P(B_1) + P(A|B_2)P(B_2) + P(A|B_3)P(B_3) = 0.9 \times 0.4 + 0.6 \times 0.5 + 0.1 \times 0.1 = 0.67$

Dependent v/s independent events

If the occurrence of one event does not influence the occurrence of the other event, then the events are called **independent events**. i.e. $P(A|B) = P(A)$ or $P(B|A) = P(B)$

If the probability of an event is affected by the occurrence of another event, then it is called a **dependent event**.

Using tree diagrams to represent an investment problem

A tree diagram helps plot the probabilities of various outcomes and depict expected values based on the paths chosen at each node.

There is a 0.6 probability of a good economy and a 0.4 probability of a poor economy. If there is a good economy, there is 0.70 probability that the stock price will be 100 and 0.3 probability that the stock price will be 90. If the economy is poor, there is a 0.2 probability that the stock price will be 80 and a 0.8 probability that the stock price will be 70. Calculate the expected stock price.

Solution:
Construct a tree diagram depicting the given scenario. The unconditional probability of stock price being 100 can be calculated by multiplying P (good economy) x P (stock price being 100 when the economy is good) = 0.6 x 0.7 = 0.42. Similarly, we can calculate the unconditional probabilities for all remaining prices.

Quantitative Methods

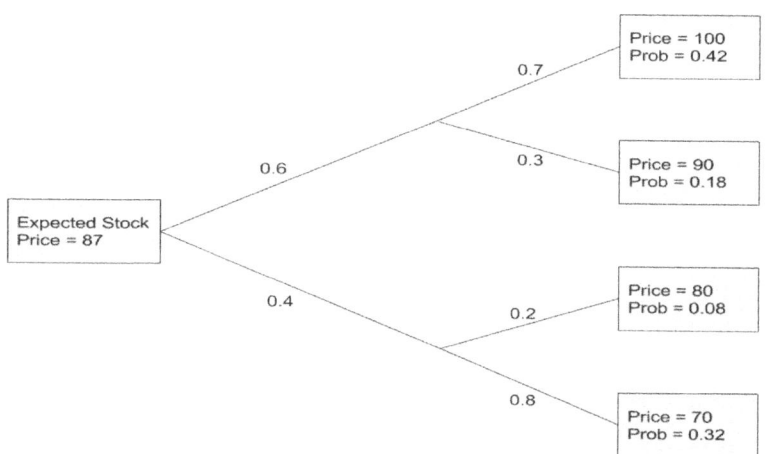

The expected stock price is 0.42 x 100 + 0.18 x 90 + 0.08 x 80 + 0.32 x 70 = 87

Covariance & correlation

Covariance is a measure of how two variables move together. **A positive covariance** indicates that the variables tend to move together in the same direction. Whereas, a **negative covariance** indicates that the variables tend to move in opposite directions. If two variables X and Y have expected values of E(X) and E(Y), then the covariance can be calculated as:

Cov (X,Y) = E[X - E(X)] [Y - E(Y)]

Calculate the covariance of two stocks A and B given two possible states of the economy. Refer to the table below.

Scenario	P(Scenario)	Expected Returns of A	Expected Returns of B
Recession	0.2	1%	3%
Expansion	0.8	8%	6%

Solution:
The expected return of A is: 0.2 x 1 + 0.8 x 8 = 6.6%
The expected return of B is: 0.2 x 3 + 0.8 x 6 = 5.4%
The covariance can be calculated as:
0.2 (1 - 6.6) (3 - 5.4) + 0.8 (8 - 6.6) (6 - 5.4) = 2.688 + 0.672 = 3.36

Correlation is a standardized measure of the linear relationship between two variables. It is obtained by dividing the covariance of two variables by the product of their standard deviations. The correlation coefficient can range from -1 to +1.

Corr (X,Y) = Cov (X,Y) / σ (X) σ (Y)

From the previous example, the covariance between Stock A and Stock B is 3.36. Calculate

Quantitative Methods

the correlation given that the standard deviation of Stock A is 2.8 and the standard deviation of Stock B is 1.2

Solution:
Corr (A,B) = 3.36/(2.8)(1.2) = 1

Expected value, variance, and standard deviation of a random variable & of returns on a portfolio

Random variable

The expected value of a random variable is the probability-weighted average of the possible outcomes of the random variable. The standard deviation / variance can be found using a financial calculator.

$E(X) = X_1 P(X_1) + X_2 P(X_2) + ... + X_n P(X_n)$

A stock's projected EPS for the upcoming year depends on the state of the economy as shown in the table below. Calculate the expected value of EPS, variance, and standard deviation.

State of Economy	Probability	EPS
Good	0.4	$9
Average	0.5	$6
Weak	0.1	$1

Solution:
$E(X) = X_1 P(X_1) + X_2 P(X_2) + X_3 P(X_3) = 9 \times 0.4 + 6 \times 0.5 + 1 \times 0.1 = \$6.7$

The expected value and standard deviation can also be directly found using a financial calculator. The keystrokes are given below. [2nd] [DATA], [2nd] [CLR WRK], 9 [ENTER], [↓] 40 [ENTER], [↓] 6 [ENTER], [↓] 50 [ENTER], [↓] 1 [ENTER], [↓] 10 [ENTER], [2nd] [STAT], [2nd] [SET] press repeatedly till you see 1-V. Keep pressing [↓] to see: N = 100, X = 6.7, Sx = 2.38, σx = 2.37.

Note: We use the population standard deviation and not the sample standard deviation because we have entered all outcomes which means that we have covered the entire population.

To calculate the population variance, we square the standard deviation.
Population variance = $2.37^2 = 5.6169$

Returns on a portfolio

The expected returns and the variance of a two-asset portfolio are given by:

$E(R_P) = w_1 E(R_1) + w_2 E(R_2)$
$\sigma^2(R_P) = w_1^2 \sigma_1^2(R_1) + w_2^2 \sigma_2^2(R_2) + 2w_1 w_2 \rho(R_1, R_2) \sigma(R_1) \sigma(R_2)$

A portfolio consists of 70% stocks and 30% bonds. The expected return on stocks is 10% and the expected return on bonds is 5%. The standard deviation of stock returns is 0.3 and

Quantitative Methods

the standard deviation of bond returns is 0.1. The correlation between stock returns and bond returns is 0.2. Calculate the expected return and the variance of the portfolio.

Solution:
Expected return = 0.7 x 10 + 0.3 x 5 = 8.5%
Variance = 0.7^2 x 0.3^2 + 0.3^2 x 0.1^2 + 2 x 0.7 x 0.3 x 0.2 x 0.3 x 0.1 = 0.04752

Calculating covariance from a joint probability function

Calculate the covariance between the returns of Stock A and Stock B, given the following joint probability table.

	R_A = 1%	R_A = 8%
R_B = 3%	0.2	0
R_B = 6%	0	0.8

Solution:
The expected return of A is: 0.2 x 1 + 0.8 x 8 = 6.6%
The expected return of B is: 0.2 x 3 + 0.8 x 6 = 5.4%
The covariance can be calculated as:
0.2 (1 - 6.6) (3 - 5.4) + 0.8 (8 - 6.6) (6 - 5.4) = 2.688 + 0.672 = 3.36

Bayes' formula

Bayes' formula is used to update the probability of an event based on new information. The formula for calculating the updated probability is:

$$P(Event|Information) = \frac{P(Information|Event)}{P(Information)} \times P(Event)$$

The probability of a recession is 0.4 and the probability of an expansion is 0.6. If there is an expansion, the probability that the stock price will increase is 0.8. If there is a recession, the probability that the stock price will increase is 0.3. It turns out that the stock price did increase, what is the probability that we are in a recession?

Solution:
P(E): The unconditional probability of recession = 0.4
P(E^c): The unconditional probability of an expansion = 0.6
P(I|E): The probability of increase in stock price given that we are in a recession = 0.3
P(I|E^c): The probability of increase in stock price given that we are in an expansion = 0.8
P(I): The unconditional probability of an increase in stock price. This can be calculated using total probability rule.
P(I) = P(I|E) x P(E) + P(I|E^c) x P(E^c)
      = 0.3 x 0.4 + 0.8 x 0.6 = 0.6
Using Bayes' formula, the probability that we are in a recession given that the stock price increased is:
P(E|I) = P(I|E) x P(E) / P(I)

Quantitative Methods

= 0.3 x 0.4 / 0.6 = 0.2

Principles of counting

Permutations is the number of ways to choose r objects from a total of n objects when the order in which the r objects are chosen is important.

$$_nP_r = \frac{n!}{(n-r)!}$$

A portfolio manager wants to sell 4 stocks from a portfolio that consist of 10 stocks. In how many ways can the 4 stocks be chosen, when the order of sale is important?
Solution:

$$_{10}P_4 = \frac{10!}{(10-4)!} = 5,040$$

Note: On the exam use the calculator function. The key strokes are:
10 [2nd] [-] 4 [=] 5,040

Combinations is the number of ways to choose r objects from a total of n objects when the order in which the r objects are chosen is <u>not</u> important.

$$_nC_r = \binom{n}{r} = \frac{n!}{(n-r)!r!}$$

A portfolio manager wants to sell 4 stocks from a portfolio that consists of 10 stocks. In how many ways can the 4 stocks be chosen, when the order of sale is <u>not</u> important?
Solution:

$$_{10}C_4 = \binom{10}{4} = \frac{10!}{(10-4)!4!} = 210$$

Note: On the exam use the calculator function. The key strokes are:
10 [2nd] [+] 4 [=] 210

R10 Common Probability Distributions

Probability distribution, discrete v/s continuous random variables

Probability distribution
A random variable is a variable whose outcome cannot be predicted. A probability distribution lists all possible outcomes of a random variable along with their associated probabilities.
Consider a probability distribution for the roll of a dice. It has six possible outcomes: 1, 2, 3, 4, 5 and 6 and each has a probability of 1/6.

Discrete random variable is one for which the number of possible outcomes can be counted. It has measurable probabilities associated with each specific outcome. The probability of each possible outcome is expressed in the form of a probability function

Quantitative Methods

P(X=x) or p(x). This is the probability that the random variable X takes on the value x. The number of days it rains in a month is a discrete random variable. The probability that it rains for 10 days can be expressed in the form of a probability function as P(X = 10) or p(10).

Continuous random variable is one for which we cannot count the number of possible outcomes. Therefore, probabilities cannot be associated with specific outcomes; instead, it has to be assigned to a particular range. The probability that a specific outcome lies within a range are expressed as a probability density function f(x).

The returns of a stock for a particular year is a continuous random variable. The probability that the return is between 10% and 20% can be expressed as f(x) = P(10 <X < 20).

Set of possible outcomes of a specified discrete random variable

The set of possible outcomes of a discrete random variable is finite.
- p(x) = 0 means that x cannot occur.
- p(x) > 0 means that x can occur.
- p(x) = 1 means that x is the only possible outcome.

Cumulative distribution function

The cumulative distribution function gives the probability that the random variable will be less than or equal to a specific value. It is denoted by F(x) = P(X ≤ x)
If you consider a roll of a dice, F(3) = probability of getting (1 or 2 or 3)
F(5) = probability of getting (1 or 2 or 3 or 4 or 5)

If we are given the cumulative distribution function for a random variable, we can use it to calculate the probability of an event. Let's understand this with the following example. The probability function and the cumulative distribution function for a dice roll is given below. Calculate P(2 ≤ X ≤ 5).

X = x	Probability Function p(x) = P(X = x)	Cumulative Distribution Function F(x) = P(X ≤ x)
1	1/6	1/6
2	1/6	2/6
3	1/6	3/6
4	1/6	4/6
5	1/6	5/6
6	1/6	6/6

Solution:
Using cumulative distribution function:

Quantitative Methods

P(2 ≤ X ≤ 5) = F(5) − F(1) = 5/6 − 1/6 = 0.667

Using probability function:
P(2 ≤ X ≤ 5) = p(2) + p(3) + p(4) + p(5) = 1/6 + 1/6 + 1/6 + 1/6 = 0.667
As you can see we get the same results for both methods.

Discrete uniform random variable, Bernoulli random variable & binomial random variable

Discrete uniform random variable is one where the probability of all the possible outcomes is equal. For example, the roll of a dice.

Bernoulli trial is an experiment that has only two possible outcomes: a success or a failure. For example, the toss of a coin.

If a Bernoulli trial is carried out n times, the number of successes (denoted by X) is called a **binomial random variable**.

The distribution that X follows is known as the **binomial distribution**.

If we toss a coin 10 times, the number of times we get a 'head' is a binomial random variable. If we repeat this experiment several times, the number of times we get a head will keep changing. If we plot this number on a graph, the distribution we get is a binomial distribution.

The expected value and the variance for a binomial variable are given by:

Expected value = np
Variance = np(1 − p)

On any given day the probability of a market up move is 0.7. What is the expected number of up moves in the market in the next 10 days? What is the variance?

Solution:
Expected value = 0.7 x 10 = 7 up moves
Variance = 10 x 0.7(1 − 0.7) = 2.1

Probabilities for discrete uniform and the binomial distribution functions

Probabilities for a discrete uniform distribution

If the total number of outcomes is n, then the probability of each outcome = 1/n

A card is drawn randomly from a deck. What is the probability of getting an ace of spades?

Solution:
Total number of outcomes = 52
Probability of each outcome = 1/52

Probabilities for a binomial distribution

The probability distribution of a binomial random variable for the probability of x successes in n trials is calculated using the following formula:

Quantitative Methods

$$P(x) = P(X = x) = {}_nC_x \, p^x (1-p)^{n-x}$$

On any given day the probability of a market up move is 0.7. What is the probability that the market will move up on 6 out of the next 10 days?

Solution:

$P(6) = P(X = 6) = {}_{10}C_6 \, 0.7^6 \, 0.3^4 = 0.2$

Binomial tree

A binomial tree can be used to model stock price movements. Refer to the tree diagram below. 'S' represents the initial stock price. 'u' represents an up move and 'd' represents a down move. The nodes show each possible value of the stock after 1, 2 and 3 time periods.

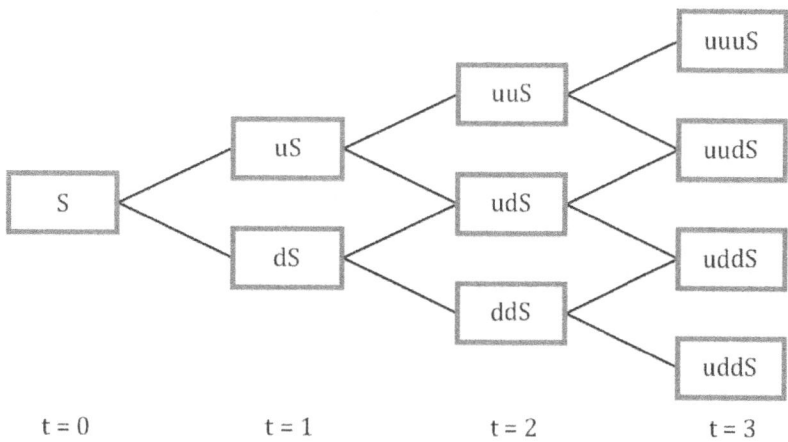

Consider an initial stock price of $100. In one time period, the stock can either rise by a factor of 1.1 or go down by a factor of 1/1.1. In any given time period, the probability of an up move is 0.6 and the probability of a down move is 0.4. After two periods, what are the possible stock prices and their respective probabilities? What is the expected stock price?

Solution:

uuS = 1.1 x 1.1 x 100 = 121 with probability 0.6 x 0.6 = 0.36
udS = 1.1 x 1/1.1 x 100 = 100 with probability 0.6 x 0.4 = 0.24
duS = 1/1.1 x 1.1 x 100 = 100 with probability 0.4 x 0.6 = 0.24
ddS = 1/1.1 x 1/1.1 x 100 = 82.64 with probability 0.4 x 0.4 = 0.16
Expected stock price = 121 x 0.36 + 100 x 0.24 + 100 x 0.24 + 82.64 x 0.16 = $104.78

Continuous uniform distribution

The continuous uniform distribution is defined over a range from a lower limit a to an upper limit b. These limits serve as the parameters of the distribution.

Quantitative Methods

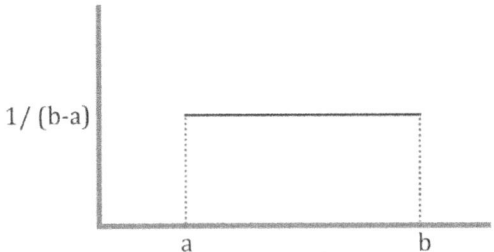

The probability of the random variable taking any set of values outside the parameters a and b is 0. The probability that the random variable will take a value between x_1 and x_2, where x_1 and x_2 both lie within the range is given by:

$P(x_1 \leq X \leq x_2) = \dfrac{x_2 - x_1}{b - a}$

X is a uniformly distributed continuous random variable between 10 and 20. Calculate the probability that X will fall between 12 and 18.

Solution:

$P(12 \leq X \leq 18) = \dfrac{18-12}{20-10} = 0.6$

The cumulative distribution function for a continuous random variable is shown below:

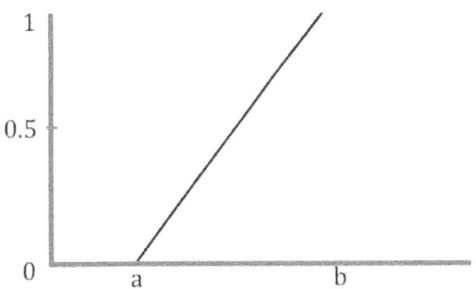

Normal distribution

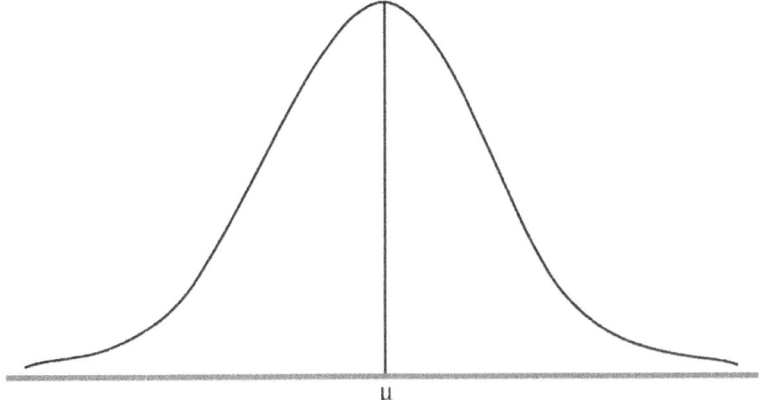

- As shown in the above figure, a normal distribution is a bell-shaped curve, with two

Quantitative Methods

identical halves.
- It is completely described by two parameters its mean (μ) and its variance (σ^2). This is stated as $X \sim N(\mu, \sigma^2)$.
- It has a skewness of 0 and a kurtosis of 3.
- A linear combination of two or more random variables is also normally distributed.

Univariate v/s multivariate distribution

Univariate distribution describes the probability distribution of a single random variable. For example, the distribution of expected return of one stock from a portfolio.

Multivariate distribution describes the probability distribution for a group of related random variables. For example, the distribution of expected return of a portfolio with multiple stocks. A multivariate normal distribution for the returns on n stocks is completely defined by following three sets of parameters:
- Mean returns on the individual stocks (n means in total).
- Variances of the individual stocks (n variances in total).
- Pairwise return correlations between the stocks (n (n - 1)/2 distinct correlations in total)

Confidence intervals for the population mean

A confidence interval represents a range within which we have a given level of confidence of finding the actual outcome of a random variable. A 90% confidence interval between 10 and 20 means that we can be 90% confident that the random variable will lie between 10 and 20. The confidence intervals for a normal distribution are:
- 90% of all observations are in the interval x ± 1.65s
- 95% of all observations are in the interval x ± 1.96s
- 99% of all observations are in the interval x ± 2.58s

The average annual return of a stock is 10% and the standard deviation is 2%. Assuming normal distribution, calculate the 95% confidence interval for the stock return for the next year.

Solution:
The 95% confidence interval is 10 ± 1.96 (2) = 6.08% to 13.92%

Standard normal distribution

The normal distribution with mean (μ) = 0 and standard deviation (σ) = 1 is called the standard normal distribution. The formula for standardizing a random variable X is:

$$Z = \frac{(X - \mu)}{\sigma}$$

The Z-table is used to find the probability that X will be less than or equal to a given value. A stock has a mean return of 10% and a standard deviation of return of 2%. What is the

probability that the return will be less than 11%?
Solution:
$Z = \frac{(11-10)}{2} = 0.5$
F(0.5) = P(Z < 0.5) = P(X < 11) = 0.6915 (from the Z table)

Safety first ratio

Shortfall risk is the risk that portfolio's return will fall below a specified minimum level of return over a given period of time.

Safety first ratio is used to measure shortfall risk. It is calculated as:

$$SF_{ratio} = \frac{E(R_P) - R_T}{\sigma_P}$$

A portfolio with higher safety first ratio is preferred over a portfolio with a lower safety first ratio.

An investor is considering two portfolios A and B. Portfolio A has an expected return of 10% and a standard deviation of 2%. Portfolio B has an expected return of 15% and a standard deviation of 10%. The minimum acceptable return for the investor is 8%. According to Roy's safety first criteria, which portfolio should the investor select?

Solution:
$SF_A = \frac{10-8}{2} = 1$
$SF_B = \frac{15-8}{10} = 0.7$

Since A has a higher safety first ratio, the investor should select portfolio A.

Roy's safety first criteria states that an optimal portfolio minimizes the probability that the actual portfolio return will fall below the target return.

Lognormal distributions

If x is a random variable that is normally distributed, then to create a lognormal distribution of x we take e^x and plot the values on a graph. The properties of a lognormal distribution are:
- It cannot be negative.
- The upper end of its range extends to infinity.
- It is positively skewed.

A lognormal distribution is often used to model asset prices because the asset prices need to be positive, they cannot be negative.

Discretely v/s continuously compounded rates of return

Discretely compounded rates of returns have defined compounding periods such as quarterly, monthly etc. As we decrease the length of the compounding period, the effective

Quantitative Methods

annual rate rises. For continuous compounding, the EAR is given by:
EAR = e^r - 1

If we are given the holding period return over any time period, we can calculate the equivalent continuously compounded rate of return for that period as:
r = ln (HPR + 1)

If the holding period return of a stock was 10% for a period of one year. What is the equivalent continuously compounded rate of return for the year?
Solution:
r = ln (0.1 + 1) = 0.0953 = 9.53%
Key strokes for calculating ln(1.1) are
1.1 [ln]

Monte Carlo simulation

Monte Carlo simulation is a computer simulation used to simulate possible security prices based on risk factors. As input, it uses randomly generated values for risk factors based on their assumed distributions. It processes this information as per the specified model and runs thousands of iterations. It gives the distribution of the expected value of the security as output.

Major applications include:
- financial planning.
- developing VAR estimates.
- valuing complex securities.

Limitations include:
- It is fairly complex and will provide answers that are no better than the assumptions.
- Simulation is not an analytical method but a statistical one.

Monte Carlo simulation v/s historical simulation

The historical simulation uses actual past distribution of risk factors as input. Whereas, Monte Carlo simulation uses randomly generated values of the risk factors based on assumed distribution.

The limitations of historical simulation are:
- It cannot take into account the effect of significant events that did not occur during the sample period.
- It cannot perform a 'what if' analysis when the 'if' scenario has not happened in the past.

Quantitative Methods

R11 Sampling and Estimation

Simple random sampling & sampling distribution

Simple random sampling is the process of selecting a sample from a larger population in such a way that each element of the population has the same probability of being included in the sample.

Sampling distribution: If we draw samples of the same size several times and calculate the sample statistic. The sample statistic will be different each time. The distribution of values of the sample statistic is called a sampling distribution.

Sampling error

Sampling error is the difference between a sample statistic and the corresponding population parameter. The sampling error of the mean is given by:

Sampling error of the mean = $\bar{x} - \mu$

You want to calculate the average returns of 10,000 stocks. You draw a sample of 100 stocks and calculate the average return of these 100 stocks as 15%. However, the actual average of the 10,000 stocks was 12%. Then the sampling error = 15% - 12% = 3%.

Simple random v/s stratified random sampling

Simple random sampling: As discussed earlier, simple random sampling is the process of selecting a sample from a larger population in such a way that each element of the population has the same probability of being included in the sample.

Stratified random sampling: Whereas, in stratified random sampling, the population is divided into sub groups based on one or more distinguishing characteristics. Samples are then drawn from each sub group, with sample size proportional to the size of the sub group relative to the population. Finally, samples from each sub group are pooled together to form a stratified random sample. The advantage of stratified random sampling is that the sample will have the same distribution of key characteristics as the overall population. This can reduce the sampling error.

You divide the universe of 10,000 stocks as per their market capitalization such that you have 5,000 large cap stocks, 3,000 mid cap stocks, and 2,000 small cap stocks. In stratified random sampling, to select a total sample of 100 stocks, you will randomly select 50 large cap stocks, 30 mid cap stocks, and 20 small cap stocks.

Time-series & cross-sectional data

Time series data consists of observations for a single subject taken at specific and equally spaced intervals of time.
The quarterly EPS of a particular stock from the S&P 500 for the last 10 years.

Cross-sectional data consists of observations for multiple subjects taken at a specific point in time.

Last quarter's EPS of all stocks from the S&P 500.

Central limit theorem

According to the central limit theorem, if we draw a sample from a population with a mean μ and a variance σ^2, then the sampling distribution of the sample mean:
- will be normally distributed (irrespective of the type of distribution of the original population).
- will have a mean of μ.
- will have a variance of σ^2/n.

Suppose the average return of the universe of 10,000 stocks is 12% and its standard deviation is 10%. Through central limit theorem, we can conclude that if we keep drawing samples of 100 stocks and plot their average returns, we will get a sampling distribution that will be normally distributed with mean = 12% and variance of $10^2/100 = 1\%$.

Standard error of the sample mean

The standard deviation of the distribution of the sample means is known as the standard error of the sample mean.

When we know the population standard deviation, the standard error of the sample mean can be calculated as:

$$\sigma_{\bar{X}} = \frac{\sigma}{\sqrt{n}}$$

When we do not know the population standard deviation (σ) we can use the sample standard deviation (s) to estimate the standard error of the sample mean:

$$s_{\bar{X}} = \frac{s}{\sqrt{n}}$$

The average returns of all large cap stocks in an economy is 10% with a standard deviation of 6%. For a random sample of 100 stocks calculate the standard error.
Solution:

$$\sigma_{\bar{X}} = \frac{\sigma}{\sqrt{n}} = \frac{6}{\sqrt{100}} = 0.6$$

Desirable properties of an estimator

The three desirable properties of an estimator are:
- **Unbiasedness:** expected value is equal to the parameter being estimated.
- **Efficiency:** has the lowest variance as compared to other unbiased estimators of the same parameter.
- **Consistency:** as sample size increases, the sampling error decreases and the

Quantitative Methods

estimates get closer to the actual value.

Point estimate v/s confidence interval estimate of a population parameter

Point estimate is a single value estimate that serves as an approximation for the actual value of the parameter.

Confidence interval is a range of values, within which the actual value of the parameter will lie with a given probability. Confidence interval is calculated as:

Confidence interval = point estimate ± (reliability factor x standard error of point estimate)
The reliability factor depends on the assumed distribution of the point estimate and the level of confidence of the interval (1 – α).

Student's t-distribution

Student's t-distribution has the following properties:
- It is symmetrical, bell-shaped and similar to a normal distribution.
- It has a lower peak and fatter tails as compared to a normal distribution.
- It is defined by a single parameter, degrees of freedom (df).

  Degrees of freedom = n - 1

  If you are given a sample size of 25, the degrees of freedom would be 25 – 1 = 24.

- As the degrees of freedom increase, the shape of the t-distribution starts approaching the shape of the normal distribution.

Calculating confidence intervals

To calculate a confidence interval for a population mean, follow these steps:

Refer to the table below and select t statistic or z statistic as per the scenario.

Sampling from		Small sample size	Large sample size
Normal distribution	Variance known	z	z
	Variance unknown	t	t (or z)
Non–normal distribution	Variance known	NA	z
	Variance unknown	NA	t (or z)

Use the following formulae to calculate the confidence interval:

Confidence interval = $\bar{X} \pm z_{\alpha/2} \frac{\sigma}{\sqrt{n}}$

Confidence interval = $\bar{X} \pm t_{\alpha/2} \frac{s}{\sqrt{n}}$

For a Z distribution,

Quantitative Methods

90% confidence → critical value = 1.65
95% confidence → critical value = 1.96
99% confidence → critical value = 2.58

You take a random sample of 100 large cap stocks. The average returns of these stocks for the past year is 12%. Assume that the average returns for all large-cap stocks in the economy follow a normal distribution with a standard deviation of 3%. Construct a 99% confidence interval for the average return all large-cap stocks for the past year.

Solution:
Since the population variance is known (the standard deviation of all large cap stocks), we will use Z statistic.
For confidence level of 99%, 1% error in both tails i.e. 0.5% (0.005) in one tail. $Z_{\alpha/2} = Z_{0.005}$ = 2.58 (From Z-table)
The confidence interval can be calculated as
Confidence interval = $12 \pm 2.58 \frac{3}{\sqrt{100}}$ = 11.226 to 12.774

You construct a sample of monthly returns of Stock A for the past two years. The stock has a mean return of 2% and a standard deviation of 8%. Compute the 95% confidence interval for the average monthly returns for this stock.

Solution:
Since the population variance is unknown (the variance of monthly returns of Stock A over its entire history, we only have data for the past two years) we will use t statistic.
Degrees of freedom = 24 – 1 = 23 (two years = 24 months)
For confidence level of 95%, 5% error in both tails, i.e. 2.5%(0.025) in one tail $t_{\alpha/2} = t_{24, 0.025}$ = 2.069
The confidence interval can be calculated as:
Confidence interval = $2 \pm 2.069 \frac{8}{\sqrt{24}}$ = −1.38% to 5.38%

Selection of sample size & sampling biases

Increasing the sample size reduces the standard error and gives us narrower confidence intervals. However, while increasing sample size we must consider two things:
- **Cost involved:** Compare the cost of getting more data to the potential benefits of increasing precision.
- **Risk of sampling from a different population:** In the process of increasing sample size if we get data from a different population, then the accuracy will not improve.

Biases observed in sampling methods are:
- **Data-mining bias**: Analyzing the same data repeatedly, till a pattern is identified. To avoid this bias test the pattern on out of sample data.
- **Sample selection bias**: Excluding certain assets from the analysis due to

Quantitative Methods

unavailability of data. A type of sample selection bias is the ***survivorship bias***, in which companies are excluded from analysis because they have gone out of business.
- **Look-ahead bias**: Analyzing past data using information that became available now.
- **Time-period bias:** If the selected time period is too short, the results may not be useful. If the time period is too long, then the results may not consider major structural changes in the economy.

R12 Hypothesis Testing

Steps of hypothesis testing

Hypothesis is a statement about the value of a population parameter developed for the purpose of testing a theory.

Hypothesis testing is the process of assessing the accuracy of a statement about a population on the basis of analysis conducted on a sample. In order to test a hypothesis, we follow the following steps:
1. State the hypothesis.
2. Identify the appropriate test statistic.
3. Specify the level of significance.
4. State a decision rule to accept or reject the hypothesis.
5. Collect sample data and calculate the test statistic.
6. Decide if the hypothesis can be accepted/rejected.
7. Make an economic or investment decision.

Null hypothesis (H_0) is the hypothesis that the researcher wants to reject. It should always include the 'equal to' condition.

Alternative hypothesis (H_a) is the hypothesis that the researcher wants to prove. If the null hypothesis is rejected, then the alternative hypothesis is considered valid.

If you want to test if the average returns of all stocks in the S&P 500 are greater than 10%.
H_0: $\mu \leq 10\%$ and H_a: $\mu > 10\%$

If you want to test if the average returns of all stocks in the S&P 500 are less than 10%.
H_0: $\mu \geq 10\%$ and H_a: $\mu < 10\%$

If you want to test if the average returns of all stocks in the S&P 500 are not equal to 10%.
H_0: $\mu = 10\%$ and H_a: $\mu \neq 10\%$

One-tailed v/s two-tailed tests

Hypothesis tests can be one-tailed or two-tailed.

In **one-tailed tests**, we are assessing if the value of a population parameter is greater than

or less than a hypothesized value.
You are testing if the average returns of all stocks in the S&P 500 are greater than 10%. Assume a 95% confidence level.
H₀: $\mu \le 10\%$ and Hₐ: $\mu > 10\%$
We will reject the null hypothesis only if the test statistic (explained later) is in the right tail (shaded portion). Hence, it is a one-tailed test.

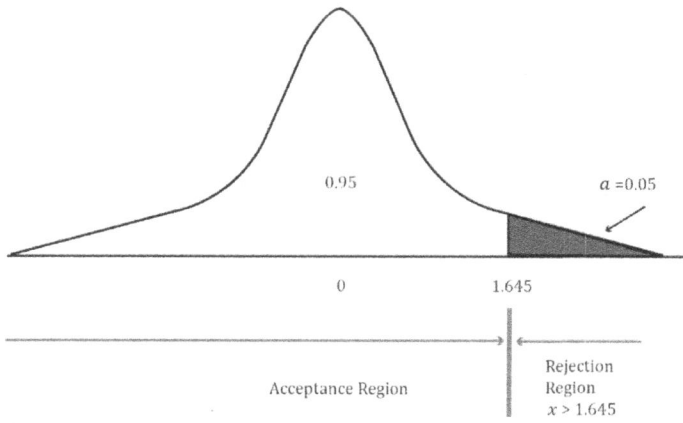

In **two-tailed tests**, we are assessing if the value of a population parameter is different from a hypothesized value.
You are testing if the average returns of all stocks in the S&P 500 are not equal to 10%. Assume a 95% confidence level
H₀: $\mu = 10\%$ and Hₐ: $\mu \ne 10\%$
We will reject the null hypothesis if the test statistic is either in the right tail or the left tail (shaded portions). Hence, this is a two-tailed test.

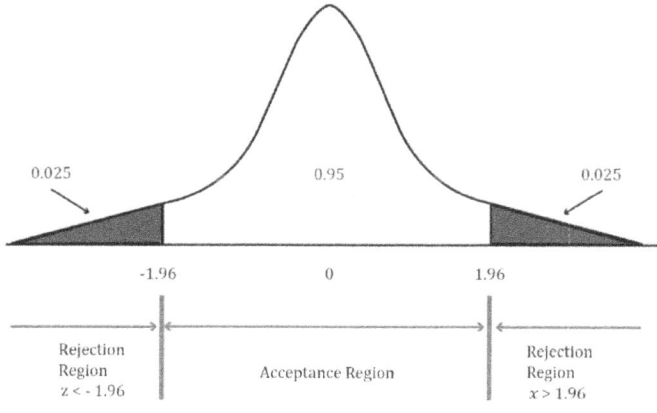

Test statistic, type I and type II errors & significance level

Test statistic is calculated from sample data and is compared to a critical value to decide whether or not we can reject the null hypothesis. Which test statistic to use depends on the properties of the population and the sample size. The two commonly used test statistics are:

$$z - \text{statistic} = \frac{\bar{X} - \mu_0}{\frac{\sigma}{\sqrt{n}}}$$

$$t - \text{statistic} = \frac{\bar{X} - \mu_0}{s/\sqrt{n}}$$

Critical values come from z and t tables and are based on the level of confidence that the researcher wants to use. If the test statistic is outside the range of the critical value, then we can reject the null hypothesis.

In reaching a statistical decision, we can make two possible errors:
- **Type I error**: We may reject a true null hypothesis.
- **Type II error**: We fail to reject a false null hypothesis.

Decision	True condition	
	H₀ true	H₀ false
Do not reject H₀	Correct decision	Type II error
Reject H₀ (accept Hₐ)	Type I error	Correct decision

Level of significance (α) of a test is the probability of making a Type I error i.e. rejecting a null when it is true.

Level of significance (α) = (1 – level of confidence)
Level of significance (α) = P (Type I error)

For example, if the level of confidence is 95%, then α = 5%. As α gets smaller, the critical value gets larger and it becomes more difficult to reject the null hypothesis.

Decision rule, power of a test, & relation between confidence intervals and hypothesis tests

Decision rule consists of comparing the computed test statistic to the critical values (rejection points) based on the level of significance to decide whether to reject or not to reject the null hypothesis.

Power of a test

Power of a test = 1 – P (Type II error)

A test that is more likely to reject a false null, is considered powerful. Similarly, a test that is less likely to reject a false null is considered weak.

Relation between confidence interval and hypothesis tests

A confidence interval gives us the range of values within which a population parameter is expected to lie. Confidence intervals and hypothesis tests are linked through critical values. The null hypothesis will be rejected only if the test statistic lies outside the confidence interval.

In the diagram below, the white portion is the confidence interval, within which the population mean is expected to lie, we will reject H₀ only if it lies outside the confidence interval.

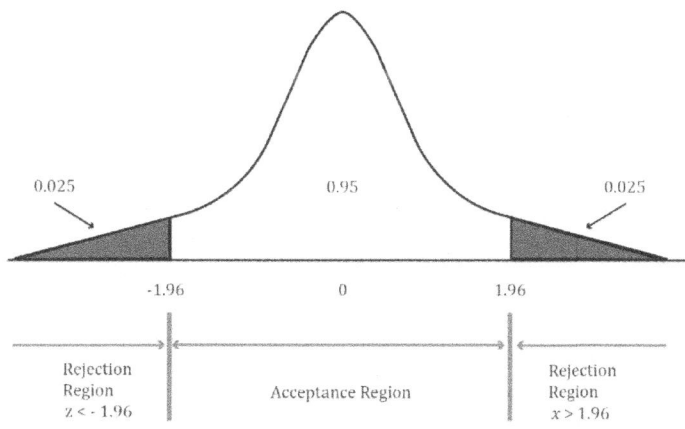

Statistical result v/s economically meaningful result

The statistical decision consists of rejecting or not rejecting the null hypothesis. The economic decision takes into consideration all economic issues relevant to the decisions such as transaction costs, risk tolerance and the impact on the existing portfolio. Sometimes a test may indicate a statistically significant result which may not be economically significant.

p-value

The p-value is the smallest level of significance at which the null hypothesis can be rejected. It can be used in the hypothesis testing framework as an alternative to using rejection points.

- If the p-value is lower than our specified level of significance, we reject the null hypothesis.
- If the p-value is greater than our specified level of significance, we do not reject the null hypothesis.

If the p-value of a test is 4% then the hypothesis can be rejected at the 5% level of significance, but not at the 1% level of significance.

Hypothesis tests concerning a single mean

We use the following table to decide which test statistic and which corresponding probability distribution to use for hypothesis testing.

Quantitative Methods

Sampling from		Small sample size	Large sample size
Normal distribution	Variance known	z	z
	Variance unknown	t	t (or z)
Non–normal distribution	Variance known	NA	z
	Variance unknown	NA	t (or z)

You believe that the average returns of all stocks in the S&P 500 is greater than 10%. You draw a sample of 49 stocks. The average return of these 49 stocks is 12%. The standard deviation of returns of all stocks in the S&P 500 is 4%. Using a 5% level of significance, determine if your belief is correct.

Solution:
Step 1: State the hypothesis
$H_0: \mu \leq 10\%$
$H_a: \mu > 10\%$

Step 2: Calculate the test statistic
The population variance is known hence we will use z-statistic.

$$z - \text{statistic} = \frac{\bar{X} - \mu_0}{\frac{\sigma}{\sqrt{n}}} = \frac{12-10}{\frac{4}{\sqrt{49}}} = 3.5$$

Step 3: Calculate the critical value
This is a one-tailed test and we will be looking at the right tail. Using the Z –table and 5% level of significance
Critical value = $Z_{0.05}$ = 1.65

Step 4: Decision
Since the test statistic (3.5) > critical value (1.65), we reject H_0. Hence at 5% level of significance, your belief that the average returns of all stocks in the S&P 500 is greater than 10% is correct.

You believe that the average returns of all stocks in the S&P 500 is greater than 10%. You draw a sample of 25 stocks. The average return of these 25 stocks is 12% and the standard deviation of their returns is 7%. Using a 5% level of significance, determine if your belief is correct.

Solution:
Step 1: State the hypothesis
$H_0: \mu \leq 10\%$
$H_a: \mu > 10\%$

Step 2: Calculate the test statistic

Quantitative Methods

The population variance is not known hence we will use t-statistic.

$$t - \text{statistic} = \frac{\bar{X} - \mu_0}{\frac{s}{\sqrt{n}}} = \frac{12-10}{\frac{7}{\sqrt{25}}} = 1.43$$

Step 3: Calculate the critical value

This is a one-tailed test and we will be looking at the right tail. Using the t–table and 5% level of significance and degrees of freedom = 25 -1 = 24

Critical value = $t_{24, 0.05}$ = 1.71

Step 4: Decision

Since the test statistic (1.43) < critical value (1.71), we cannot reject H_0. Hence at 5% level of significance, your belief that the average returns of all stocks in the S&P 500 is greater than 10% is incorrect.

Hypothesis tests concerning differences between means

(Note: This section has high difficulty and low probability of being tested. Do this section once you have mastered all remaining topics)

Unknown but equal variance

When we can assume that the two populations are normally distributed and that the unknown population variances are equal, the t-test based on independent random samples is given by:

$$t = \frac{(\bar{X}_1 - \bar{X}_2) - (\mu_1 - \mu_2)}{\left(\frac{s_p^2}{n_1} + \frac{s_p^2}{n_2}\right)^{1/2}}$$

The term s_p^2 is known as the pooled estimator of the common variance. It is calculated by the following formula:

$$s_p^2 = \frac{(n_1 - 1)s_1^2 + ((n_2 - 1)s_2^2}{n_1 + n_2 - 2}$$

The number of degrees of freedom is $n_1 + n_2 - 2$.

Unknown and unequal variance

When we can assume that the two populations are normally distributed and that the unknown population variances are unequal, an approximate t-test based on independent random samples is given by:

$$t = \frac{(\bar{X}_1 - \bar{X}_2) - (\mu_1 - \mu_2)}{\left(\frac{s_1^2}{n_1} + \frac{s_2^2}{n_2}\right)^{1/2}}$$

In this formula, we use the tables of the t-distribution using the 'modified' degrees of freedom. The 'modified' degrees of freedom are calculated using the following formula:

$$df = \frac{\left(\frac{s_1^2}{n_1} + \frac{s_2^2}{n_2}\right)^2}{\frac{(s_1^2/n_1)^2}{n_1} + \frac{(s_2^2/n_2)^2}{n_2}}$$

Quantitative Methods

Hypothesis tests concerning mean differences

(Note: This section has high difficulty and low probability of being tested. Do this section once you have mastered all remaining topics)

If the samples of the populations whose means we are comparing are dependent, then the paired comparison test is used. The hypothesis is structured as the difference between means of two populations.

$H_0: \mu_d = \mu_{d0}$

$H_a: \mu_d \neq \mu_{d0}$

where:

μ_d stands for the population mean difference and

μ_{d0} stands for the hypothesized value for the population mean difference, which is usually zero.

In order to arrive at the test statistic, we first determine the sample mean difference using:

$$\bar{d} = \frac{1}{n}\sum_{i=0}^{n} d_i$$

The standard error of the mean difference as follows:

$$s_{\bar{d}} = \frac{s_d}{\sqrt{n}}$$

Once we have these two values, we can calculate the test statistic using a t-test. This is calculated using the following formula using n - 1 degrees of freedom:

$$t = \frac{\bar{d} - \mu_{d0}}{s_{\bar{d}}}$$

The value of calculated test statistic is compared with the t-distribution values in the usual manner to arrive at a decision on our hypothesis.

Hypothesis tests concerning variance

(Note: This section has high difficulty and low probability of being tested. Do this section once you have mastered all remaining topics)

Single population variance

In tests concerning the variance of a single normally distributed population, we use the chi-square test statistic, denoted by χ^2.

After drawing a random sample from a normally distributed population, we calculate the test statistic using the following formula with n - 1 degrees of freedom:

$$\chi^2 = \frac{(n-1)(s^2)}{\sigma_0^2}$$

where:

n = sample size

s = sample variance

We then determine the critical values using the level of significance and degrees of freedom. The chi-square distribution table is used to calculate the critical value.

Two population variance

In order to test the equality or inequality of two variances, we use an F-test which is the ratio of sample variances.

The formula for the test statistic of the F-test is:

$$F = \frac{s_1^2}{s_2^2}$$

where:

s_1^2 = the sample variance of the first population with n observations
s_2^2 = the sample variance of the second population with n observations

A convention is to put the larger sample variance in the numerator and the smaller sample variance in the denominator.

$df_1 = n_1 - 1$ numerator degrees of freedom
$df_2 = n_2 - 1$ denominator degrees of freedom

The test statistic is then compared with the critical values found using the two degrees of freedom and the F-tables.

Finally, a decision is made whether to reject or not to reject the null hypothesis.

Types of Test Statistics	
Hypothesis test of	**Use**
One population mean	t-statistic or z-statistic
Two population mean	t-statistic
One population variance	Chi-square statistic
Two-population variance	F-statistic

Parametric v/s nonparametric tests

Parametric tests like a t-test, F-test or chi-square test are based on specific assumptions about the distribution of the population from which samples are drawn.

Nonparametric tests are either not concerned with a parameter or make minimal assumptions about the population from which the sample comes. A nonparametric test is primarily used in three situations:

- when data does not meet distributional assumptions.
- when data is given in ranks.
- when we are concerned about quantities other than the parameters of the distribution.

R13 Technical Analysis

Principles & assumptions of technical analysis

Technical analysis is a form of security analysis that involves examination of past price and volume data to predict future behavior of the market or individual security.

Assumptions:
- Market prices are determined by supply and demand.
- Market prices reflect both rational and irrational investor behavior.
- Investor behavior is reflected in trends and patterns that tend to repeat.
- Price and volume information can be used to understand investor sentiment and make investment decisions.

Technical analysis can also be used on assets such as commodities, currencies and futures that do not have underlying income streams or financial statements.

Charts

Line charts
- Graphic display of prices over time.
- Only one data point per time interval – the closing price.
- Price is plotted on the Y-axis and time on the X-axis.
- The closing prices for each trading period are connected by a line.

Bar charts
- Four data points per time interval – opening price, highest and lowest price, and closing price.
- Price is plotted on the Y-axis and time on the X-axis
- They give a better sense of the trend in the market.
- A short bar indicates low volatility, a long bar indicates high volatility

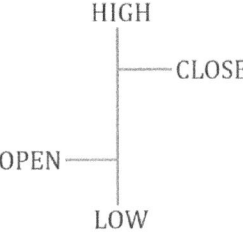

Candlestick charts
- Has the same four data points per time interval as a bar chart– opening price, highest and lowest price, and closing price.
- Price is plotted on the Y-axis and time on the X-axis

- If the market closed up, the body of the candle is clear.
- If the market closed down, the body of the candle is shaded.

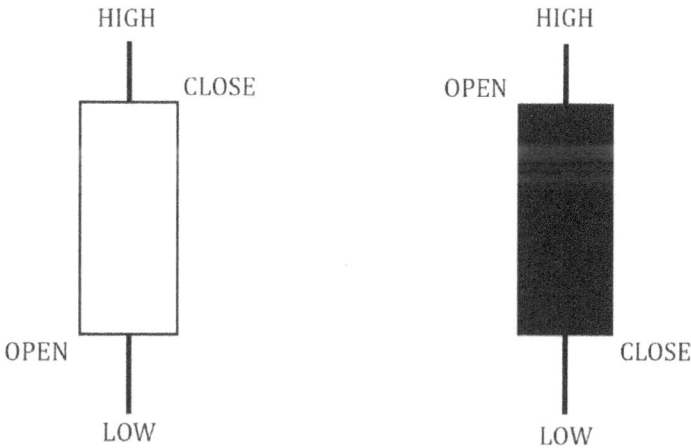

White body means market closed UP
Close > Open

Dark body means market closed DOWN
Close < Open

Volume charts
- Often displayed below a line, bar or candlestick chart.
- Number of units of the security traded is plotted on the Y-axis and time on the X-axis.

Point and figure charts
- Drawn as a grid consisting of columns of X's alternating with columns of O's. X represents an increase in price while an O represents a decrease in price.
- Y-axis measures box size increments in price whereas X-axis measures the number of price changes.
- To construct this chart, you need to specify a box size and a reversal size.

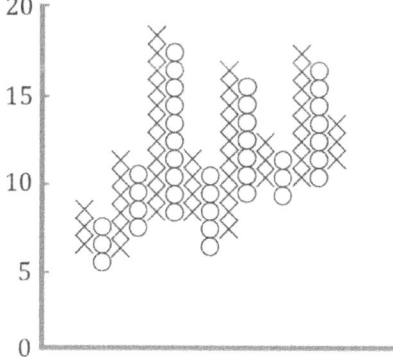

Trends

Uptrend: A security is said to be in an uptrend if prices are reaching higher highs and higher lows. An upward trendline can be drawn by connecting the increasing low points with a straight line.

Downtrend: A security is said to be in a downtrend if prices are reaching lower highs and lower lows. A downward trendline can be drawn by connecting the decreasing high points with a straight line.

Support is the price level at which there is sufficient buying pressure to stop further decline in prices.

Resistance is the price level at which there is sufficient selling pressure to stop the further increase in prices.

Change in polarity: Once a support level is breached, it often becomes a new resistance level. Similarly, once a resistance level is breached; it often becomes a new support level.

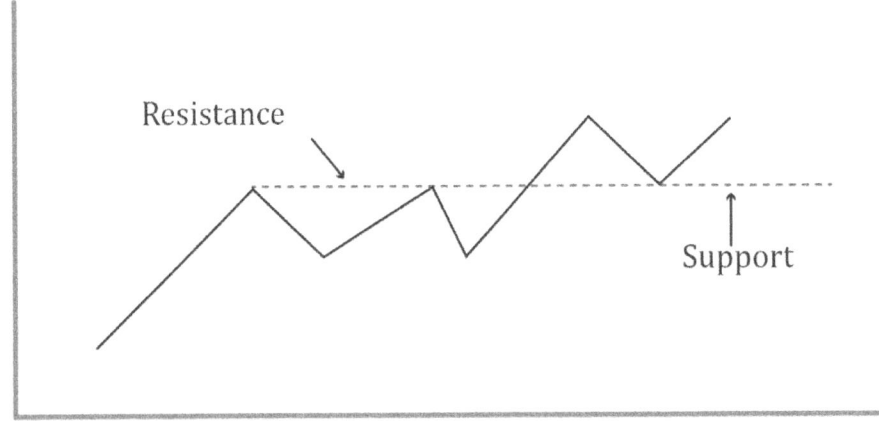

Common chart patterns

Reversal Patterns signal the end of a trend. The four kinds of reversal patterns are:

Head and shoulders pattern:
- Consists of the left shoulder, the head, and the right shoulder.
- Indicates the end of an uptrend.
- You can profit by going short on the security, the price target is:
  Price target = neckline – (head – neckline)

Inverse head and shoulders pattern:
- Is a mirror image of the head and shoulders pattern.
- Indicates the end of a downtrend.
- You can profit by going long on the security, the price target is:
  Price target = neckline + (head – neckline)

Double tops and bottoms:
- A double top is formed when prices hit the same resistance level twice and fall

down. It indicates the end of an uptrend.
- A double bottom is formed when prices bounce back from the same support level twice. It indicates the end of a down-trend.

Triple tops and bottoms:
- Triple tops are formed when prices hit the same resistance level thrice.
- Triple bottoms are formed when prices bounce back from the same support level thrice.

Continuation patterns signal a temporary pause in the trend, and that the trend will continue in the same direction as before. The four kinds of continuation patterns are:

Triangles:
- There are three forms - symmetrical triangles, ascending triangles and descending triangles.
- One trendline connects the highs and a second trendline connects the lows.
- As the distance between the highs and lows narrows, the trendlines converge, forming a triangle.

Rectangles:
- One trendline connects the highs and a second trendline connects the lows.
- As the distance between the highs and lows is constant, the trendlines are parallel to each other and form a rectangle.

Flags:
- Is similar to a rectangle and is formed by two parallel trendlines.
- However, it forms over a much shorter time interval.

Pennants:
- Is similar to a triangle and is formed by two converging trend lines.
- However, it forms over a much shorter time interval.

Technical indicators

Price-based indicators incorporate information contained in the current and past market prices. The common types are:

Moving average:
- Average of the closing prices over a specified number of periods.
- Used to smooth out short-term price fluctuations and helps identify the trend.

Bollinger bands:
- They are drawn at a given number of standard deviations above and below a moving average.
- Price are expected to reverse when they touch the upper/lower band.

Quantitative Methods

Momentum oscillators help to identify changes in the market sentiment. The common types are:

Rate of change (ROC) oscillator:
- Oscillates around 0 (or around 100 if an alternative formula is used for calculation)
- When the ROC oscillator crosses zero into the positive territory, it is considered bullish.
- When the ROC oscillator crosses zero into the negative territory, it is considered bearish.

Relative strength index (RSI):
- RSI graphically compares a security's gains with its losses over a given period. The popular time period is 14 days.
- The value of the RSI is always between 0 and 100. A value above 70 represents an overbought situation while a value below 30 suggests that an asset is oversold.

Stochastic oscillator:
- Based on the observation that in uptrends, prices tend to close at or near the high end of their recent range. Similarly in downtrends, they tend to close near the low end.
- Composed of two lines, called %K and %D.
- Has a default setting of 14-days.
- Oscillates between 0 and 100. A value above 80 indicates overbought situation and value below 20 indicates oversold situation.

Moving-average convergence/divergence oscillator:
- Difference between a short-term and a long-term moving average of the security's price.
- Composed of two lines - MACD line and signal line.
- Oscillates around 0 and has no upper or lower limit.

Sentiment indicators gauge investor activity for signs of bullishness or bearishness. The common types are:

Opinion polls:
- Regular polls are conducted of investors and investment professionals to gauge the overall market sentiment.

Calculated statistical indices:
- The ***put/call ratio*** is the volume of put options traded divided by the volume of call options traded. A high ratio indicates that the market is bearish. Whereas, a low ratio indicates that the market is bullish.
- The ***CBOE volatility index (VIX)*** is a measure of near-term market volatility calculated from option prices of S&P 500 stocks. The VIX rises when market

participants become fearful of a market decline.
- ***Margin debt*** is loans taken by individual investors to fund their stock purchases. When stock margin debt is increasing, investors are aggressively buying and the stock prices will rise because of increased demand.
- ***Short interest*** refers to the number of shares of a particular security that are currently sold short. The short interest ratio is calculated as:

$$\text{Short interest ratio} = \frac{\text{Short interest}}{\text{Average daily trading volume}}$$

A high ratio suggests an overall negative outlook on the security.

Flow-of-funds indicators indicate the change in potential demand and supply. The common types are:

The arms index :(also known as TRIN)
- Calculated as:

$$\text{Arms index} = \frac{\text{number of advancing issues} \div \text{number of declining issues}}{\text{volume of advancing issues} \div \text{volume of declining issues}}$$

- When this index is near 1, the market is in balance. A value above 1 means that there is more volume in declining stocks and that the market is in a selling mood. A value below 1 means that there is more volume in increasing stocks and that the market is in a buying mood.

Margin debt:
- Margin loans may increase the purchases of stocks and declining margin balances may force the selling of stocks.

Mutual funds cash position:
- Mutual funds must hold some of their assets in cash to pay for miscellaneous expenses and to fund redemptions.
- During a bullish market, the cash positions tend to be low.
- During a bearish market, the cash positions tend to be high.

New equity issuance:
- IPOs are often timed with bullish markets to get the best valuations.
- A large number of IPOs may indicate that a market is near its peak.

Secondary offerings:
- Like IPOs, technicians also monitor secondary offerings to gauge potential changes in the supply of equities.

Cycles

Kondratieff wave (K-wave):
- States that western economies have a 54-year old cycle.

Quantitative Methods

<u>18-year cycle</u>:
- Three 18-year cycles make up the longer 54-year Kondratieff Wave.
- This cycle is often mentioned in real estate markets, but it can also be found in equities and other markets.

<u>Decennial pattern</u>:
- This pattern links average stock market returns with the last digit of the year.
- Years ending in 0 have shown poor performance whereas years ending in 5 have shown good performance.

<u>Presidential cycle</u>:
- This cycle connects the performance of the U.S. market with the U.S. presidential elections.
- Historically, the third year following an election has shown the best performance.

Elliott wave theory

- According to this theory, the market moves in regular waves or cycles.
- In a bull market, the market moves up in five waves in the following pattern: 1 = up, 2 = down, 3 = up, 4 = down and 5 = up.
- Each wave can be broken into smaller waves over a shorter time period.
- Market waves follow patterns that are ratios of the numbers in the Fibonacci sequence. Hence, ratios of the numbers in the Fibonacci sequence can be used to set price targets while trading.
The Fibonacci Sequence is the series of numbers: 0, 1, 1, 2, 3, 5, 8, 13, 21, 34, ... The next number is found by adding up the two numbers before it.

Intermarket analysis

- Inter-market analysis is based on the principle that different markets such as stocks, bonds, commodities, currencies etc. are interrelated and influence each other.
- Technicians often use relative strength analysis to look for the inflection point in one market as a warning sign to start looking for a change in another related market.
- The relative strength analysis can also be used to identify attractive asset classes and attractive sectors within these classes to invest in.

R14 Topics in Demand and Supply Analysis

Price, income, and cross-price elasticities of demand

Elasticity of demand is measured as a ratio of percentage change in quantity demanded to a percentage change in other variables.

Own-price elasticity

- Own price elasticity = $\frac{\text{\% change in quanitity demanded}}{\text{\% change in own price}}$
- Own-price elasticity of demand is usually always negative.
- If |own price elasticity| > 1, then demand is elastic.
- If |own price elasticity| < 1, then demand is inelastic.
- If own price elasticity = -1, then demand is unit, or unitary, elastic.

Income elasticity

- Income elasticity = $\frac{\text{\% change in quanitity demanded}}{\text{\% change in income}}$
- If income elasticity > 0, then the good is a normal good.
- If income elasticity < 0, then the good is an inferior good.

Cross price elasticity

- Cross price elasticity = $\frac{\text{\% change in quanitity demanded}}{\text{\% change in price of related good}}$
- If cross price elasticity > 0, then the related good is a substitute.
- If cross price elasticity < 0, then the related good is a complement.

A demand function for chairs is as follows:
$Q_{chairs} = 200 - 2P_{chairs} + 0.05\text{Income} - 0.8P_{tables} + 1.2P_{stools}$
At current average prices, a chair costs $50, a table costs $100 and a stool costs $30. Average income is $5,000. Calculate the income elasticity of demand for chairs.

Solution:

Substitute current values for the independent variables (except income)
$Q_{chairs} = 200 - 2(50) + 0.05\text{Income} - 0.8(100) + 1.2(30)$
$Q_{chairs} = 56 + 0.05\text{Income}$

The slope of income is 0.05
For an income of $5,000; Q_{chairs} = 306
Income elasticity = $\frac{I_0}{Q_0} \times \frac{\Delta Q}{\Delta I} = \frac{5,000}{306} \times 0.05 = 0.82$

Factors impacting the own price elasticity of demand for a product include:
- Substitutes: If the number of substitutes for this product is high, then elasticity will be high.
- Portion of total budget: If the portion of total budget spent on this product is high, then

elasticity will be high.
- Time horizon: If the time horizon we consider is long, then elasticity will be high. This is because consumers will have enough time to respond to changes in the price of this product.
- Discretionary (optional) versus non-discretionary (necessary): If the product is discretionary rather than non-discretionary, then the elasticity will be high.

Substitution and income effects.

Substitution effect
- When a good's price falls, due to substitution effect consumers buy more of this good as compared to other goods for which the prices have remained the same.
- Substitution effect is always positive.

Income effect
- When a good's price falls, real income rises.
- If the good is a normal good, the income effect will be positive and more of this good will be purchased.
- If the good is an inferior good, the income effect will be negative and less of this good will be purchased.

Giffen goods
- Giffen goods are highly inferior for which the negative income effect outweighs the positive substitution effect.
- Therefore even though price falls, the quantity demanded still decreases.
- Giffen goods have a positively sloped demand curve (which means that as price decreases the quantity demanded also decreases).

Veblen goods
- Veblen goods are "high status" goods.
- If price increases, this makes the goods even more desirable and quantity demanded increases.
- Veblen goods also have a positively sloped demand curve (which means that as price increases the quantity demanded also increases).

Diminishing marginal returns.

- Marginal returns refer to the additional output than can be obtained by adding one more unit of a productive input, while keeping the quantities of other inputs constant.
- As the first few units of an input are added, marginal returns may increase. However, as we keep increasing the input quantity, we reach a point where marginal returns start to decrease.
- Inputs beyond this point produce diminishing marginal returns.

Economics

Breakeven and shutdown points of production

Under perfect and imperfect competition we have:
- Breakeven quantity is the quantity for which TR = TC.
- If TR < TC, then the firm should shut down in the long run.
- If TR < TVC, then the firm should shut down in the short run.

Under perfect competition, we can additionally state the following:
- Breakeven quantity is the quantity for which price (P) = average total cost.
- If P < ATC, then the firm should shut down in the long run.
- If P < AVC, then the firm should shut down in the short run.

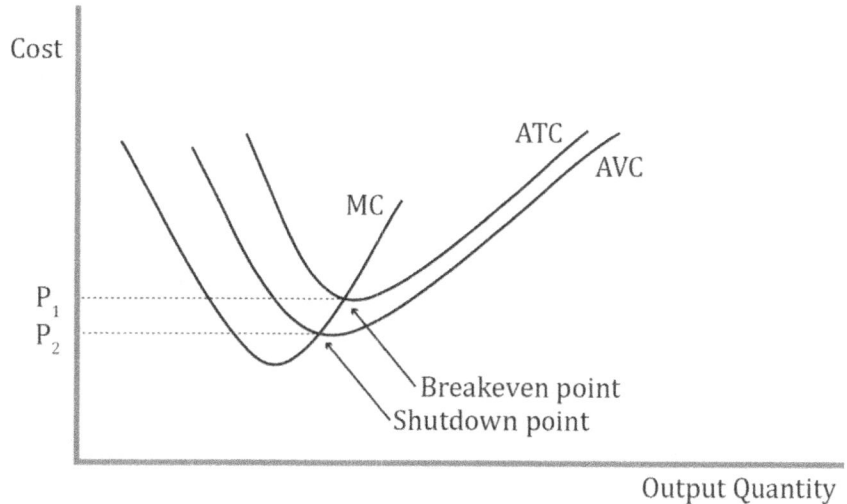

Economies and diseconomies of scale

Economies of scale: As output increases, the long-run cost per unit decreases. Factors contributing to economies of scale include:
- Increase in output larger than increase in input
- Specialization
- More expensive but more efficient equipment
- Lower waste and lower costs
- Better use of market information
- Volume discounts from suppliers

Diseconomies of scale: As output increases, the long-run cost per unit increases. Factors contributing to diseconomies of scale include:
- Increases in output are less than increases in input
- Company size becomes too large to manage efficiently
- Duplication
- Higher labor costs

Economics

- Higher resource costs

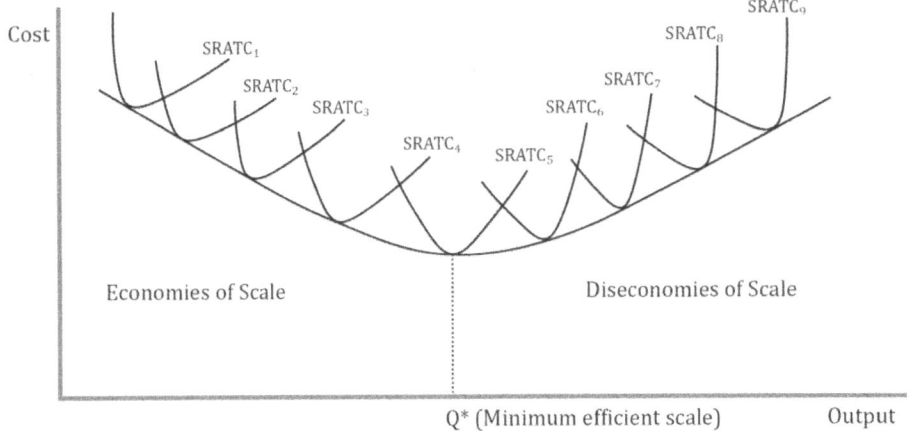

R15 The Firm and Market Structures

Perfect competition, monopolistic competition, oligopoly & monopoly

	Perfect competition	**Monopolistic competition**	**Oligopoly**	**Monopoly**
Number of firms	Many firms	Many firms	Few firms	Single firm
Barriers to entry	Very low	Low	High	Very high
Nature of substitute products	Very close substitutes	Substitutes but differentiated	Very close substitutes or differentiated	No good substitutes
Nature of competition	Price only	Price, marketing & features	Price, marketing & features	Advertising
Pricing power	None	Some	Some to significant	Significant
Demand curve for the firm	Perfectly elastic (Horizontal)	Downward sloping, yet elastic	Downward sloping	Downward Sloping
Example	Rice market	Soap	Aircraft manufacturers	Utility companies

Economics

Key points	Overall market supply and demand, determine the prices.	Branding creates differentiation in otherwise very similar products.	Firms are interdependent, i.e. they must consider actions and reactions of each other.	May be regulated by the government.

Characteristics of different market structures

Perfect competition
- Perfectly elastic demand curve for individual firms.
- A firm's short-run supply curve is the portion of MC curve above the AVC.
- Industry supply curve is simply the sum of supply curves of all the competing firms.
- Zero economic profit in equilibrium.
- Any economic profit or loss in the short-run; will be eliminated by more firms entering or leaving the market.
- Long-run equilibrium output level will be at MR = MC = ATC, where ATC is minimum.

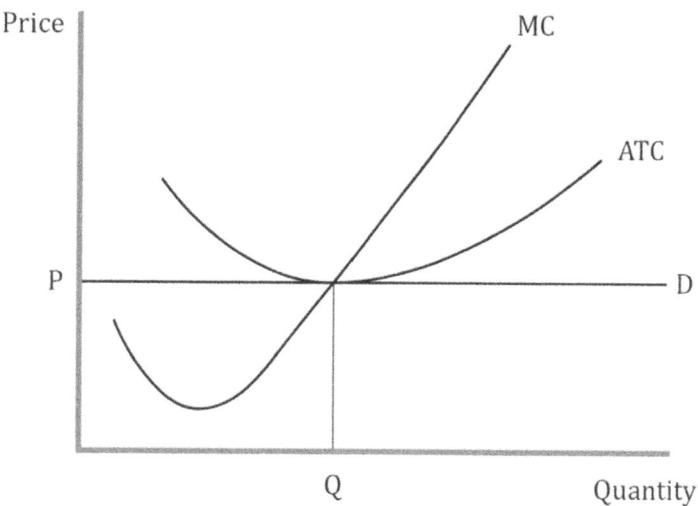

Monopolistic Competition
- In equilibrium, price > marginal revenue = marginal cost.
- Downward sloping firm demand curve.
- Price is derived from the demand curve at the point where MR = MC.
- At this point, ATC is not at its lowest point suggesting inefficiencies or underutilized capacity.
- Price will be slightly higher as compared to perfect competition.
- Zero economic profit in long-run equilibrium.
- Product innovation, advertising and brand names offer some competitive advantage.

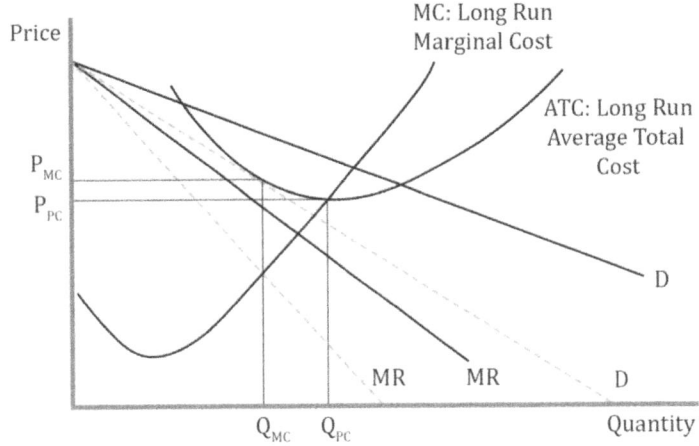

Oligopoly

- In equilibrium, price > marginal revenue = marginal cost.
- Downward sloping firm demand curve.
- May earn positive economic profit in long-run equilibrium, which trends towards zero over time.

Four models for oligopoly pricing and profits:

Kinked demand curve model:
- Firms will not follow a price increase but will cut their prices in response to a price decrease by a competitor.
- The point of kink is the profit maximizing amount of production and price.
- Kink in the demand curve also creates a gap in the MR curve for the firm.

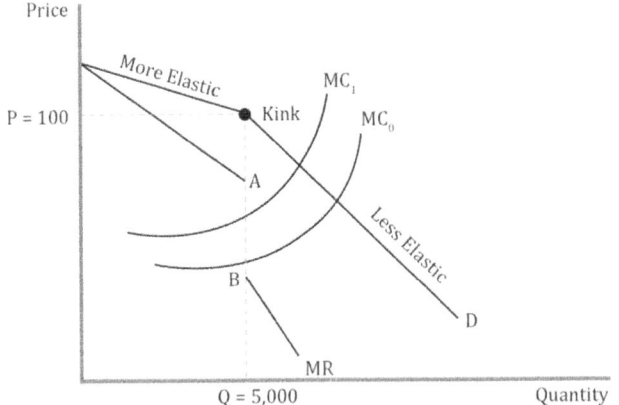

Cournot duopoly model:
- Each firm determines profit-maximizing quantity assuming other firms' output will not change.
- In the long-run, change in price or quantity will not increase profits.
- As the number of firms increases the equilibrium point moves towards perfect

competition.

Nash equilibrium model:
- Each firm acts in its own best interest and does not collude.
- No firm can increase profits by changing its price/output choices.

Consider a two-firm oligopoly where both have agreed to charge a higher price.

	Firm Y respects	Firm Y cheats
Firm X respects	X earns 200 Y earns 200	X earns 50 Y earns 350
Firm X cheats	X earns 350 Y earns 50	X earns 150 Y earns 150

Solution:

Nash equilibrium is for both firms to charge a lower price i.e. cheat on their agreement. Either of the firm can improve their profits from 200 to 350 by cheating. However, the non-cheating firm can increase its profit from 50 to 150, giving both the firms an incentive to cheat.

Stackelberg dominant firm model:
- One firm is assumed to have the lowest cost structure and a significant proportion of the market.
- Dominant firm essentially sets the price for the industry.
- All other firms are price takers and set their output quantities according to this price.

Monopoly

- In equilibrium, price > marginal revenue = marginal cost.
- Downward sloping firm demand curve.
- May have positive economic profit in long-run equilibrium.
- Profits may tend towards zero as expenses are incurred to preserve monopoly.
- For a firm whose marginal cost of production is constant, price discrimination can be used to reduce the deadweight loss and further maximizing profits.

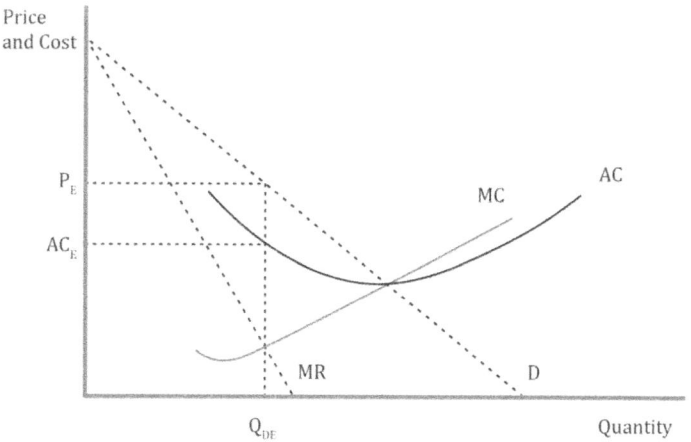

- Monopoly creates deadweight loss relative to perfect competition as the optimum level of production that maximizes consumer and producer surplus is not reached.
- Due to this deadweight loss some monopolies may be regulated. Commonly used regulations are:

  Average cost pricing
  - Output and pricing at intersection of ATC and market demand curve.
  - Ensures a normal profit as Price = ATC.

  Marginal cost pricing
  - Output and pricing at intersection of MC and market demand curve.
  - Monopolist needs to be subsidized for the difference in the ATC and MC.

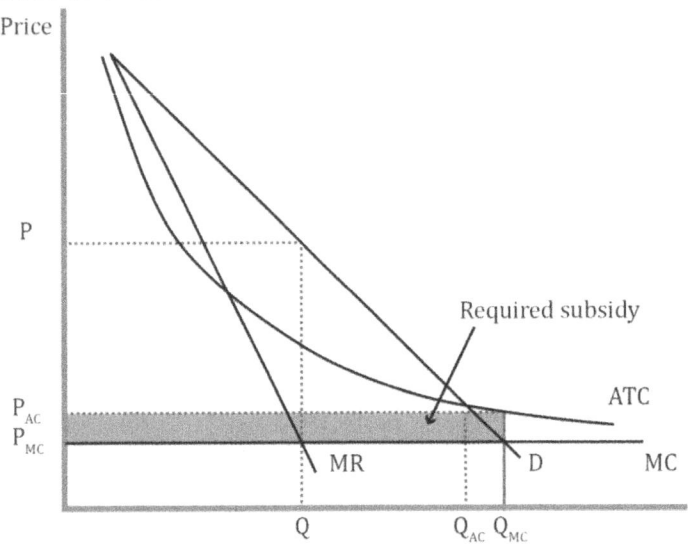

Supply functions under different market structures

Perfect competition
- A firm's short-run supply curve is the portion of its short-run marginal cost curve above its average variable cost.
- Market's short-run supply curve is the sum of the supply curves of all the competing firms.
- A firm's long-run supply curve is the portion of its long-run marginal cost curve above its average total cost.

Monopolistic competition, oligopoly and monopoly market:
- Supply functions are not well-defined.
- Neither marginal cost curves nor average cost curves are supply curves.
- The quantity to be produced is determined through intersection of marginal revenue and marginal cost curves and the price to be charged is determined through the demand curves that they face.

Factors affecting long-run equilibrium

In the long run,
- perfectly competitive and the monopolistically competitive firms cannot make economic profits.
- oligopoly firm can make economic profit but history shows that the dominant firm's market share declines.
- unregulated monopoly firm can make economic profit.

Concentration measures

The two concentration ratios used to measure the market power of the firm.

N-Firm Concentration Ratio
- Sum of the market shares of the N largest firms in an industry.
- Market share = firm revenue / total market revenue.
- **Advantage**: Simple to calculate and understand.
- **Disadvantages:** Ignores barriers to entry, does not directly measure market power or elasticity of demand.

Herfindahl-Hirschman Index (HHI)
- HHI = sum of squared market shares of N largest firms in a market.
- Ranges from 0 to 1: where 0 indicates perfect competition and 1 indicates a perfect monopoly.

Consider the market share of the following firms:

Firm	Revenue/Total market revenue
Bruce	30%
Clark	20%
Flash	15%
Peter	10%
Xavier	10%
James	5%

Compute the following 4-firm concentration ratio and the HHI.
1. 4-firm concentration ratio prior to and post the merger of Bruce and Clark.
2. HHI prior to and post the merger of Bruce and Clark.

Solution:

1. Prior to the merger,

Four $-$ firm concentration ratio $= 30 + 20 + 15 + 10 = 75\%$

Post the merger, Bruce and Clark become one entity having a market share of 50%.

Four $-$ firm concentration ratio $= 50 + 15 + 10 + 10 = 85\%$

Four-firm concentration ratio fails to capture the large increase in market share of the most dominant firm which has gone up from 30% to 50%, while the measure has only gone up by 10%.

2. Prior to the merger,
HHI = $0.30^2 + 0.20^2 + 0.15^2 + 0.10^2 = 0.1625$
Post the merger,
HHI = $0.50^2 + 0.15^2 + 0.10^2 + 0.10^2 = 0.2925$
HHI shows a larger increase, better reflecting the increase in the market share of the new large firm.

R16 Aggregate Output, Prices and Economic Growth

Gross domestic product (GDP)

Gross domestic product refers to the market value of all final goods and services produced in a country over a specific time period, usually one year; government transfers and goods/services without market value are not included.

There are two approaches to calculate GDP:
- The **income approach** computes GDP as the total income earned by households, businesses and the government in the country during a time period.
- The **expenditure approach**
  - Can be computed through the ***sum-of-value-added*** approach where GDP is calculated by summing the additions to value created at each stage of production & distribution
  - Can be computed through the ***value-of-final-output*** approach where GDP is calculated by summing the values of all final goods and services produced during the period

The expenditures approach can also be stated as:
GDP = C + I + G + (X − M)
where:
C = consumption spending,
I = business investments (includes capital equipment and inventories),
G = government purchases,
X = exports,
M = imports

Theoretically, the GDP derived from the two methods should match. Practically, there are some discrepancies due to measurement issues.

Nominal v/s real GDP

Nominal GDP values goods and services at their current prices. It includes inflation, which

Economics

can increase GDP even if there is no real growth in the output.

Real GDP measures current-year output of economy using prices from a base year. It eliminates the impact of inflation.

GDP deflator is a price index that can be used to convert nominal GDP into real GDP by removing the effects of changes in prices.

$$\text{GDP deflator} = \frac{\text{nominal GDP}}{\text{real GDP}} * 100$$

1. GDP in 2013 is $2.08 billion at 2013 prices and $1.93 billion when year 2012 is taken as base. Calculate the GDP deflator for 2013 using 2012 as the base period.
2. Nominal GDP in 2014 was $798 billion and $576 billion in 2009. If the 2014 GDP deflator using 2009 as the base year was 116.4, compute the real GDP for 2014. Also calculate the real GDP growth rate over 2009-2014.

Solution:

1. GDP deflator for 2013 using 2010 as base year $= \frac{2.08}{1.93} = 107.77$

    This shows that the prices have risen by 7.77% over the year.

2. Real GDP for 2014 $= \frac{798}{1.164} = \$685.57$

    Real GDP over the five-year period is computed as follows:

    Real annual GDP growth rate $= \left(\frac{685.57}{576}\right)^{\left(\frac{1}{5}\right)} - 1 = 3.54\%$

GDP, national income, personal income, and personal disposable income

GDP using income approach

GDP = national income + capital consumption allowance (CAA) + statistical discrepancy

- As the name suggests, it includes all the income items at the national level.
- CAA refers to depreciation of physical capital and represents the maintenance amount that needs to be invested to maintain production.
- Statistical discrepancy is an adjustment to match the GDP derived using the expenditure and income approach.

National income is the total income received by all the factors of production for producing the final output.

National income = wages and benefits to employees + corporate & government enterprise profits before taxes + interest income + unincorporated business income + rent + indirect business taxes-subsidies

Personal income is pre-tax income received by households.

Personal income = national income + transfer payments to households - indirect business taxes – corporate income taxes - undistributed corporate profits

Note: a transfer payment is a redistribution of income by the government which does not entail the exchange of any good or service; examples: welfare, social security and government subsidies.

Personal disposable income is the households' after tax income. Each period, individuals decide whether to save or consume disposable income.

Personal disposable income = personal income − personal taxes

Relationship between saving, investment, the fiscal balance, and the trade balance

In a given economy, the household savings go into investments, covering the government deficit and net exports.

$$S = I + (G - T) + (X - M)$$

where:
S = household and business savings,
I = investments
(G − T) is difference between government spending and tax receipts and is also known as **fiscal balance.** A positive value implies budget deficit. A negative value implies budget surplus.
(X − M) is the difference between exports and imports and is also known as **trade balance.** A positive value implies trade surplus. A negative value implies trade deficit.

The above equation can be rearranged as,

$$(S - I) = (G - T) + (X - M)$$

IS and LM curves

IS (Income Savings) curve

- The IS curve represents combinations of income and the real interest rate at which planned expenditure equals income.
- The income = savings (IS) curve states that the (S − I) = (G − T) + (X − M) condition holds when income = planned expenditure.
- IS curve shows a negative relationship between real interest rates and income.

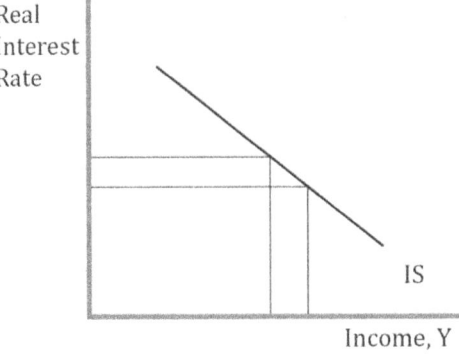

Economics

LM (Liquidity Money) Curve

- Shows the positive relationship between the real interest rate and aggregate income at which demand and supply of real money balances are equal.
- Quantity theory of money gives us the demand and supply for money.
  $MV = PY$
  $\frac{M}{P} = kY$ (Assuming the velocity is constant)
- Demand for real money increases as real income increases.
- If price level decreases, then real money increases and LM curve shifts to the right. This is illustrated in the figure below.

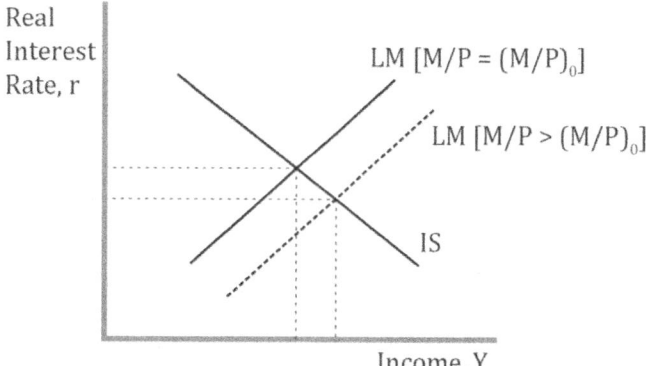

- Demand for real money is a decreasing function of interest rates. If interest rates are high people would rather invest money than hold money.

Aggregate demand curve

Intersection of IS and LM curves for different price levels gives us the aggregate demand curve. The aggregate demand curve shows the negative relationship between GDP (real output) and the price level.

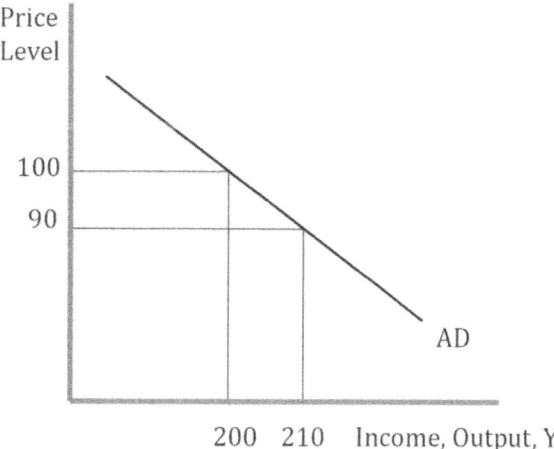

Movements along the AD curve:

Points on this curve satisfy two equilibrium conditions: aggregate income = planned expenditure (IS curve) and supply of money = demand for money (LM curve).

Shifts in the AD curve:

Shifts in AD are caused by changes in household wealth, business and consumer expectations, capacity utilization, fiscal policy, monetary policy, currency exchange rates and global economic growth rates. The equation GDP = C + I + (G - T) + (X - M), is useful in determining the direction of the shift.

Aggregate supply curve

The **aggregate supply curve** shows the positive relationship between GDP and the price level

- In the **very short run,** companies change output to some degree without changing prices.
- In the **short run** input prices are fixed so businesses expand real output when output prices increase.
- In the **long run** aggregate supply is perfectly inelastic (vertical) and represents the **potential GDP** which is the full-employment level of economic output.

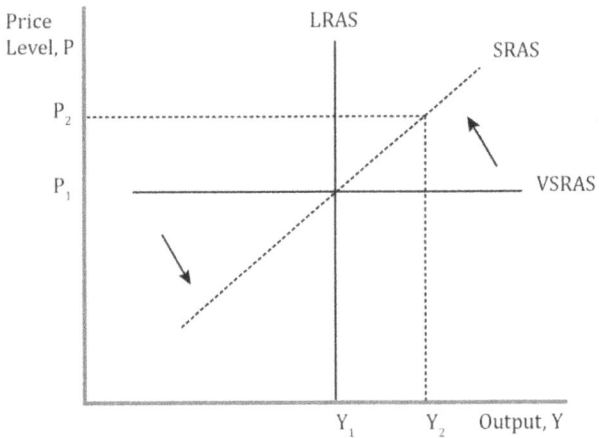

Shifts in the SRAS are cause by changes in input prices, expectations about the future, changes in business tax rates, changes in subsidies, currency exchange rates.

Shifts in the LRAS are caused by changes in labor supply, availability of natural resources, stock of physical capital, changes in productivity and technology

Macroeconomic equilibria

Short-run recessionary gap
- Refers to a situation where real GDP (as determined by the intersection of AD and SRAS) is ***less than*** potential GDP (as determined by the intersection of AD and LRAS)
- Results in a downward pressure on input prices which causes an increase in SRAS back

towards long-run equilibrium

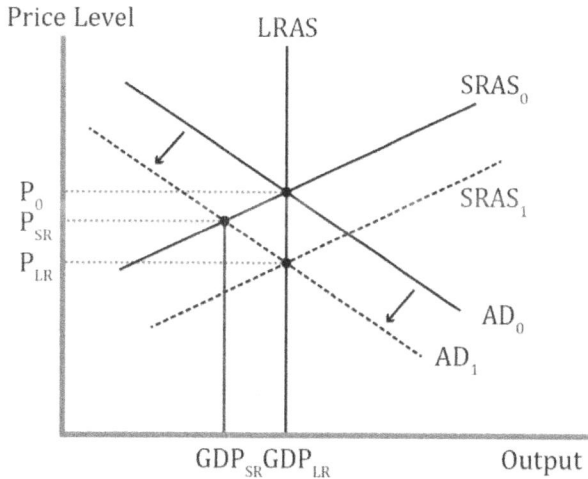

Short-run inflationary gap
- Refers to a situation where real GDP (as determined by the intersection of AD and SRAS) is *more than* potential GDP (as determined by the intersection of AD and LRAS)
- Results in an upward pressure on input prices which causes a decrease in SRAS back towards long-run equilibrium.

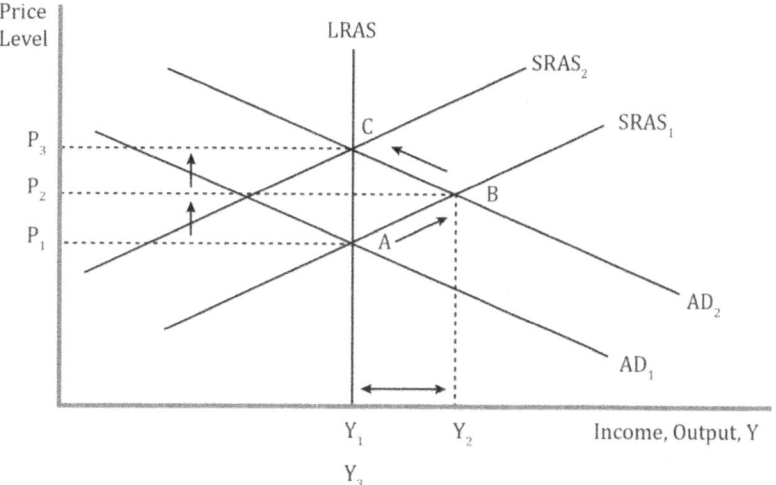

Short-run stagflation gap (Stagnant economy with inflation)
Stagflation refers to simultaneous high inflation and weak economic growth which results from a sudden decrease in short-run aggregate supply.

Economics

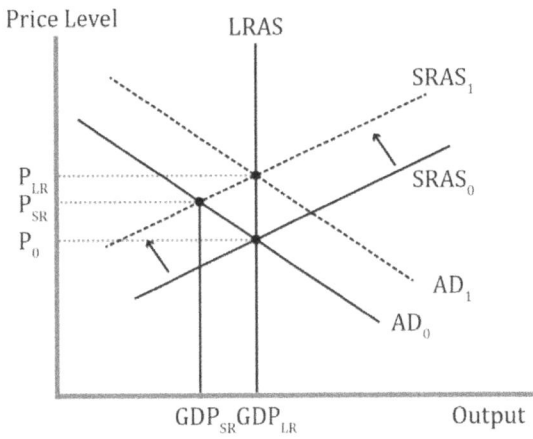

Sources of economic growth

The sources of economic growth are:
- Increase in factors of production: labor, human capital, physical capital, natural resources.
- Advances in technology.

Potential GDP = total hours worked * labor productivity

Potential GDP growth = technology growth + W_L(labor growth) + W_C(capital growth)
where:
W_L = Labor's percentage share of national income
W_C = Capital's percentage share of national income

Growth in per capita potential GDP = Growth in technology + Wc (Growth in K/L ratio)

Production function approach

Production function describes the relationship between output and labor, capital stock and productivity.

$Y = A * f(L, K)$
where:
Y = aggregate economic output,
L = size of labor force,
K = capital available,
A = total factor productivity

Total factor productivity accounts for the amount of output that cannot be explained by capital and labor increases. It relates to technological advances.

R17 Understanding Business Cycle

Business cycle

Business cycles refer to the fluctuation in economic activity where the real GDP and unemployment vary through time. The four stages of the business cycle are: expansion, peak, contraction and trough.

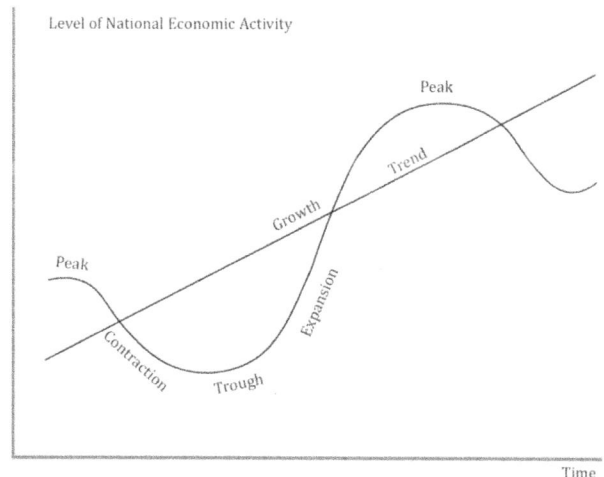

Business cycle characteristics

Trough:
- GDP growth rate changes from negative to positive.
- High unemployment rate and a moderate or declining inflation.
- Increasing production to meet the pickup in sales with more flexible methods like overtime or increasing utilization levels.
- Housing activity starts to pick up coupled with an increase in consumer spending.

Expansion:
- GDP growth rate increases.
- Reduction in unemployment rate as hiring rises.
- Inflation may begin to rise.
- Increasing production needs are met with investments and labor force additions.
- Housing demand leads to a rise in construction activity.
- Import increases as the domestic GDP increases.

Peak:
- GDP growth rate decreases.
- Unemployment rate decreases but firms cut back on hiring.
- Business and consumer confidence declines, slowing the growth rates in investments and consumer spending.
- Inflation rate increases.

Contraction (Recession):
- GDP growth rate is declining.
- Unemployment rate increases as firms cut back on production.

- Inflation decreases with a lag.
- Decline in consumer and business confidence lowers the investment and consumer spending.
- Housing activity starts to decline.
- Import decreases as the domestic GDP decreases.

Theories of the business cycle

Theory	Causes of Business Cycles	Recommended Policy
Neoclassical	Changes in technology.	No action is necessary; wages and prices adjust through demand-supply characteristics pulling or pushing the economy form expansion or recession level to its full-employment level.
Keynesian	Shifts in AD due to changes in business expectations can lead to over or under investments. Downward sticky wages prevent a self-recovery from contraction (SRAS curve is slow to move down).	Authorities should use fiscal and/or monetary policy to shift the AD curve directly to get the GDP to its full employment level.
New Keynesian	In addition to Keynesian beliefs, this theory believes other factors of production are also downward sticky, presenting additional barriers to self-recovery.	Same as Keynesian (use fiscal and/or monetary policy to shift the AD curve directly to get the GDP to its full employment level).
Monetarist	Inappropriate changes in money supply growth rate.	Monetary authorities should follow policies of steady, predictable growth rate of money supply.
Austrian	Government intervention in economy.	Policymakers shouldn't keep interest rates at artificially low levels. Markets should be allowed to self-correct.
New Classical (RBC Theory)	Changes in technology and external shocks.	Policymakers shouldn't try to counteract business cycles, as expansions and contractions are rational market reactions to external shocks. Theory assumes that individuals and firms try to maximize their utility functions.

Economics

Unemployment

Unemployment types
- **Frictional unemployment** is caused by the time lag necessary to match employees seeking work with employers seeking their skills.
- **Structural unemployment** is caused by long-run changes in the economy that eliminate some jobs and require workers to gain new skills to be capable of the available jobs.
- **Cyclical unemployment** is caused by changes in the business cycle.

Measures of unemployment
- To be considered unemployed, a person must be actively searching for work.
- **Labor force** includes employed and unemployed people.
- **Participation ratio (Activity ratio)** = Labor Force / working-age population (Age group: 16 - 64).
- Unemployment rate is the percentage of labor force that is unemployed; unemployment rate = unemployed people / labor force.
- **Discouraged workers** are those who are available for work but are neither employed nor actively seeking employment.
  - They are not considered in the labor force, not counted as unemployed.
  - With better job prospects in an expansion, these workers start actively seeking work. This adds to the labor force and makes the unemployment ratio a lagging indicator of business cycle.
- **Underemployed** individual is a person who is employed at a low-paying job despite being qualified for a significantly higher-paying one or works part time despite his preference for full time work.

Inflation, hyperinflation, disinflation & deflation

- **Inflation** is the persistent increase in general price levels over time. The inflation rate refers to the percentage increase in price level over a period.
- **Disinflation** refers to the decrease in the inflation rate over time i.e. price levels are increasing at a lower rate (e.g. from 6% to 4%).
- **Deflation** is the persistent decrease in general price levels over time.
- **Hyperinflation** refers to out of control acceleration of inflation which can destroy a country's monetary system and bring about social and political upheavals.

Construction of indices used to measure inflation

- **Price index** serves as proxy of price levels and is measured as the average price of defined basket of goods and services.
- **Inflation rate** is calculated as the price change in percentage for a basket of goods and

Economics

services from a base year.
- **Consumer price index (CPI)** uses a basket that is based on the purchasing patterns of a typical household.
  - The basket typically includes food, energy and other items.
  - Basket used in calculation varies significantly form countries to countries.
  - *Inflation rate* is calculated as the price change in the basket of goods and services from a base year.
  - *Headline inflation* is calculated for the entire basket.
  - *Core inflation* includes all the items except food and energy as they are relatively volatile.
- **Wholesale price index (WPI) or Producer price index (PPI)** uses basket of raw materials, intermediate goods and finished goods to get an earlier indication of the price increase.

Inflation measures

Laspeyres index is the most common type of index; which uses a constant basket of goods and services. The three factors that cause the index to biased upwards are:
- New goods: Older goods are replaced by newer goods that are initially more expensive.
- Quality changes: Quality improvements can cause the increase in basket price without any inflation.
- Substitution: Consumers prefer substitute products.

Paasche index uses the current weights of basket to derive the base year basket price while determining the rate of change. It is used to address the issue arising from substitution.

Fischer index is a geometric mean of Laspeyres and Paasche index.

Compute the Paasche index for the following simple basket of goods:

Item	Base period quantity	Base period price	Current period quantity	Current price
Apparel	100	25.00	105	30.00
Burgers	50	3.50	40	4.50
Gasoline	80	2.00	95	3.50
Books	65	4.00	50	3.00

Solution:
Base period:
Apparel = 105 * 25 = 2,625
Burgers = 40 * 3.5 = 140

Gasoline = 95 * 2 = 190
Books = 50 * 4 = 200
Cost of basket = 3,155

Current period:
Apparel = 105 * 30 = 3,150
Burgers = 40 * 4.5 = 180
Gasoline = 95 * 3.5 = 332.5
Books = 50 * 3 = 150
Cost of basket = 3,812.5

Paasche index $= \dfrac{3,812.5}{3,155} * 100 = 121$

Cost-push and demand-pull inflation

Cost-push inflation
- Results from a decrease in aggregate supply caused by an increase in the real price of an important factor of production, such as labor or energy.
- Initially decreases the GDP.

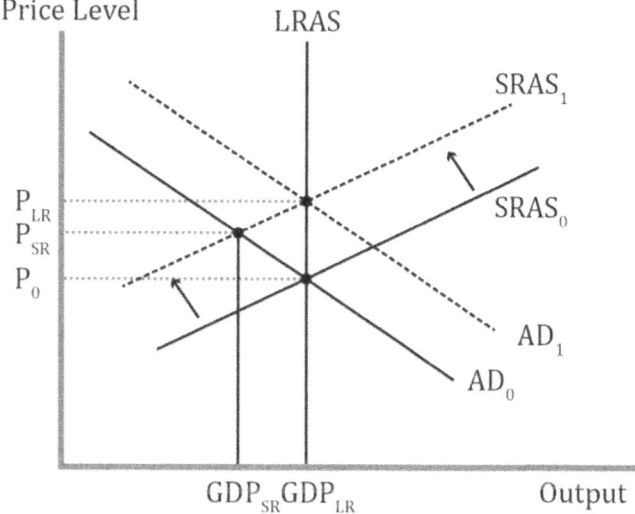

- Increased wages push the SRAS curve upwards, leading to drop in the output to GPD$_{SR}$.
- To combat the fall in GDP and increase in the unemployment levels, policymakers adopt measures to increase the AD curve. This results in further increase in the price levels.

Demand-pull inflation
- Results from persistent increase in aggregate demand that increase the price level and temporarily increase economic output above its potential or full-employment level.

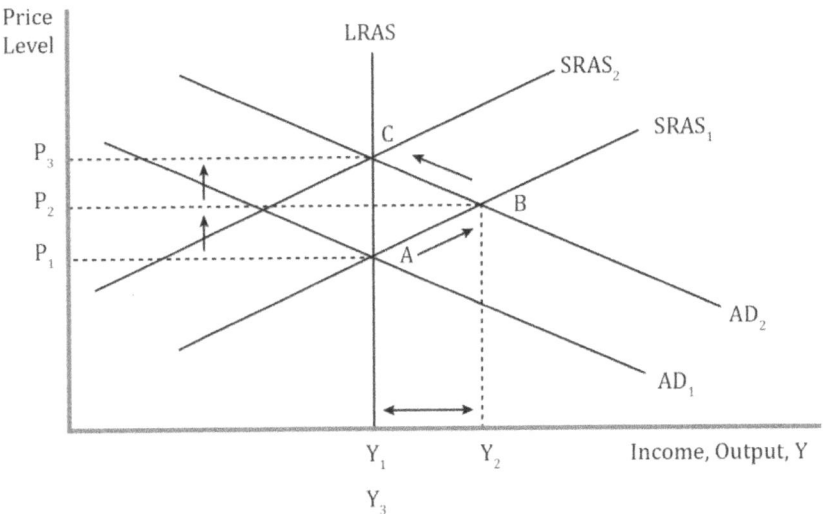

- Initially raises the GDP.
- Increase in money supply or government spending can pull the AD curve upwards, temporarily increasing the overall output and price levels.
- However, lower unemployment rates at the GDP_{SR} level can push the wages higher (shifting the SRAS curve upwards).
- This will restore the economy at its full-employment level, however at higher prices.

Non-accelerating inflation rate of unemployment (NAIRU) is the lowest unemployment rate that will not induce wage-push (cost-push) inflation. It is also known as the natural rate of unemployment (NARU).

Economic indicators

Economic indicators are used to assess the current state of the economy by analysts and to provide information about future economic activity. The three types of indicators are:

Leading indicators have turning points that tend to precede those of the business cycle. For example, weekly hours in manufacturing, S&P 500 return, private building permits, initial unemployment claims, and real M2 money supply.

Coincident indicators have turning points that tend to coincide with those of the business cycle and are used to indicate the current phase of the business cycle. For example, manufacturing activity, personal income, number of non-agricultural employees.

Lagging indicators have turning points that tend to occur after those of the business cycle. For example, bank prime lending rate, inventory-to-sales ratio, average duration of unemployment, change in unit labor costs.

R18 Monetary & Fiscal Policy

Monetary v/s fiscal policy

Both policies are used to maintain stable prices and promote positive economic growth.

Monetary policy: Refers to central bank actions aimed at influencing the money supply and credit in an economy through interest rates, repo rates, open market operations and other methods.

- Expansionary or accommodative or easy monetary policy: Increases money supply and credit in the economy.
- Contractionary or restrictive or tight monetary policy: Decreases money supply and credit in the economy.

Fiscal policy: Refers to government actions aimed at influencing economic activity through taxation and spending.

- Balanced budget: Tax revenues equal government spending.
- Budget surplus: Tax revenues exceed government spending.
- Budget deficit: Tax revenues are less than government spending.

Functions and definitions of money

Money serves as the most generally accepted medium of exchange. It has the following three functions:

- Medium of exchange: Accepted as a means of payments for goods or services.
- Unit of account: Prices of all goods and services can be expressed in units of money.
- Store of value: Money earned now for goods and services can be used later to purchase other goods and services.

Definitions of money

Narrow money: Includes the amount of notes and coins in circulation plus the balances of checkable bank deposits.

Broad Money: In addition to narrow money, it also includes other liquid assets that can be used to make purchases.

Federal Reserve Bank of New York classification:
- M1 = Currency in circulation + traveller's checks + demand deposits + checkable deposits
- M2 = M1 + savings accounts + time deposits (<$100,000) + amount in retail money market mutual funds

Economics

Money creation process

- A **fractional reserve banking system** refers to the money multiplying effect which results from the operations of the banks.
- For each $100 deposited in a bank, it must maintain certain portion of it as reserves to meet the withdrawal requests. Let us assume the reserve requirement is 20% i.e. $20.
- Since not all deposits are likely to be withdrawn at the same time, the non-reserved amount of deposits is lent out. ($80)
- The borrowing entity then spends this money which ends up in the sellers' bank. ($80)
- Sellers bank in turn lends out $64 and maintains $16 as reserves.
- If this process of lending and borrowing continues, then each dollar will eventually create a money supply that will be greater by a factor called the **money multiplier.**
- Money multiplier $= \frac{1}{\text{reserve requirement}} = \frac{1}{0.2} = 5 \; times$
- For our example, $100 will create a money supply of $500 (which is 5 times).

Quantity theory of money

- Quantity theory of money states that total spending (in money terms) is proportional to the quantity of money.
- money supply * velocity = price * real output. (MV=PY)
- Velocity is the average number of times per year each unit of money is used.
- **Money neutrality:**
  o Real variables like real GDP and velocity are not affected by monetary variables like money supply and prices. They change slowly and hence can be considered as constant.
  o Thus any change in money supply will have a proportionate change in the price level. For example, a 3% increase in money supply will lead to 3% increase in average prices.

Theories of the demand for and supply of money

Demand for money refers to the amount that households and business entities are likely to hold in money. Three factors influencing demand for money are as follows:

- Transaction demand: Money needed to undertake transactions. As GDP level increases, the number and the sizes of transaction increases, this increases demand for money.
- Precautionary demand: Money needed to meet unexpected events. As GDP level increases, the money required to address unexpected events increases, this increases demand for money.
- Speculative demand: Money needed to take advantage of investment opportunities that might arise. It is directly proportional to the perceived risk in the market i.e. with higher perceived risk demand for money will increase.

Supply and demand for money

- Supply of money in the economy is determined by central bank of the country which is a perfectly inelastic curve (vertical).
- Demand for money is inversely related to the interest rates i.e. at lower rates of returns in financial asset like bonds and stocks, demand for money would be high.
- Increase in money supply will switch the supply curve to the right and lower the equilibrium interest rates as entities invest the surplus cash in financial assets. This will increase security prices and lower interest rates.
- Decrease in money supply will switch the supply curve to the left and increase the equilibrium interest rates as entities withdraw investments from financial assets to maintain cash balances. This will decrease security prices and increase interest rates.

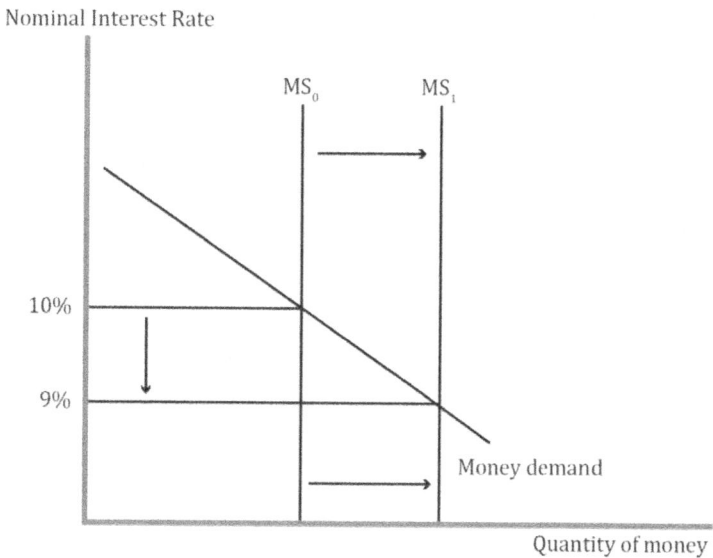

Fisher effect

The **Fischer effect** states that a nominal risk-free interest rate is equal to the real interest rate plus the expected inflation rate.

$R_{Nominal} = R_{Real} + E[I]$

where:

$R_{Nominal}$ = nominal interest rate
R_{Real} = real interest rate
$E[I]$ = expected inflation

Roles and objectives of central banks

Roles of central bank

- <u>Supply currency</u>: Central banks have the sole authority to supply money.
- <u>Banker to government and other banks</u>: Central banks provide banking services to the

government and other banks in the country.
- Regulate risk and supervise payment system: Central banks regulate the risk standards in the banking systems and monitor the payment system to ensure smooth transactions.
- Lender of last resort: Central banks can print money when the need arises.
- Repository of gold and foreign exchange reserves: Holds a country's gold and foreign exchange reserves.
- Conducts monetary policy: Central bank controls the money supply in an economy.

Objectives of central bank
- Control inflation (primary objective): A controlled inflation level promotes price stability which is conducive to a stable economic development.
- Exchange rate stability: Countries that have their domestic currency pegged to another currency must make an effort to match its inflation rate with that country.
- Full employment: Take measures that move the economy to its full potential level of employment.
- Sustainable positive economic growth.
- Moderate long-term interest rates.

Costs of expected and unexpected inflation

Costs of expected inflation
- Menu costs: Due to high inflation, businesses constantly have to change the advertised prices of their goods and services. This is known as menu cost.
- Shoe leather costs: In times of high inflation, people would naturally tend to hold less cash and would therefore wear out their shoe leather in making frequent trips to the banks to withdraw cash. This is known as shoe leather cost.

Costs of unexpected inflation
- Higher risk premiums: Lenders will demand higher rates if there is high uncertainty in inflation; the borrowing costs for firms goes up which negatively impacts the economy.
- Lower information content of market prices: Information about supply and demand from changes in prices becomes less reliable.
- Inequitable transfers of wealth between borrowers and lenders: If inflation is higher than expected then borrowers benefit at the expense of lenders, because the real value of borrowing declines. Similarly, if inflation is lower than expected, then lenders benefit at the expense of borrowers because the real value of the payment on debt increases.

Tools used to implement monetary policy

The three tools available to central banks to control the money supply are:

Policy rates

- **Borrowing from central bank:**
    - Banks can borrow from central bank to meet shortfall in reserves at a rate called discount rate or refinancing rate or repo rate. This is facilitated through **repurchase agreements**.
    - A lower repo rate increases money supply and encourages lending, this lowers interest rates.
    - On the other hand, a higher repo rate decreases money supply and reduces lending, this increases interest rates.
- **Interbank lending:**
    - Banks can lend to each other overnight loan reserves at a rate called federal funds rate (for US banks).
    - Fed uses open market operations to move it to the targeted rate.

Open market operations

- Central bank buys securities → Investors and banks get cash → increases banks excess reserves → increases money supply and encourages lending → lowers interest rates.
- Central bank sells securities → Investors and banks pay cash → lowers bank excess reserves → decreases money supply and reduces lending → increases interest rates.
- Frequently used in US.

Reserve requirements

- Represents the deposits to be maintained to meet withdrawal limits.
- Increase in reserve requirement → decreases money supply and reduces lending → increases interest rates.
- Decrease in reserve requirement → increases money supply and encourages lending → decreases interest rates.

Monetary transmission mechanism

Monetary transmission mechanism: mechanism through which a central bank's interest rate gets transmitted through the economy and ultimately affects inflation.

Contractionary monetary policy in which money supply is reduced will have the following impact:

- Banks short-term lending rates will increase.
- Asset prices of bonds and equities will decrease.
- Expectation of future economic growth will decrease.
- Domestic currency may appreciate relative to foreign currency.

The overall impact of increase in interest rates is to decrease aggregate demand and put downward pressure on the price level.

The opposite holds true for an expansionary monetary policy.

Qualities of effective central banks

Effective central bank should have the following three qualities to achieve the desired inflation rate:
- **Independence:** Central banks should be free from political interference.
- **Credibility:** A central bank should follow through on its stated policy intentions thereby making its inflation targets a self-fulfilling prophecy.
- **Transparency:** Makes public the interest rate determining policy and the economic indicators it relies on, so that its decisions are easier to anticipate.

Inflation, interest rate, and exchange rate targeting by central banks

Central banks can use the following ideologies while determining its monetary policy decisions:

Interest rate targeting:
- Measures are taken to keep the interest rates within acceptable range.
- Money supply is increased and decreased when the interest rates rise above and fall below a target range.

Inflation targeting:
- Measures are taken to keep the inflation rates within acceptable range.
- Most commonly acceptable range is 1% to 3%.
- Usually central banks do not target 0% inflation, as any variations might lead to negative inflation rates (deflation) which is highly disruptive to the economic growth.

Exchange rate targeting:
- Measures are taken to keep exchange rates within acceptable range.
- Money supply is increased by buying foreign currency with domestic currency and vice versa.

Expansionary or contractionary monetary policy

Real trend rate is an economy's long-term sustainable growth rate.

Neutral interest rate refers to the growth rate of money supply that neither increases nor decreases the economic growth rate.

neutral interest rate = real trend rate of economic growth + inflation target

- If policy rate > neutral interest rate → contractionary monetary policy.
- If policy rate < neutral interest rate → expansionary monetary policy.

Limitations of monetary policy

The will of the monetary authority does not necessarily transmit seamlessly through the economy.

This is because central banks cannot control:

- The amount of money households and corporations put in banks on deposits
- The willingness of banks to create money by expanding credit.

It is relatively easy for central banks to influence short-term rates but long term rates depend on expectations of interest rates and are not easy to control.

Roles and objectives of fiscal policy

Fiscal policy refers to the use of the government expenditures and tax revenues to influence the overall output (GDP), economic growth and employment.

- **Budget deficit** is when government expenditures exceed tax revenues and is used to tackle recession.
- **Budget surplus** is when tax revenues exceed government expenditures and is used to tackle high inflation in the expansion phase.
- Budget deficit is decreased in the expansion phase and increased in the recession phase.
- Policy measures can be either of the two:
  - Discretionary: Measures taken to tackle that particular situation.
  - Automatic: For example: When the economy slows and unemployment rises, government spending on social insurance and unemployment benefits will rise. If the economy is at full employment, taxes collected will be high and there will be a budget surplus.

Objective of fiscal policy

- Influencing economic activity and aggregate demand.
- Wealth and income distribution among segment of society.
- Resource allocation among sectors in economy.

Fiscal policy tools

Fiscal policy tools include::
Spending tools:

- Current expenditure: On-going spending on goods and services by government. For e.g. salaries of government personnel, national defense expenditure etc.
- Transfer payments: Primarily aimed at redistributing wealth. For e.g. unemployment insurance benefits, social security etc.
- Capital expenditure: Government spending on infrastructure projects to boost economic productivity. For e.g. bridges, road networks etc.

Revenue tools:

- Direct taxes: Taxes levied on wealth and income. Includes income taxes, corporate

taxes, wealth taxes capital gains taxes etc.
- Indirect taxes: Taxes levied on goods and services. Includes sales taxes, value-added taxes, excise taxes etc.

Advantages and disadvantages of fiscal policy

Advantages:
- Indirect taxes can be implemented swiftly and start generating revenue for the government immediately without incurring additional costs.
- Indirect taxes like VAT can influence spending behavior instantly and can be used to discourage consumption of sin products like alcohol and tobacco.

Disadvantages:
- Implementation of changes in direct taxes and transfer payments policies is time consuming, thereby delaying the impact of the fiscal policy.
- Capital expenditure projects like road construction have long gestation periods; delaying the impact of the fiscal policy.

Size of a national debt relative to GDP

Arguments regarding size of national debt relative to GDP:

Concerning arguments:
- Higher debt ratio → higher future taxes → discourages entrepreneurship and work → lower economic growth.
- Higher debt ratio → weakens market confidence → makes refinancing of loans difficult.
  - Debt issued in foreign currency → default.
  - Debt issued in local currency → printing money to repay → increases inflation.
- Increase in government borrowings to finance deficit → increases interest rates → private players hesitate from borrowing and investing spending decreases → lowers the overall impact of government spending (is also called as **crowding-out effect**).

Comforting arguments:
- Majority of the debt holders are domestic citizens.
- Future profits of projects executed will be sufficient to repay the debt.
- Ricardian equivalence holds i.e. private sector savings increase in anticipation of future tax liabilities which balances the government deficit.
- Tax revenues could be increased in future.
- An economy in recession can be aided by the increase in fiscal deficits.

Implementation of fiscal policy

Fiscal policy (includes the discretionary policy decisions) is difficult to execute because it suffers from the following lags:
- **Recognition lag:** Time taken to recognize the state of the economy.

Economics

- **Action lag:** Time taken by governments to determine and enact required fiscal policy changes.
- **Impact lag:** Time taken for fiscal policy to affect economic activity.

Expansionary or contractionary fiscal policy

Fiscal policy can be evaluated by two methods:

Changes in surplus or deficits:
- If surplus increases → contractionary.
- If surplus decreases → expansionary.
- If deficit increases → expansionary.
- If deficit decreases → contractionary.

Changes in revenue or spending item:
- If revenue item increases → contractionary (for e.g. VAT increases).
- If revenue item decreases → expansionary.
- If spending item increases → expansionary (for e.g. road constructions).
- If spending item decreases → contractionary.

Interaction of monetary and fiscal policy

	Easy/Expansionary Fiscal Policy	Tight Fiscal Policy
Easy/Expansionary Monetary Policy	AD up Low rates → private sector demand up Growing private and public sector	AD down Low rates → private sector stimulated The public sector will become a smaller percentage of the economy.
Tight Monetary Policy	AD up High interest rates → private sector down Public spending will become a higher percentage of GDP.	AD down High interest rates → private sector demand down Shrinking private and public sectors

R19 International Trade and Capital Flows

Gross domestic product (GDP) v/s gross national product (GNP)

Gross domestic product represents the total value of all goods and services produced within a nation's border over a period (usually a year).

Gross national product represents the total value of all goods and services produced by a nation's citizens.

GNP = GDP - contribution from foreign citizens working within the nation's border + contribution by nation's citizens to other countries across the globe.

Benefits and costs of international trade

Benefits

- Importing countries get lower-cost goods and exporting country gets better prices than domestic prices.
- Increased competition results in efficient allocation of resources and economies of scale lowers costs.
- Countries having competitive advantage will become a dominant player in that sector.
- Employment opportunities and profits in the exporting country increase.

Costs

- Workers in importing country will lose their job in the short-run and will have to obtain the necessary skill set for jobs in other sectors.
- Less efficient firms will go out of business.

Net impact: in the long-run the benefits outweigh the costs.

Comparative advantage v/s absolute advantage

- **Absolute advantage** in production of good is when a country can produce that good in lower cost in terms of resources compared to other country.
- **Comparative advantage** in production of a good is when a country can produce that good at a lower opportunity cost (amount of other good produced, if we gave up the production of this good, is low) compared to other country.
- A country will still benefit from trade even if it does not have an absolute advantage in the production of a good but does have a comparative advantage in it.

Consider the following example where costs of producing two goods - food and machine for two countries India and Japan are given.

	Food	Machine
India	70	80
Japan	100	90

Determine which country has absolute and comparative advantage in producing food.

Solution:

India has absolute advantage in producing both food and machine (Since costs for both goods are lower than that of Japan's).

In India, opportunity cost of one unit of food = 70/80 = 0.88 units of machine

In Japan, opportunity cost of one unit of food = 100/90 = 1.11 units of machine

Since the opportunity cost for food in units of machine is low for India (0.88 units) compared to Japan (1.11 units), India has comparative advantage in food.

If India has comparative advantage in food, then Japan will have a comparative advantage in machines.

In India, opportunity cost of one unit of machine = 80/70 = 1.14 units of food

In Japan, opportunity cost of one unit of machine = 90/100 = 0.90 units of food

Ricardian and Heckscher-Ohlin models of trade

Ricardian model of trade
- There is only one factor of production – labor.
- Goods are produced with varying combinations of labor.
- Differences in labor productivity due to technology is the key source of comparative advantage.

Heckscher-Ohlin model of trade
- There are two factors of production - capital and labor.
- Goods are produced with varying combinations of labor and capital.
- Differences in the relative endowment of these factors are the key source of comparative advantage.
- Countries with relatively high labor will focus on labor-intensive industries while countries with high capital will focus on capital-intensive industries.
- Income distribution will happen as price of more abundant factor of production increases. In our example, owners of capital in Japan will earn more (at the expense of labor) as price of machine increases (exports to India) and food decreases (imports from India). In India, labor will earn more (at the expense of capital) as the price of food increases (exports to Japan) and machine decreases (imports from Japan).

Trade restrictions

Types of trade restrictions
- <u>Tariffs</u>: Taxes imposed on imported goods by the government.
- <u>Quotas</u>: Restricts the absolute amount of imports allowed in a country over some period.
- <u>Export subsidies</u>: Government incentives to exporting firms which artificially reduce cost of production.
- <u>Voluntary Export Restraint</u>: Agreements by exporting countries to voluntarily restrict exported amount to avoid tariffs or quotas imposed by trading partners.

- Minimum domestic content: Restrictions imposed to ensure certain portion of the product content is produced in the country.

Effects of trade policies:

	Tariff	Quota	Export Subsidy	VER
Impact on	Importing country	Importing country	Exporting country	Importing country
Producer surplus	Increases	Increases	Increases	Increases
Consumer surplus	Decreases	Decreases	Decreases	Decreases
Government revenue	Increases	Increases if quota rent is captured.	Decreases as spending increases.	No impact
National welfare	Decreases for a small country Could increase for a large country.	Decreases for a small country Could increase for a large country.	Decreases	Decreases
Price	Increases	Increases	Increases	Increases
Domestic consumption	Decreases	Decreases	Decreases	Decreases
Domestic production	Increases	Increases	Increases	Increases
Trade	Imports decrease	Imports decrease	Exports increase	Imports decrease

Capital restrictions

Capital Restrictions refer to the restriction of flow of financial capital across countries. Types of capital restrictions include:
- Outright prohibition of investment in domestic country by foreigners.
- Prohibition of or imposing tax on income from foreign investments by domestic citizens.
- Prohibition of foreign investment in certain domestic industries.
- Restrictions on repatriation of earnings of foreign entities operating in a country.

Objectives of capital restrictions:
- Strategic reasons: Capital investments might be restricted to protect strategic or defense-related industries.
- Reduce asset price volatility: If capital inflows and outflows are high relative to the size

of the economy, macro-economic events can induce greater asset price volatility in the country.
- Maintaining exchange rate: Limiting inflows and outflows make it easier for countries with scarce foreign exchange to maintain a fixed exchange rate.
- Limiting global influences on monetary and fiscal policy: Countries can pursue monetary policy independent from concerns of the global economy.

Over the long-term, capital restrictions reduce welfare.

Types of trading blocs and regional trading agreements

- **Free-Trade Area:** All barriers to import and export of goods and services among member countries are removed. For e.g. North American Free Trade Agreement (NAFTA).
- **Customs Union:** Free-trade area + all member countries adopt a common set of trade restrictions with non-members.
- **Common Market:** Customs union + all barriers to the movement of labor and capital goods among member countries are removed.
- **Economic Union:** Common market + member countries establish common institutions and economic policy. For e.g. European Union (EU).
- **Monetary Union:** Economic union + member countries adopt a single currency. For e.g. European Zone.

Balance of payments accounts

Balance of payments (BOP) summarizes a country's transactions with the rest of the world. It has the following three components:

Current account: represents the flows related to goods and services. It includes:
- Merchandise and services:
  o Raw materials and manufactured goods sold or bought from foreign entities.
  o Charge for services rendered or sought from foreign entities.
  o Fees paid or earned from use of patents and copyrights.
- Income receipts:
  o Dividends earned on foreign stock investments.
  o Interest earned on foreign debt investments.
- Unilateral transfers of assets:
  o Remittances from labor force working abroad.
  o Direct foreign aid.

Capital account: represents acquisition and disposal of non-produced, non-financial assets. It includes:

- Capital transfers:
  - Debt forgiveness.
  - Financial assets brought in or taken out by migrants.
  - Sale or purchase of overseas fixed (physical) assets.
  - Flows related to sale or purchase of overseas fixed assets like gift & inheritance taxes, death duties and uninsured damages to fixed assets.
- Sales & purchases of non-financial assets:
  - Rights to natural resources.
  - Intangible assets like patents, copyrights, franchises, trademarks and leases.

Financial account: represents investment flows. It includes:
- Government-owned assets abroad:
  - Gold, foreign currencies and securities held abroad.
  - IMF reserve position.
  - Foreign direct investment (FDI) in foreign entities etc.
- Foreign-owned assets in the domestic country:
  - FDI in domestic entities.
  - Investments by foreign entities in the domestic country's government and corporate securities.

Influences on BOP position

Influences on the BOP position: $(X - M) = (S - I) - (G - T)$
$(X - M) = S + (T - G) - I$ = private savings + government savings − investments.
This indicates that lower private and government savings in relation to the domestic investments will increase current account or trade deficit.
This current account deficit will need to be financed from a surplus in capital account (foreign investments or borrowing).

Current account surplus can be because of:
- High private savings.
  - Government surplus $((T - G) > 0)$.
- Low private investment.

Conversely, current account deficit can be because of:
- Low private savings.
- Government deficit $((T - G) < 0)$.
- High private investment.

World Bank, International Monetary Fund, and the World Trade Organization

International Monetary Fund
- Lends foreign currencies to member states in times of significant external deficits.

- Promotes international monetary cooperation and exchange rate stability.
  - Assists in setting up international payment systems.
  - Makes resources available to member countries with balance of payments problems.

World Bank
- Help developing countries fight poverty and promote sound economic growth.
- Provides low-interest loans, interest-free credits, and grants to developing countries for many specific purposes.

World Trade Organization
- Ensures that trade flows freely and works smoothly.
- Main focus: institute, interpret, and enforce a number of multilateral trade agreements which detail global trade policies for a large majority of the world's trading nations.

R20 Currency Exchange Rates

Nominal and real exchange rates

Exchange rate is the price or cost of one currency expressed in terms of another currency. Stated otherwise, it is the number of units of the price currency needed to buy/sell one unit of the base currency.

Consider an exchange rate quote of 1.4500 USD/EUR. The numerator currency (USD) is called the price currency and the denominator currency (EUR) is called the base currency. It implies that one EUR is exchangeable with 1.45 USD.

From an investor's perspective, if the price of a currency is mentioned in his domestic currency then it is a direct quote; else it is an indirect quote. The above mentioned quote is a direct quote for the US-based investor and an indirect quote for the euro-based investor.

Nominal exchange rate is the quoted currency exchange rate at any point in time.

Real exchange rate adjusts the nominal exchange rate for inflation in each country compared to a base period.

Real exchange rate $_{P/B}$ = nominal exchange rate $_{P/B}$ x (base currency CPI / price currency CPI).

Spot exchange rate is the currency exchange rate for immediate delivery.

Forward exchange rate is the currency exchange rate for an exchange to be done in the future.

Participants in the foreign exchange market

- In terms of value of daily transactions, currency markets are the largest markets globally.

Economics

- Forex and currency swaps are the most used instrument followed by the spot transactions.
- Speculative and hedging transactions exceed international trade transactions.

Hedgers vs. speculators
- Hedgers are entities that have an existing foreign exchange risk which they want to reduce/eliminate through transactions in the forex market.
- Speculators enter into transactions that increase their foreign exchange risk with the expectation of earning a profit.

Buy side vs. sell side participants
- Sell side includes: market makers, large multinational banks.
- Buy side includes: corporations, investment fund managers, hedge fund managers, investors, governments, sovereign wealth funds and central banks.

Percentage change in a currency relative to another currency

Consider the change in USD/EUR exchange rate from 1.4560 to 1.4210.
1. Determine which currency has appreciated/depreciated.
2. Determine the percentage appreciation/depreciation in EUR.
3. Determine the percentage appreciation/depreciation in USD.

Solution:
1. Since EUR is the base currency and the quotation in terms of USD has decreased, EUR has depreciated relative to USD. In other words, USD has appreciated relative to EUR.
2. Percentage depreciation in EUR relative to USD = (1.4210/1.4560 − 1) = −2.40%.
3. For percentage appreciation in USD, we need quotes where USD is the base currency. So, 1.4560 USD/EUR → (1/1.4560) EUR/USD = 0.6868 EUR/USD
   1.4210 USD/EUR → (1/1.4210) EUR/USD = 0.7037 EUR/USD
   Percentage appreciation in USD relative to EUR = (0.7037/0.6868 − 1) = 2.46%.

Note: In a currency pair, the percentage appreciation in one currency does not equal the percentage depreciation in other currency.

Currency cross-rates

Cross rate is the exchange rate between two currencies derived from their exchange rate with a common third currency.

Consider the following exchange rates:

	Spot rate	Expected spot rate
USD/EUR	1.3690	1.3457
CHF/USD	0.9164	0.9020
USD/GBP	1.5160	1.5100

Determine the following:

Economics

1. CHF/EUR cross rates.
2. GBP/EUR cross rates.
3. CHF/GBP cross rates.
4. Does EUR appreciate/depreciate against CHF and by how much.
5. The strongest currency over the next year.

Solution:

1. Spot rate:
$$\frac{CHF}{EUR} = \frac{CHF}{USD} * \frac{USD}{EUR} = 0.9164 * 1.3690 = 1.2546$$
Expected spot rate:
$$\frac{CHF}{EUR} = \frac{CHF}{USD} * \frac{USD}{EUR} = 0.9020 * 1.3457 = 1.2138$$

2. Spot rate:
$$\frac{GBP}{EUR} = \frac{GBP}{USD} * \frac{USD}{EUR} = \left(\frac{1}{1.5160}\right) * 1.3690 = 0.9030$$
Expected spot rate:
$$\frac{GBP}{EUR} = \frac{GBP}{USD} * \frac{USD}{EUR} = \left(\frac{1}{1.5100}\right) * 1.3457 = 0.8912$$

3. Spot rate:
$$\frac{CHF}{GBP} = \frac{CHF}{USD} * \frac{USD}{GBP} = 0.9164 * 1.5160 = 1.3893$$
Expected spot rate:
$$\frac{CHF}{GBP} = \frac{CHF}{USD} * \frac{USD}{GBP} = 0.9020 * 1.5100 = 1.3620$$

4. As the quoted rate for CHF/EUR drops from 1.2546 to 1.2138, the EUR depreciates relative to CHF.
Percentage depreciation in EUR relative to CHF = (1.2138/1.2546 – 1) = -3.25%

5. From the change in quoted exchange rates we can see that USD strengthens relative to both EUR and GBP.
Whereas USD depreciates relative to CHF.
Hence, the strongest currency is CHF.

Forward quotations expressed on a points or percentage basis

- The difference between forward quote and spot quote is mentioned in points.
- For example, a quote of +100 points for a 180-day forward quote means that the forward rate is 0.0100 more than the spot rate. So, if the spot rate is 1.3000 USD/EUR the forward quote becomes 1.3100.
- To convert points to decimal divide by 10,000: 100/10,000 = 0.01.

The USD/EUR spot exchange rate is 1.4345 with 90-day forward rate quoted at -50 and 1-year forward rate quoted at -0.78%. Compute the 90-day and 1-year forward rate.

Solution:
90-day forward rate = 1.4345 - 0.0050 = 1.4295 USD/EUR
1-year forward rate = 1.4345 (1 - 0.0078) = 1.4233 USD/EUR

Arbitrage relationship between spot rates, forward rates, and interest rates

Forward rates must have the following relationship with spot rates to ensure that there is no arbitrage. This equation is also known as the interest rate parity relation.

Forward rate $_{P/B}$ = Spot rate $_{P/B}$ (1 + Interest rate$_P$) / (1 + Interest rate$_B$)

- The currency with the higher (lower) interest rate will always trade at a discount (premium) in the forward market.
- Interest rate differential = $i_{\text{Price currency}} - i_{\text{Base currency}}$
- Percentage change in spot rates is proportional to the interest rate differential.

The exchange rate between AUD/HKD is 0.1526 and the one-year riskless HKD interest rate is 7% while one-year riskless AUD interest rate is 3%. What will be the one-year forward exchange rate that prevents arbitrage?

Solution:
For there to be no arbitrage, interest rate parity must hold:

$$F_{AUD/HKD} = S_{AUD/HKD} * \frac{(1+\text{interest}_{AUD})}{(1+\text{interest}_{HKD})} = 0.1526 * \frac{(1+0.03)}{(1+0.07)} = 0.1469$$

Since HKD has higher interest rate, it should trade at a discount in forward market.
Discount in HKD = (0.1469/0.1526 − 1) = -3.74%
Interest rate differential = interest$_{AUD}$ − interest$_{HKD}$ = 3% − 7% = −4%
Hence the currency with higher interest rate should depreciate over time by approximately the interest rate differential.

If the 180-day LIBOR rates (annualized) for the EUR and GBP are 1.280% and 1.175% respectively and the spot GBP/EUR exchange rate is 0.8128. Compute the forward points for 180-day forward rate for GBP/EUR.

Solution:

$$F_{GBP/EUR} = S_{GBP/EUR} * \frac{\left(1+\text{interest}_{GBP}*\frac{n}{360}\right)}{\left(1+\text{interest}_{EUR}*\frac{n}{360}\right)} = 0.8128 * \frac{\left(1+0.01175*\frac{180}{360}\right)}{\left(1+0.01280*\frac{180}{360}\right)} = 0.8124$$

Forward points = (Forward rate − Spot rate) * 10,000 = (0.8124 - 0.8128) * 10,000 = -4 points

Intuition:
Since the EUR interest rate is higher, EUR trades at a discount compared to the GBP.

Exchange rate regimes

Exchange rate regimes for countries that do not have their own currency:
- **Formal dollarization**: A country uses the currency of another currency, typically the

US dollar.
- **Monetary Union**: Several countries use a common currency.

Exchange rate regimes for countries that have their own currency:
- **Currency board system**: An explicit commitment to exchange domestic currency for a specified foreign currency at a fixed exchange rate.
- **Fixed parity**: A country pegs its currency within margins of 1% vs. another currency.
- **Target zone**: Like fixed parity but with wider bands (+/- 2%); gives monetary authority more flexibility.
- **Crawling peg**: Exchange rate is adjusted periodically, typically to adjust for higher inflation versus the currency used in the peg.
- **Managed float**: Monetary authority attempts to influence the exchange rate in response to specific indicators – balance of payments, inflation rates, or employment – without any specific target exchange rate.
- **Independently float**: Exchange rate is entirely market-driven.

Effects of exchange rates on countries' international trade and capital flows

The effect of a depreciation of the domestic currency on a country's trade balance can be analysed using either the elasticities approach or the absorption approach.

Elasticities approach: For a depreciation of the domestic currency to reduce an existing trade deficit, the elasticities (ε) of export and import demand must meet the Marshall-Lerner Condition: $\omega_X \varepsilon_X + \omega_M (\varepsilon_M - 1) > 0$. Where ε = elasticity; ω = the proportion of total trade for imports or exports.

The J-Curve Effect: In the short-run, existing contracts make exports and imports relatively inelastic – therefore, currency depreciation initially leads to a larger trade deficit; but in the long run, elasticities increase and the currency depreciation leads to trade deficit reduction.

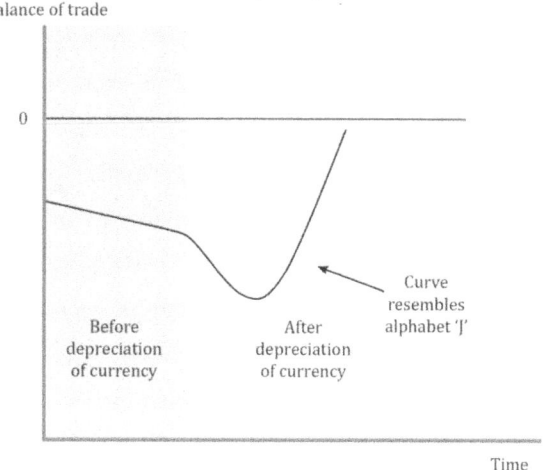

Absorption approach: National income must increase relative to national expenditure in order to decrease a trade deficit. In other words, national saving must increase relative to domestic investment in order to decrease a trade deficit.

$X - M = (S - I) + (T - G)$

$X - M = (C + S + T) - (C + I + G)$ → Balance of trade = national income – total expenditure

Financial Reporting and Analysis

R21 Financial Statement Analysis: An Introduction

Role of financial reporting and financial statement analysis

Financial reporting: The role of financial reporting is to provide information about a firm's performance and financial position. Financial reports include: balance sheet, income statement, cash flow statement, statement of changes in equity.

Financial statement analysis: The role of financial statement analysis is to use the financial reports in combination with other sources of information to decide whether to invest in a firm.

Role of financial statements

Balance sheet reports the firm's financial position at a specific point in time. It has the following elements:
- Assets – what the company owns.
- Liabilities – what the company owes.
- Owner's equity – what the owners own.

The relationship between the elements can be shown as:

Assets = liabilities + owner's equity

Income statement reports the financial performance of the firm over a period of time. It has the following elements:
- Revenues – income generated by selling goods and services.
- Expenses – costs incurred for producing goods and services.
- Net income – resulting profit or loss.

The relationship between the elements can be shown as:

Net income = revenues - expenses

Cash flow statement reports the sources and uses of cash for the firm over a period of time. It has the following elements:
- Operating cash flows – cash flows from day-to-day activities.
- Investing cash flows - cash flows associated with the acquisition and disposal of long-term assets, such as property and equipment.
- Financing cash flows - cash flows from activities related to obtaining or repaying capital to be used in the business.

Statement of changes in owner's equity reports the changes in the owners' investment in the firm over time. It has the following elements:
- Paid in capital – amount raised from owners.
- Retained earnings – amount of firm's profits that have been retained.

Financial Reporting and Analysis

Financial statement notes and supplementary information

Footnotes provide additional details about the information presented in financial statements. This includes important information about the accounting methods, estimates and assumptions. They also contain information regarding acquisitions and disposals, commitments and contingencies, legal proceedings, employee stock options and other benefits, related party transactions and business and geographic segments.

Management's commentary provides an assessment of the data reported in the financial statements from the management's perspective. Examples of content include trends and significant events affecting the company's operations, liquidity and capital resources, off-balance sheet obligations and planned capital expenditures.

Audits of financial statements

Audit is an independent review of a firm's financial statements. It enables the auditor to express an opinion on the fairness and reliability of the financial reports. An audit report can contain one of the following opinions:
- Unqualified opinion - reasonable assurance that financial statements are fairly presented.
- Qualified opinion - some misstatement or exception to accounting standards.
- Adverse opinion - financial statements are not presented fairly.

Effective internal controls are important to ensure the accuracy of financial statements. A firm's management is responsible for maintaining an effective internal control system.

Other information sources

Apart from the financial statements, other information sources available for an analyst are:
- **Interim reports** – quarterly or semiannual reports prepared by the firm.
- **Proxy statements** - statements distributed to shareholders about matters that are to be put to a vote.
- **Press releases, conference calls, websites** – firms often provide current information via these mediums.
- **External sources** – information about the economy, industry and the firm's competitors.

Financial statement analysis framework

The financial statement analysis framework consists of the following six steps:
1. Define the purpose and context of the analysis.
    - Define the context of the analysis based on your function, client inputs and organizational guidelines.
    - Determine the time frame and the resources available for the task.

Financial Reporting and Analysis

2. Collect data.
    - Collect data from financial statements and other information sources.
3. Process the data.
    - Make adjustments to financial statements.
    - Create graphs, ratios, common-sizes statements, etc.
4. Analyze and interpret the processed data.
5. Develop and communicate conclusions.
6. Follow up.
    - Conduct periodic reviews to check if previous conclusions are still valid.

R22 Financial Reporting Standards

Objective of financial statements

Objective of financial statements is to provide useful information about a firm's financial performance to existing and potential investors, lenders and other creditors. This will help them in making decisions like – buying and selling equity and debt instruments of the firm.

Importance of financial reporting standards in security analysis and valuation:
Financial reporting standards ensure that there is consistency in the preparation of financial reports. This ensures that financial reports of different firms are comparable to one another. A firm's management uses estimates and assumptions to prepare financial reports. Financial reporting standards ensure that the assumptions and estimates are within a narrow reasonable range. This makes financial reports useful in security analysis and valuation. If there were no standards, the financial reports prepared by different firms would be very different from one another. This would make them less useful to an analyst.

Financial reporting standard-setting bodies and regulatory authorities

Standard-setting bodies are private sector organizations that help develop financial reporting standards. The two important standard-setting bodies are:
- <u>Financial Accounting Standards Board (FASB)</u> – For U.S. The standards developed by FASB are called U.S. GAAP (Generally accepted accounting principles).
- <u>International Accounting Standards Board (IASB)</u> – For rest of the world. The standards developed by IASB are called IFRS (International Financial Reporting Standards).

Desirable attributes of standard-setting bodies
- Clearly define responsibilities of all parties involved.
- Observe high professional and ethical standards.
- Have adequate authority, resources and competencies.
- Have a clear and consistent process.
- Have a well-articulated framework for guidance.

Financial Reporting and Analysis

- Seek inputs from stakeholders, but still operate independently.
- Should not succumb to pressure from external forces.
- Final decisions should be made in the public interest.

Regulatory authorities are government entities that have legal authority to enforce the financial reporting standards. The two important regulatory authorities are:
- Securities and Exchange Commission (SEC) – For US
- Financial Services Authority (FSA) – For UK

Regulatory authorities are also responsible for the regulation of capital markets under their jurisdiction.

The International Organization of Securities Commission (IOSCO) itself is not a regulatory authority but various regulatory authorities are members of IOSCO. Its members together regulate a significant portion of the financial capital markets. The core objectives of IOSCO are:
- Protect investors.
- Ensure fairness, efficiency, and transparency in markets.
- Reduce systemic risk.

Global convergence of accounting standards

IFRS is in the process of being adopted in many countries. The different standard setting bodies are working with IASB to converge their standards with IFRS. The challenges in full convergence are:
- Difference of opinion among standard-setting bodies and regulatory authorities from different countries.
- Political pressure from industry lobbying groups that will be affected by the change.

International Accounting Standards Board's (IASB) conceptual framework

Objective of financial statements: As per the IFRS framework, the objective of financial statements is 'to provide financial information about the reporting entity that is useful to existing and potential investors, lenders and other creditors in making decisions about providing resources to the entity'.

Qualitative characteristics: The two fundamental qualitative characteristics are:
- <u>Relevance</u>: Financial statements should be useful both for making forecasts as well as to evaluate past forecasts. They should be timely and sufficiently detailed and important facts should not be omitted.
- <u>Faithful representation</u>: Information presented should be complete, neutral and free from errors.

The four supplementary qualitative characteristics are:

- Comparability: Financial statements should be consistent over time and across firms to facilitate comparisons.
- Verifiability: Independent observers should be able to verify that information reflects true economic reality.
- Timeliness: Information should be available in a timely manner.
- Understandability: Information should be presented in simple manner, such that even users with basic business knowledge can understand it.

Constraints
- Tradeoff between reliability and timeliness. If a firm tries to make statements that have no errors and are highly reliable it will need a lot of time. Similarly, if a firm tries to make statements in the least amount of time they will have more errors and be less reliable.
- Cost: The benefit that the users gain from using the reports should be more than the cost of preparing the reports
- Intangible aspects: Intangible information such as brand name and customer loyalty cannot be captured directly in financial statements.

Assumptions
- Accrual basis: Revenue should be recognized when earned and expenses should be recognized when incurred, irrespective of when the cash is actually paid.
- Going concern: Assumption that the company will continue operating for the foreseeable future.

Reporting elements
- Elements related to measurement of financial position are: assets, liabilities, equity.
- Elements related to measurement of financial performance are: income, expenses.

General requirements under International Financial Reporting Standards (IFRS)

Required financial statements are: balance sheet, income statement, cash flow statement, statement of changes in owner's equity, explanatory notes.

General features for preparing financial statements are:
- Fair presentation: Faithful representation of transactions.
- Going concern: Assume firm will continue to exist for foreseeable future.
- Accrual basis: Recognize revenue when earned and expense when incurred.
- Materiality and aggregation: Important information should not be omitted. Similar information should be grouped together.
- No offsetting: Assets and liabilities, Income and expenses should not be offset against each other
- Frequency of reporting: Prepare statements at least annually.

- Comparative information: Comparable information for prior periods should be included.
- Consistency: Prepare reports in the same manner every period.

Structure and content requirements: Firms should use the classified balance sheet structure (which shows current and non-current assets and liabilities separately). Certain minimum information must be presented in the notes and on the face of the financial statements.

Key concepts of IFRS and US GAAP reporting systems

U.S. GAAP uses standards issued by FASB while IFRS uses standards issued by IASB. The two organizations are working towards conversion but still have some differences:

Performance Elements: IASB lists income and expenses as performance elements, whereas the FASB lists revenue, expenses, gains, losses and comprehensive income.

Financial position elements: IASB defines asset as a resource from which future economic benefit is expected to flow. Whereas, FASB defines an asset as a future economic benefit.

Recognition of elements: IASB uses the word 'probable' in its revenue recognition criteria. Whereas, FASB does not use it.

Measurement of elements: IASB allows upward revaluation of assets whereas FASB does not.

Characteristics of a coherent financial reporting framework

The characteristics of a coherent financial reporting framework are:
- **Transparency**: Full disclosure and fair presentation.
- **Comprehensiveness:** All transactions should be recorded, including those already in existence and those that will emerge with time.
- **Consistency:** Similar transactions should be recorded in similar ways, irrespective of industry type, geography and time period.

The barriers to single coherent framework are differences in:
- **Valuation:** Tradeoff between reliability and relevance.
  If historical cost is used which requires less judgment then asset values will be more reliable but less relevant. If fair value is used which requires more judgment then asset values will be more relevant but less reliable.
- **Standard setting approach:** Reporting standards can be based on one of the following approaches
  - Principles-based approach: Relies on a broad framework, provides limited guidance on how to report specific transactions.
  - Rules-based approach: Gives detailed rules on how to report specific

transactions.
- ○ <u>Objectives-oriented approach</u>: Combination of the two.

IFRS has a principles-based approach. US GAAP historically followed a rules-based approach, but is recently moving towards objectives-oriented approach.

- **Measurement:** Tradeoff between asset/liability approach and revenue/expense approach.

  Asset/liability approach focuses on proper valuation of elements at a point in time, i.e. it focuses on the balance sheet. If we use this approach, we will get more reliable balance sheet but less reliable income statement. Revenue/ expense approach focuses on proper valuation of changes in the elements over a period of time, i.e. it focuses on the income statement. If we focus on this approach, we will get more reliable income statement but less reliable balance sheet.

Monitoring developments in financial reporting standards

It is important for analysts to be aware that reporting standards are evolving rapidly. They need to monitor developments in financial reporting standards and assess their implications for security analysis and valuation. To do this, an analyst can monitor three sources:

- New products or transactions in capital markets.
- Actions of standard setting bodies.
- Company's disclosures regarding critical accounting policies and estimates.

Company disclosures of significant accounting policies

Both IFRS and U.S. GAAP, require companies to disclose their accounting policies and estimates in the footnotes and management commentary. Companies are also required to disclose the likely impact of recent change in accounting standards on their financial statements. These disclosures can alert analysts to significant changes that could affect security valuation.

R23 Understanding Income Statements

Components of the income statement

Components of income statement: Income statement is also called 'profit and loss statement', 'statement of earnings' or 'statement of operations'. The components of income statement are:

- <u>Revenues</u>: Income generated from the sale of goods and services in the normal course of the business. Net revenue is the total revenue minus products that were returned and amounts that are unlikely to be collected.

Financial Reporting and Analysis

- Expenses: Costs incurred to generate revenues. They are grouped together by their nature or function. Costs of similar nature like depreciation of building and depreciation of equipment are grouped together. Costs associated with the same function such as production (e.g. raw materials and labor) are grouped together.
- Gains and losses: Amounts generated from non-operating activities.
- Net income: Net income can be calculated as:

Net income = revenues – expenses + gains - losses

Presentation formats: Income statements can be presented in the following two formats:
- Single-step: All revenues and all expenses are grouped together. There are no sub-totals.
- Multi-step: It includes subtotals such as gross profit and operating profit.

Gross profit = revenue – cost of goods sold
Operating profit = gross profit – operating expenses

Single-step format	
Revenue	$100,000
Cost of goods sold	$60,000
Selling, general and administrative expenses	$10,000
Depreciation expense	$10,000
Interest expense	$5,000
Taxes (10%)	$1,500
Net income	$13,500

Multi-step format	
Revenue	$100,000
Cost of goods sold	$60,000
Gross profit	**$40,000**
Selling, general and administrative expenses	$10,000
Depreciation expense	$10,000
Operating profit	**$20,000**
Interest expense	$5,000
Earnings before taxes	$15,000
Taxes (10%)	$1,500
Net income	$13,500

Revenue recognition

Criteria for revenue recognition: According to the accrual method of accounting, revenue is recognized when earned and expenses are recognized when incurred. Accrual accounting

Financial Reporting and Analysis

allows firms to manipulate net income through their choices about revenue and expense recognition. Hence to reduce manipulation, standard setting bodies have defined a criteria for revenue recognition. As per U.S. GAAP, revenue can be recognized if the following conditions are met:
- There is evidence of an arrangement between the buyer and seller.
- The product has been delivered or the service has been rendered.
- The price is determined or determinable.
- The seller is reasonably sure of collecting money.

There is a similar criteria for IFRS. From an exam perspective, knowing the U.S. GAAP criteria is good enough.

Long-term contracts extend beyond one accounting period. For example, the construction of a building that takes five years. The revenue recognition methods to be used for long-term contracts are:
- If costs and revenues can be reliably measured: Both IFRS and U.S. GAAP require **percentage of completion method.** The revenue to be recognized in a year is given by:

$$\text{Revenue recognized in a year} = \frac{\text{costs incurred in that year}}{\text{total cost of the project}} \times \text{total revenue}$$

Company ABC has a contract to construct a building. This project will take 5 years to complete. The expected total revenue from the project is $10 million and the expected total cost is $8 million. In year 1, the cost incurred by the company was $2 million. In year 2, the cost incurred by the company was $1 million. Using the percentage of completion method, what amount of revenue will the company recognize in year 1 and year 2?

Solution:

Revenue recognized in year 1 $= \frac{\$2 \text{ million}}{\$8 \text{ million}} \times \$10$ million $= \$2.5$ million

Revenue recognized in year 2 $= \frac{\$1 \text{ million}}{\$8 \text{ million}} \times \$10$ million $= \$1.25$ million

- If costs and revenues cannot be reliably measured: IFRS states that revenue can be recognized to the extent of contract costs incurred.

Company ABC has a contract to construct a building. This project will take 5 years to complete. The expected total revenue from the project is $10 million and the expected total cost is $8 million. In year 1, the cost incurred by the company was $2 million. In year 2, the cost incurred by the company was $1 million. The costs and revenues cannot be reliably measured and the company follows IFRS standards, what amount of revenue will the company recognize in year 1 and year 2?

Solution:

Revenue recognized in year 1 $= \$2$ million
Revenue recognized in year 2 $= \$1$ million

Financial Reporting and Analysis

U.S. GAAP requires the **completed contract method** in which the company does not report any income until the contract is complete.

Company ABC has a contract to construct a building. This project will take 5 years to complete. The expected total revenue from the project is $10 million and the expected total cost is $8 million. In year 1, the cost incurred by the company was $2 million. In year 2, the cost incurred by the company was $1 million. The costs and revenues cannot be reliably measured and the company follows U.S. GAAP standards, what amount of revenue will the company recognize in year 1 and year 2?

Solution:
Revenue recognized in year 1 = $0 million
Revenue recognized in year 2 = $0 million

Installment sales: In installment sales the company finances a sale and the sales proceeds are paid in installments over multiple accounting periods. For example, sale of an apartment in which the customer will pay the sale price in installments over the next 10 years. The revenue recognition methods to be used for installment sales are:

- <u>If the company is reasonably sure of collecting payments</u>: Separate installments into two components: Sales price (present value of installments) and interest component. Revenue attributable to the sales price is recognized immediately, and revenue attributable to the interest component is recognized over time.
- <u>If the collectability cannot be reasonably estimated</u>, the **installment method** is used. The profit for a period is calculated as:

$$\text{Profit for a period} = \frac{\text{cash collected in that period}}{\text{total revenue}} \times \text{total profit}$$

Company ABC sold a property at a sales price of $100,000. The cost of the property to the company was $80,000. The buyer made a down payment of $25,000 in year 1. He will be paying the remaining amount in installments over the next 10 years. For year 1, how much profit can be recognized using the installment method?

Solution:

$$\text{Proift for year 1} = \frac{\$25,000}{\$100,000} \times \$20,000 = \$5,000$$

- <u>If the collectability is highly uncertain</u>, the **cost recovery method** is used. Under this method, profits are recognized only once the total cash collections exceed total costs.

Company ABC sold a property at a sales price of $100,000. The cost of the property to the company was $80,000. The buyer made a down payment of $25,000 in year 1. He will be paying the remaining amount in installments over the next 10 years. For year 1, how much profit can be recognized using the cost recovery method?

Solution:
Profit for year 1 = $0.

Since the total cash collected ($25,000) did not exceed the total cost ($80,000), we cannot recognize any profits in year 1.

Note: We can start recognizing profits only from year 8 onward, when the total cash collected ($85,000) exceeds the total cost.

Cash collected till year 8: $85,000 → Profit for year 8 = $5,000.
Cash collected till year 9: $92,500 → Profit for year 9 = $7,500.
Cash collected till year 10: $100,000 → Profit for year 10 = $7,500

Barter transaction: In a barter transaction, two parties exchange goods or services without any cash payment. A round trip transaction is a special type of barter transaction in which the goods/services exchanged are identical to each other. Under IFRS, revenue from barter transactions can be measured using the fair value from a similar non-barter transaction with an unrelated party. Under U.S. GAAP, revenue can be recognized at fair value only if the firm has historically received cash payments for such goods.

Gross v/s net revenue reporting: Under gross revenue reporting, the selling firm reports sales revenue and cost of goods sold separately. Under net revenue reporting, only the difference between sales and cost of goods sold is reported. Thought the profit reported is the same under both methods, using gross reporting gives us higher reported sales. Gross reporting can only be used if:

- The company is the primary obligor under the contract.
- The company bears inventory and credit risk.
- The company can choose its suppliers.
- The company has reasonable latitude to establish price.

For example, an airline company would use gross reporting for tickets sold, whereas a travel agent who sells airline ticket will use net reporting.

Implications for financial analysis: Companies disclose their revenue recognition policies in the footnotes. An analyst should be able to determine the policies as conservative or aggressive. An aggressive policy would recognize revenue sooner rather than later. An analyst should also determine how difference in policies of two similar companies can impact their financial ratios.

Converged accounting standards for revenue recognition

In May 2014, the IASB and FASB issued a converged standard for revenue recognition. The standards take a principles-based approach and require the application of a five step process for recognizing revenue. The steps are:
1. Identify the contract(s) with a customer.
2. Identify the performance obligations in the contract.
3. Determine the transaction price.
4. Allocate the transaction price to the performance obligations in the contract.

Financial Reporting and Analysis

5. Recognize revenue when (or as) the entity satisfies a performance obligation.

Expense recognition

Matching principle: The most important principle of expense recognition is the matching principle, under which the expenses incurred to generate revenue are recognized in the same period as revenue.

If some goods bought in the current year remain unsold at the end of the year, they are not included in the cost of goods sold for the current year. If they are sold in the next year, they will be included in the cost of goods sold for the next year.

Periodic costs: Expenses that cannot be tied directly to generation of revenues are called periodic costs. They are expensed in the period incurred.

The rent paid for office premises are simply expensed in the period for which the rent was paid.

Inventory methods: Accounting standards permit the use of following methods to assign inventory expenses:

- 'First in first out (FIFO)' assumes that the earliest items purchased are sold first.
- 'Last in first out (LIFO)' assumes that the most recent items purchased are sold first.
- 'Weighted average cost' averages total cost over total units available.
- 'Specific identification' identifies each item in the inventory and uses its historical cost for calculating COGS, when the item is sold.

Issues in expense recognition: Some issues in expense recognition are:

- Doubtful accounts: When sales are made on credit, there is a chance that some customers will default. There are two methods of recognizing credit losses. The first one is to wait for a customer to default and then recognize a loss. This is called the direct write-off method. The second is to record an estimate of credit losses (using historical data) at the time of revenue recognition. The matching principle requires this method.
- Warranties: When a company provides warranty, there is a chance that some defective product may need to be replaced or repaired. There are two methods of recognizing warranty expense. The first one is to recognize warranty expense when warranty is claimed. The second is to estimate a warranty expense (using historical data) at the time of revenue recognition. The matching principle requires this method.
- Depreciation: It is the process of allocating costs of long-lived assets over the period during which the assets are expected to provide economic benefits. The first method is called straight line method, where we expense an equal amount of depreciation in each year of the asset's useful life. The second method is declining balance method, where a greater proportion of deprecation is allocated in the initial years and a lower proportion is allocated in later years.
- Amortization: It is the process of allocating costs of intangible assets (a non-physical

asset) over its useful life. Intangible assets with identifiable useful lives (for example a patent) are amortized evenly over their lives. Intangible assets with indefinite lives (for example goodwill) are not amortized. They are tested for impairment annually. If the asset value has come down, an expense is recorded in the income statement to bring its value down to the current value.

Implications for financial analysis: Companies disclose their expense recognition policies in the footnotes. An analyst should be able to determine the policies as conservative or aggressive. An aggressive policy would delay the recognition of expenses. An analyst should also determine how difference in policies of two similar companies can impact their financial ratios.

Non-recurring items & changes in accounting policies

Non-recurring items: A company needs to separate revenues and expenses into items that are likely to continue in the future and items that are not likely to continue in the future. This helps analysts to predict future earnings of the company. Items that are not likely to continue can be classified as:

- Discontinued operations: An operation that the company has disposed in the current period or is planning to dispose in future. On the income statement, discontinued operations are shown as a separate line item, net of tax, after net income from continuing operations.
- Extraordinary items: IFRS does not allow this classification. Under U.S. GAAP an item is extraordinary if it is both unusual in nature and infrequent in occurrence. For example, destruction of property in an earthquake. On the income statement, extraordinary items are shown as a separate line item, net of tax, after net income from continuing operations.
- Unusual or infrequent items: These items are either unusual in nature or infrequent in occurrence, but not both. For example, gains or losses from selling a manufacturing equipment. On the income statement, they are shown as a separate line item, but before tax, and are included in the income from continuing operations.

Changes in accounting standards

- Change in accounting policy: This refers to change from one accounting method to another. For example, changing inventory valuation method from LIFO to FIFO. It requires retrospective application, i.e. all prior period financial statements need to be restated as per the new method.
  A retrospective application, helps maintain comparability of the statements across different time periods.
- Changes in accounting estimate: This refers to change in the management's estimate. For example, changing the useful life of a depreciable asset. It requires prospective

application, i.e. no need to restate prior period financial statements, only statements presented going forward reflect this change.
- Correction of prior-period error: This refers to an adjustment done to correct a prior period accounting error. All prior period statements should be restated. In addition, disclosure of the nature of the adjustment is required in footnotes. Frequent errors may point to weakness in the company's accounting system or internal controls.

Operating and non-operating components of the income statement

Operating income is generated from the firm's normal business operations. Non-operating income is generated from activities outside the firm's normal business operations. For a computer manufacturer, income generated from selling computers is operating income. Interest income from investments is a non-operating income.

IFRS does not define operating activities, so companies use judgment to classify income as operating or non-operating. Under U.S. GAAP, operating activities generally involve producing and delivering goods and providing services. All other activities are non-operating.

Earnings per share (EPS)

Earnings per share is a very important profitability measure. It depicts the earnings per ordinary share. Some basic terminology related to EPS are:
- **Potentially dilutive securities:** Securities that can be converted into ordinary share are called potentially dilutive securities. This includes convertible bonds, convertible preferred stock, and employee stock options.
- **Simple capital structure:** If a company has no potentially dilutive securities, it is said to have a simple capital structure.
- **Complex capital structure:** If a company has potentially dilutive securities, it is said to have a complex capital structure.
- **Dilutive securities:** A potentially dilutive security that decreases EPS when exercised is called a dilutive security.
- **Anti-dilutive security:** A potentially dilutive security that increases EPS when exercised is called an anti-dilutive security.

Basic EPS: In this calculation, we do not consider the effect of any potentially dilutive securities. Basic EPS is calculated as:

$$\text{Basic EPS} = \frac{\text{net income} - \text{preferred dividends}}{\text{weighted average number of shares outstanding}}$$

Weighted average number of shares outstanding is the number of shares outstanding during the year, weighted by the portion of the year they were outstanding. Stock splits and stock dividends are applied retroactively to the beginning of the year, so the old shares are

Financial Reporting and Analysis

converted to new shares for consistency.

During 2001, Company ABC had a net income of $100,000. It paid $22,000 dividends to its preference shareholders and $12,000 dividends to its common shareholders. The number of common shares outstanding during 2001 were as follows:

Shares as of January 1, 2001: 10,000
Additional shares issue on July 1, 2001: 2,000

Calculate the basic EPS of the company for 2001.

Solution:

We had 10,000 shares outstanding for the first 6 months and 12,000 shares outstanding for the last 6 months.

Therefore weighted average number of shares outstanding = 10,000 x 6/12 + 12,000 x 6/12 = 11,000 shares.

Basic EPS = $\frac{\$100,000 - \$22,000}{11,000} = \$7.09$

Note: We ignore dividend paid to common shareholders.

Diluted EPS: In this calculation, we consider the effect of potentially dilutive securities. If a firm has a complex capital structure it has to report both basic and diluted EPS. Diluted EPS is calculated as:

Diluted EPS = $\frac{\text{NI} + \text{conv debt int } (1-t) - \text{pref div} + \text{conv pref div}}{\text{wt avg shares} + \text{new shares issued}}$

- For <u>preference shares</u>, we need to subtract preference share dividends from the numerator and add new shares issued from conversion to the denominator.

  During 2001, Company ABC had a net income of $100,000. It paid $22,000 dividends to its preference shareholders and $12,000 dividends to its common shareholders. It had 2,200 preference share and 11,000 common shares outstanding during 2001. Each preference share is convertible into 2 shares of common stock. Calculate the diluted EPS for the company.

  Solution:

  Number of common shares issued upon conversion = 2,200 x 2 = 4,400

  Diluted EPS = $\frac{\text{NI} + \text{conv debt int } (1-t) - \text{pref div} + \text{conv pref div}}{\text{Wt avg shares} + \text{New shares issued}}$

  Diluted EPS = $\frac{\$100,000 + 0 - \$22,000 + \$22,000}{11,000 + 4,400} = \$6.5$

- For <u>convertible bonds</u>, we need to add the after tax interest cost savings to the numerator and new shares issued from conversion to the denominator.

  During 2001, Company ABC had a net income of $100,000. The capital structure of the company for 2001 was as follows:

  11,000 common shares

  1,000 convertible bonds with par value of $100 and 10% coupon; convertible to 5,000

116

shares.
The tax rate of the company is 30%.
Calculate diluted EPS.
Solution:
Number of common shares issued upon conversion = 5,000
Interest payable on the bonds = 100 x $1,000 x 10% = $10,000

$$\text{Diluted EPS} = \frac{\text{NI+conv debt int (1-t)-pref div+conv pref div}}{\text{Wt avg shares+New shares issued}}$$

$$\text{Diluted EPS} = \frac{\$100,000+\$10,000 \times 0.7-\$0+\$0}{11,000+5,000} = \$6.69$$

- For <u>stock options</u> we use the **'Treasury Stock Method'**, which assumes that the hypothetical funds received by the company from the exercise of options are used to purchase shares of the company's common stock at the average market price over the reporting period. Thus, the numerator is unchanged and the number of shares to be added to the denominator = the number of shares created by exercising the options – number of shares hypothetically repurchased with the proceeds of the exercise.

During 2001, Company ABC had a net income of $100,000. It paid $22,000 dividends to its preference shareholders and $12,000 dividends to its common shareholders. The capital structure of the company for 2001 was as follows:

11,000 common shares
1,000 stock options outstanding, that have an exercise price of $20.
During 2001, the average market price for the company's share was $25.
Calculate the diluted EPS.

Solution:
Number of common shares issued upon conversion = 1,000
Cash proceeds from the exercise of options = 1,000 x 20 = $20,000
Number of shares that can be purchased at the average market price with these funds = $20,000/25 = 800
Net increase in common shares outstanding = 1,000 – 800 = 200

$$\text{Diluted EPS} = \frac{\text{NI+conv debt int (1-t)-pref div+conv pref div}}{\text{Wt avg shares+New shares issued}}$$

$$\text{Diluted EPS} = \frac{\$100,000+\$0-\$22,000+\$0}{11,000+200} = \$6.96$$

Common-size income statements

Common-size income statement presents each line item on the income statement as a percentage of revenue. This format standardizes the income statement and helps remove the effect of company size. They are useful to comparisons across time periods and across companies. The income statement is used to calculate ratios to evaluate a firm's profitability. The commonly used ratios are:

Gross profit margin = gross profit / revenue

Financial Reporting and Analysis

Operating profit margin = operating profit / revenue
Net profit margin = net profit / revenue

High margin ratios are desirable. A firm can increase its margins either by increasing selling price or by lowering costs, or both.

	2001	%	2002	%
Revenue	$100,000	100%	$110,000	100%
Cost of goods sold	$60,000	60%	$65,000	59%
Gross profit	**$40,000**	**40%**	**$45,000**	**41%**
Selling, general and administrative expenses	$10,000	10%	$11,000	10%
Depreciation expense	$10,000	10%	$11,000	10%
Operating profit	**$20,000**	**20%**	**$23,000**	**21%**
Interest expense	$5,000	5%	$5,500	5%
Earnings before taxes	$15,000	15%	$17,500	16%
Taxes (10%)	$1,500	1.5%	$1,750	1.6%
Net income	**$13,500**	**13.5%**	**$15,750**	**14.3%**

Looking at the above common sized statement we can conclude that, the profitability margins of this company have improved in 2002 as compared to 2001.

Financial ratios based on the income statement

Common-size income statements are useful in examining a firm's business strategies. Popularly used ratios are:

- **Net profit margin**: It is calculated as: net income / sales. This indicates how much income a company was able to generate for each dollar of revenue.
- **Gross profit margin**: It is calculated as: gross profit / sales. Where gross profit is calculated as revenue minus cost of goods sold.
- **Operating profit margin**: It is calculated as: operating profit / sales.

A firm can achieve higher profit margins by differentiating its products from the competitors.

Comprehensive income & other comprehensive income

Other comprehensive income includes transactions that are not included in net income. Four types of items treated as other comprehensive income under both IFRS and U.S. GAAP are:

- Unrealized gains /losses from available for sale securities.
- Foreign currency translation adjustments.
- Unrealized gains/losses on derivative contracts used for hedging.

- Adjustments for minimum pension liability.

Note: At Level I, you need to remember these four items, these are explained in detail at Level II.

Comprehensive income is the sum of net income and other comprehensive income. It measures all changes to equity apart from those resulting from transactions with shareholders (for example, dividends paid, and stocks repurchased are not included in comprehensive income).

Company ABC's beginning shareholder equity was $100 million; its net income for the year was $10 million. Cash dividends of $2million were paid to shareholders during the year. The company's actual ending shareholder equity is $113 million. Calculate OCI.

Solution:
Amount that has bypassed the income statement = OCI = $113 – ($100+$10-$2) = $5 million.

R24 Understanding Balance Sheets

Elements of the balance sheet

Assets are the resources controlled by the company as a result of past events, which are expected to provide future economic benefits to the entity.

Liabilities are the obligations of a company as a result of past events, which are expected to result in an outflow of economic benefits from the entity in future.

Equity represents the owner's residual interest in the company's assets after deducting its liabilities. Equity = assets – liability.

Limitations of the balance sheet in financial analysis

A balance sheet provides useful information regarding a company's financial position. However, the elements of a balance sheet cannot be viewed as a measure of either the market or the intrinsic value of a company's equity for the following reasons:

- Some assets and liabilities are measured based on historical cost while some are measured based on current value. These differences can have significant impact on reported figures.
- The value of an item reported on the balance sheet is the value at the end of the reporting period. If we are analyzing the company at a later date, these values may have changed.
- Some assets and liabilities are difficult to quantify and are not reported on the balance sheet. For example, brand, customer loyalty, and human capital.

Financial Reporting and Analysis

Alternative formats of balance sheet presentation

There are two ways of presenting balance sheet:

Classified balance sheet: In this format, assets are separated into current assets and non-current assets. Similarly, liabilities are separated into current liabilities and non-current liabilities. Both IFRS and U.S. GAAP require this format.

Liquidity-based format: In this format, the assets and liabilities are presented in a decreasing order of liquidity. This method is often used in banking industry. Only IFRS permits this method.

Current and non-current assets & liabilities

Current assets are those assets that are expected to be used up or converted to cash within one year or in one operating business cycle, whichever is greater. Examples: Cash and cash equivalents, marketable securities, trade receivables, inventories, etc.

Non-current assets include all assets that cannot be classified as current assets. Examples: Property, plant and equipment, investment property etc.

Current liabilities are those liabilities which are expected to be settled within one year or in one operating business cycle, whichever is greater. Examples: Accounts payable, notes payable, income tax payable etc.

Non-current liabilities include all liabilities that cannot be classified as current liabilities. Examples: long term financial liabilities, deferred tax liabilities etc.

Measurement bases for different types of assets and liabilities

Measurement bases

- <u>Historical cost</u> – Cost at which the item was actually purchased. Historical cost is highly reliable, but its relevance to an analyst declines as values change.
- <u>Fair value</u> – Cost at which an item can be purchased now, in an arm's length transaction. Fair value is more relevant to an analyst but is less reliable compared to historical cost, because it involves some level of judgment.

Different types of assets and liabilities

Current assets

- <u>Cash and cash equivalents</u> – Highly liquid, low risk securities with maturity less than 90 days. They are reported at either fair value or amortized cost.
- <u>Accounts receivable</u> – Amount owed to a company for goods and services sold. They are reported at net realizable value.
- <u>Inventories</u> – Items held for sale or to be used for manufacture of goods to be sold. Inventories are measured at the lower of cost or net realizable value under IFRS, and at the lower of cost or market under U.S. GAAP.
- <u>Marketable securities</u> – Liquid securities which are publicly traded in market. Example,

Financial Reporting and Analysis

bonds and stocks.

Non-current assets

- Property, plant and equipment - Tangible assets that are used in company operations and are expected to be used over more than one fiscal period. IFRS allows companies to report PPE using either a cost model or a revaluation model. U.S. GAAP allows only the cost model.
- Investment property - Refers to property not used in the regular operations of a company. This is an IFRS concept. Investment properties need to be valued using either the cost model or the fair value model.
- Intangible assets - These are long term assets which lack physical substance. For e.g. patents, goodwill etc.
  - Unidentifiable intangible assets – These cannot be purchased separately and may have infinite life. These assets are tested for impairment on annual basis. For e.g. goodwill is an unidentifiable intangible asset. It is created when one company is purchased by another company. If the purchase price is greater than fair value at acquisition, then goodwill is created in the acquirers' balance sheet.
  - Identifiable intangible assets – These assets last only for a definite period (For e.g. patents) and are amortized over lifetime of the asset
- Financial assets include investment securities, derivatives, loans and receivables. The following table summarizes measurement of different categories of financial assets:

Asset Category	Treatment
Held-for-trading (HFT)	- Measured at fair value - Unrealized gains shown on Income Statement
Available-for-sale (AFS)	- Measured at fair value - Unrealized gains/losses shown in Other Comprehensive Income (OCI)
Held-to-maturity (HTM)	- Measured at cost or amortized cost - Unrealized gains not recorded anywhere

Current liabilities:

- Accounts payable - Amount that a company owes to its vendors for goods/services purchased on credit.
- Notes payable - Amount to be paid by company for short term borrowings like commercial papers.
- Income taxes payable - Taxes recognized in the income statement but have not yet been paid.
- Accrued expenses - Expenses that have been recognized on a company's income statement but which have not yet been paid as of the balance sheet date.

- Unearned revenue - Revenue for which cash has been collected but goods or service are yet to be provided. For e.g. receipt of advance rent payments will fall under this category.

Non-current liabilities:
- Long-term financial liabilities - Include loans, notes and bonds payable. These are usually reported at amortized cost on the balance sheet.
- Deferred tax liabilities - Result from temporary timing difference between a company's taxable income and reported income. They are defined as the amounts of income taxes payable in future periods in respect of taxable temporary differences.

Components of shareholders' equity

The six components of equity are:
- **Contributed capital:** Total amount paid in by common and preferred shareholders.
- **Treasury shares:** These are shares that have been repurchased by the company, but not yet retired.
- **Retained earnings:** Cumulative income of firm since inception that has not been distributed as dividends.
- **Accumulated other comprehensive income:** These include items which lead to changes in equity but are not part of income statement or from issuing stock, reacquiring stock, and paying dividends.
- **Non-controlling interest (minority interest):** It is the portion of a subsidiary not owned by parent company. For example, if a firm owns 80% of a subsidiary, then it will report 20% of net assets of the subsidiary as minority interest.

Common-size balance sheets

The statement of changes in equity gives information about all transactions that increases or decreases the company's equity over a period. Balance sheet analysis can help us evaluate a company's liquidity and solvency. Balance sheet can also be used to analyze a company's capital structure and ability to pay liabilities.

Common-size balance sheets: In a common size balance sheet, all balance sheet items are expressed as a percentage of total assets. Firms of different sizes can be compared using common size balance sheet as elements are presented in terms of percentage. Similarly individual elements on balance sheets can be compared over time to find any increasing or decreasing trend.

Liquidity and solvency ratios

Liquidity ratios measure a company's ability to meet current liabilities. The higher the liquidity ratio, the more likely the firm will be able to meet its short term obligations.

Financial Reporting and Analysis

- Current ratio - It is the most widely used measure of liquidity.
$$\text{Current ratio} = \frac{\text{current assets}}{\text{current liabilities}}$$

- Quick ratio - It is a more conservative measure of liquidity. It excludes inventories and less liquid assets from the numerator
$$\text{Quick ratio} = \frac{\text{cash} + \text{marketable securities} + \text{receivables}}{\text{current liabilities}}$$

- Cash ratio - It is the most conservative measure of liquidity. Even receivables are excluded from the numerator.
$$\text{Cash ratio} = \frac{\text{cash} + \text{marketable securities}}{\text{current liabilities}}$$

Solvency ratios measure a company's ability to meet long-term obligations. A high ratio indicates high leverage and a high financial risk.

- Long term debt to equity ratio – It measures long term financing sources relative to total equity.
$$\text{Long term debt to equity} = \frac{\text{total long term debt}}{\text{total equity}}$$

- Debt to equity ratio – It measures total debt relative to total equity.
$$\text{Debt to equity} = \frac{\text{total debt}}{\text{total equity}}$$

- Total debt to assets ratio – It measures the extent to which assets are financed by liabilities.
$$\text{Debt to assets} = \frac{\text{total debt}}{\text{total assets}}$$

- Financial leverage ratio – It measures total assets relative to total equity.
$$\text{Financial leverage ratio} = \frac{\text{total assets}}{\text{total equity}}$$

R25 Understanding Cash Flow Statements

Classification of cash flow items

Under both IFRS and U.S. GAAP, cash flows in the cash flow statement are categorized as:
- **Operating activities:** These are inflows and outflows of cash from a firm's day-to-day business activities.
- **Investing activities:** These are inflows and outflows of cash associated with acquisition and disposal of long-term assets.
- **Financing activities:** These are inflows and outflows of cash generated from issuance and repayment of capital.

US GAAP Cash Flow Classification

Operating Activities

Inflows

- Cash collected from customers
- Interest and dividends received
- Proceeds from sale of securities held for trading

Outflows

- Cash paid to employees
- Cash paid to suppliers
- Cash paid for other expenses
- Acquisition of trading securities
- Interest paid
- Taxes paid

Investing Activities

Inflows

- Sale proceeds from fixed assets
- Sale proceeds from long-term investments
- Repayment of loan made to others

Outflows

- Purchase of fixed assets
- Purchase of long-term investments.
- Loans made to others

Financing Activities

Inflows

- Proceeds from issuing debt
- Proceeds from issuing stock

Outflows

- Repayment of debt
- Repurchasing stock
- Dividends paid to shareholders

IFRS Cash Flow classification is similar to US GAAP, but IFRS allows more flexibility on classification.

Non-cash investing and financing activities

Non-cash investing and financing activities do not result in any cash inflows or outflows. Hence these are not reported in cash flow statement. For example, conversion of convertible bonds to common shares will not result in any cash inflow or outflow. Non-cash transactions should either be reported in the footnote or in a supplemental schedule to cash flow statement.

IFRS v/s US GAAP

The differences between the two standards are shown in the table below:

Topic	IFRS	U.S. GAAP
Interest received	Operating or investing	Operating
Interest paid	Operating or financing	Operating
Dividends received	Operating or investing	Operating
Dividends paid	Operating or financing	Financing
Bank overdrafts	Considered part of cash equivalents	Not considered part of cash equivalents and classified as financing
Taxes paid	Generally operating, but a portion can be allocated to investing or financing if it can be specifically identified with these categories	Operating
Format of statement	Direct or indirect; direct is encouraged	Direct or indirect; direct is encouraged. A reconciliation of net income to cash flow from operating activities must be provided.

Direct v/s indirect methods of presenting cash from operating activities

Two methods of presenting cash flow statements are permitted under U.S. GAAP and IFRS – Direct Method and Indirect Method. Only cash flow from operating activities is presented differently under the two methods. Presentation of cash flow from investing activities and cash flow from financing activities is the same under both methods.

In the **direct method,** we take each item from the income statement and convert it to its cash equivalent by removing the impact of accrual accounting. The main advantage of the direct method is that it provides more information that the indirect method.

Financial Reporting and Analysis

XYZ Company
Cash Flow from Operating Activities
Direct Method

	Sales	$ 300,000
+	Decrease in Account Receivable	10,000
	Cash Collections	**310,000**
	Less	
	Cost of goods sold	167,000
+	Increase in inventories	25,000
−	Increase in Accounts Payable	(10,000)
	Cash Payment for Purchases	**182,000**
	SG&A	30,000
	Cash expenses related to R&D	1,500
+	Increase in Prepaid expenses	2,000
	Cash Payment for Operations	**33,500**
	Interest expense	5,000
−	Increase in interest payable	(2,500)
	Cash Interest	**2,500**
	Income taxes	28,150
	Increase in income tax payable	(1,500)
	Cash payment for income taxes	**26,650**
	Net cash flow from operating activities	**65,350**

Indirect method shows how cash flow from operations can be obtained from reported net income as a result of a series of adjustments. The main advantage of indirect method is that it focuses on the differences between net income and operating cash flow.

XYZ Company
Cash Flow from Operating Activities
Indirect Method

Net income	$ 66,800
Adjustments:	
Depreciation and amortization	2,000
Deferred taxes	50
Decrease in accounts receivable	200
Increase in inventories	(4,000)
Increase in accounts payable	1,150
Increase in accrued interest receivable	(350)
Increase in accrued interest payable	100
Gain on sale of property	(600)
Net cash flow from operating activities	65,350

Total cash flow from operating activities is the same under both methods.

Link between cash flow statements, and income statements and balance sheets

Change in cash: The balance sheet at the start of the year shows the firm's cash position at

Financial Reporting and Analysis

the start of the year. The cash flow statement shows the net change in cash during the year. The balance sheet at the end of the year will show that the firm's cash position at the end of the year changed by the same amount as the net change depicted by the cash flow statement.

At the start of the year, the balance sheet shows cash of $2,000. The cash flow statement shows that cash increased by $200 during the year. Calculate the cash at the end of the year.

Solution:
Ending cash balance = beginning cash balance + net change during the year
= $2,000 + $200 = $2,200

Other relationships: CFO is calculated from net income and from changes in the current assets and current liabilities. CFI is calculated from changes in non-current assets. CFF is calculated from changes in non-current liabilities and equity.

Steps in the preparation of direct and indirect cash flow statements

Operating Cash Flow

Direct method: In the direct method, we take each item from the income statement and convert it to its cash equivalent by removing the impact of accrual accounting. The rules to adjust are:

- Increase in asset is use of cash (-ve adjustment) and decrease in asset is source of cash (+ve adjustment)
- Increase in liability is source of cash (+ve adjustment) and decrease in liability is use of cash (-ve adjustment)

Cash collected from customers: Adjust sales for changes in accounts receivables and unearned revenue.
Cash for inputs: Adjust COGS for changes in inventory and accounts payable.
Cash operating expenses: Adjust SG&A for changes in related accrued liabilities or prepaid expenses.
Cash interest paid: Adjust interest expense for change in interest payable.
Cash taxes paid: Adjust tax expense for changes in tax payable and changes in deferred tax assets and liabilities.

Consider a company which reported sales of $10 million. Accounts receivable for the year went up from $2 million to $4 million. Unearned revenue went up from $1 million to $2 million. Calculate cash collected from customers.

Solution:
Δ Accounts receivable = $2 million. This is an asset and increase in asset is use of cash so –ve adjustment.

Δ Unearned revenue = $1 million. This is a liability and increase in liability is source of cash so +ve adjustment.
Cash collected from customers = + $10 million - $2 million + $1 million = $9 million

Consider a company with COGS of $20 million for a particular period. During this period, inventory increased by $4 million and accounts payable went up by $2 million. Calculate the cash paid to suppliers.

Solution:
Δ Inventory = $4 million. This is an asset and increase in asset is use of cash so –ve adjustment.
Δ Accounts payable = $2 million. This is a liability and increase in liability is source of cash so +ve adjustment.
Cash paid to suppliers = - $20 million - $4 million + $2 million = - $22 million

Indirect method shows how cash flow from operations can be obtained from reported net income as a result of a series of adjustments. The steps are:
- Begin with net income.
- Add back all non-cash charges to income and subtract all non-cash components of revenue (For example: add depreciation and amortization).
- Subtract any gains that resulted from financing or investing cash flows (For example: Gain on the sale of an equipment).
- Add or subtract changes to related balance sheet operating accounts.
  Decrease in operating assets (source of cash) should be added and increase in operating assets (use of cash) should be subtracted.
  Similarly, increase in current liabilities (source of cash) should be added and decrease in current liabilities (use of cash) should be subtracted.

Consider a company with net income of $100 million in 2001. Depreciation expense is $10 million. Gain on sale of equipment is $4 million. Increase in A/R is $8 million. Increase in A/P is $4 million. Increase in inventory is $10 million. Calculate CFO using the indirect method.

Solution:

Net Income	100
Add non-cash charges (depreciation)	+ 10
Less gain on sale of equipment	- 4
Less increase in A/R	-8
Add increase in A/P	+4
Less increase in inventory	-10
Total	**92**
CFO = $92 million	

Financial Reporting and Analysis

Investing cash flows: CFI is calculated by determining changes in the gross asset account that result from the purchase or sale of equipment. It can be calculated by using the following formulae:

(1) Cash paid for new equipment = ending gross equipment balance + gross cost of equipment sold – beginning gross equipment balance
(2) Cash from sale of old equipment = book value of equipment sold + gain (or - loss) on sale of equipment

Financing cash flows: CFF is the sum of net cash flows from creditors and net cash flows from shareholders. It can be calculated using the following formulae:

(1) CFF = net cash flow from creditors + net cash flow from shareholders
(2) Net cash flow from creditors = new borrowings – principal repaid
(3) Net cash flow from shareholders = new equity issued – shares repurchased – cash dividends

The following information is available about company ABC for 2001.

New borrowings	$10 million
Principal repaid	$5 million
New equity issued	$5 million
Shares repurchased	-
Dividends paid	$2 million

Calculate CFF.

Solution:
Net cash flow from creditors = new borrowings – principal repaid = 10 – 5 = $5 million
Net cash flow from shareholders = new equity issued – shares repurchased – cash dividends = 5 – 0 – 2 = $3 million.
CFF = net cash flow from creditors + net cash flow from shareholders = 5 + 3 = $8 million

Converting cash flows from the indirect to direct method

The operating cash flow from indirect method can be converted to direct by using the three-step process:
- Aggregate all the revenues and expenses.
- Remove all non-cash items from aggregated revenues and expenses and break up remaining items into relevant cash flow items.
- Convert accrual amounts to cash flow amounts by adjusting for changes in corresponding working accounts.

Note: The probability of getting tested on this material on the exam is low.

Analyzing reported cash flows and common-size cash flow statements

Operating cash flow: A healthy firm should generate positive cash flows from operating

Financial Reporting and Analysis

activities (This is not applicable for startups). Positive operating cash flow generated by liquidating noncash working capital items (like liquidating inventory and receivables or increasing payables) is not sustainable. Earnings that are significantly greater than operating cash flows, indicate that aggressive accounting policies are being followed.

Investing cash flow: Cash outflows can result from investments in property, plant & equipment or other assets. Increasing outflows is an indication of growth. Decreasing outflows may indicate a reduction of capital expenditure and reduction in growth.

Financing cash flow: Tells us if the company is generating cash by issuing debt or equity. Also tells us if the company is using cash to repay debt, reacquire stock or pay dividends.

Common-size format: There are two approaches:
- In the first approach, we express each line item of cash inflow (outflow) as a percentage of total inflows (outflows).
- In the second approach, we express each line item as a percentage of revenue.

Common size cash flow statement makes it easier to identify trends in cash flows. It also helps us in forecasting future cash flows.

Free cash flow to firm (FCFF), Free cash flow to equity (FCFE) & Cash flow ratios

Free cash flow to the firm (FCFF) is the cash available to all investors (both equity and debt holders) after covering the firm's capital expenditures and working capital requirements. It can be calculated as:

FCFF = NI + NCC + Int (1 - Tax rate) – FCInv – WCInv
FCFF = CFO + Int (1 - Tax rate) – FCInv

The following selected data is available for a firm:

	$ millions
Net income	45.0
Non-cash charges	12.3
Interest expense	2.6
Capital expenditures	15.0
Working capital expenditures	8.1

If the firm's tax rate is 30%, Calculate the free cash flow to the firm (FCFF):

Solution:

FCFF = net income + non-cash charges + interest expense * (1 – tax rate) – capital expenditures – working capital expenditures

FCFF = 45 + 12.3 + 2.6*(1 – 0.3) – 15 – 8.1 = $36.02 million

Free cash flow to equity (FCFE) is the free cash available to equity holders after all obligations have been paid. It can be calculated as:

FCFE = CFO – FCInv + net borrowing

Financial Reporting and Analysis

The following information has been provided about a firm.

CFO	$200 million
Fixed capital investment	$50 million
Net borrowing	-$80 million

Calculate FCFE.

Solution:

FCFE = CFO − FCInv + net borrowing = 200 − 50 − 80 = $70 million

Cash flow ratios

Performance ratios: They measure a firm's efficiency.

Ratio	Formula	What It Measures
Cash flow to revenue	CFO ÷ net revenue	ability of a firm to convert revenues to cash flows.
Cash return on assets	CFO ÷ average total assets	cash flow generated from operations which can be attributed to all capital providers.
Cash return on equity	CFO ÷ average shareholders' equity	cash flow generated from operations which can be attributed to equity capital providers.
Cash to income	CFO ÷ operating income	ability of a firm to convert operating income to cash flows.
Cash flow per share	(CFO − preferred dividends) ÷ number of common shares outstanding	operating cash flow on a per-share basis.

Coverage ratios: They measure a firm's liquidity and solvency.

Ratio	Formula	What It Measures
Debt coverage	CFO ÷ total debt	ability of a firm to cover debt obligations using cash generated from operating activities.
Interest coverage	(CFO + interest paid + taxes paid) ÷ interest paid	ability of a firm to cover interest obligations using cash generated from operating activities.

Financial Reporting and Analysis

Reinvestment	CFO ÷ cash paid for long-term assets	ability of a firm to meet investing and financing flows using cash generated from operating activities.
Debt payment	CFO ÷ cash paid for long-term debt repayment	ability of a firm to repay debt using cash generated from operating activities.
Dividend payment	CFO ÷ dividends paid	ability of a firm to pay dividends using cash generated from operating activities.

R26 Financial Analysis Techniques

Tools and techniques used in financial analysis

Tools and techniques used in financial analysis include:

Ratio analysis

Uses
- Evaluation of operational efficiency and financial flexibility of a firm.
- Comparing company performance relative to industry and other peer companies
- Evaluating management performance.

Limitations
- Not useful when used in isolation.
- Comparisons among companies is difficult because of differences in accounting methods.
- It may be difficult to find comparable companies for a company that operates in multiple industries.
- Requires judgment to interpret.

Common size analysis normalizes the balance sheets and income statements and allows for easy comparison among different-sized firms. The vertical common-size balance sheet expresses each balance sheet account as a percentage of total assets. The horizontal common-size balance sheet expresses each account as a ratio to its base year value. The vertical common-sized income statement expresses each item as a percentage of sales.

Graphical analysis is a pictorial representation of the analysis done (ratio or trend). It helps in quick comparison of financial performance and structure over time.

Regression analysis is a statistical method of analyzing relationships between variables.

Financial Reporting and Analysis

Financial ratios

Activity ratios measure the efficiency of a company's operations, such as collection of receivables or management of inventory.

Activity ratios	Numerator	Denominator
Inventory turnover	Cost of goods sold	Average inventory
Days of inventory on hand	Number of days in period	Inventory turnover
Receivables turnover	Revenue	Average receivables
Days of sales outstanding	Number of days in period	Receivables turnover
Payables turnover	Purchases	Average trade payables
Number of days of payables	Number of days in period	Payables turnover
Working capital turnover	Revenue	Average working capital
Fixed asset turnover	Revenue	Average net fixed assets
Total asset turnover	Revenue	Average total assets
Cash conversion cycle (net operating cycle) = days of inventory on hand (DOH) + days of sales outstanding (DSO) – number of days of payables		

Company ABC's payable turnover is 8 times, the receivable turnover is 9 times and the inventory turnover is 6 times. What is ABC's cash conversion cycle?
Solution:
Cash conversion cycle = Days of sales outstanding + Days of inventory on hand – Number of days of payable = 365/9 + 365/6 – 356/8 = 55.76 days

Liquidity ratios measure the ability of a company to meet short-term obligations.

Liquidity ratios	Numerator	Denominator
Current ratio	Current assets	Current liabilities
Quick ratio	Cash + short term marketable investments + receivables	Current liabilities
Cash ratio	Cash + short term marketable investments	Current liabilities
Defensive interval ratio	Cash + short term marketable investments + receivables	Daily cash expenditures

Solvency ratios measure the ability of a company to meet long-term obligations.

Solvency ratios	Numerator	Denominator
Debt to assets ratio	Total debt	Total assets
Debt to capital ratio	Total debt	Total debt + total shareholder's equity

Financial Reporting and Analysis

Debt to equity ratio	Total debt	Total shareholder's equity
Financial leverage ratio	Average total assets	Average total equity
Interest coverage ratio	EBIT	Interest payments
Fixed charge coverage ratio	EBIT + lease payments	Interest payments + lease payments

Profitability ratios measure the ability of a company to generate profits from revenue and assets.

Profitability Ratios	Numerator	Denominator
Gross profit margin	Gross profit	Revenue
Operating profit margin	Operating income	Revenue
Pre-tax margin	EBT (earnings before tax but after interest)	Revenue
Net profit margin	Net profit	Revenue
Operating ROA	Operating income	Average total assets
Return on assets (ROA)	Net income	Average total assets
Return on total capital	EBIT	Short and long term debt and equity
Return on equity (ROE)	Net income	Average total equity
Return on common equity	Net income – preferred dividend	Average common equity

Company ABC's sales and COGS during the year were $100,000 and $40,000 respectively. Its balance sheet shows total assets of $70,000 and an average inventory balance of $10,000. Calculate ABC's total asset turnover and gross margin.

Solution:
Total asset turnover = Sales / Total assets = $100,000 / $70,000 = 1.43 times
Gross profit = Sales – COGS = $100,000 - $40,000 = $60,000
Gross margin = Gross profit / Sales = $60,000 / $100,000 = 60%

Valuation ratios express the relation between the market value of a company and its equity.

Valuation Ratios	Numerator	Denominator
P/E	Price per share	Earnings per share
P/CF	Price per share	Cash flow per share
P/S	Price per share	Sales per share
P/BV	Price per share	Book value per share

Evaluation of a company using ratio analysis

To evaluate the overall position and performance of a company, an analyst cannot simply examine a single ratio or a single category of ratios in isolation. An analyst should be able to use an appropriate combination of different ratios to evaluate a company over time and relative to comparable companies. The most accurate overall picture comes from assimilating information from different ratios.

DuPont analysis

DuPont analysis decomposes a firm's ROE to better analyze a firm's performance.

Start with ROE

$$ROE = \left(\frac{net\ income}{equity}\right)$$

Traditional DuPont equation is:

$$ROE = \left(\frac{net\ income}{sales}\right)\left(\frac{sales}{assets}\right)\left(\frac{assets}{equity}\right)$$

ROE = (net profit margin)(asset turnover)(leverage ratio)

Extended DuPont equation is:

$$ROE = \left(\frac{net\ income}{EBT}\right)\left(\frac{EBT}{EBIT}\right)\left(\frac{EBIT}{revenue}\right)\left(\frac{revenue}{total\ assets}\right)\left(\frac{total\ assets}{total\ equity}\right)$$

ROE = (tax burden)(interest burden)(EBIT margin)(asset turnover)(financial leverage)

An analyst has gathered the following information about a company:
- Operating profit margin = 12%
- Average tax rate = 30%
- Asset turnover ratio = 2 times
- Financial leverage multiplier = 1.5 times
- Interest burden = 0.6 times

Calculate the company's ROE.

Solution:

$$ROE = \frac{Net\ income}{EBT} \times \frac{EBT}{EBIT} \times \frac{EBIT}{Revenue} \times \frac{Revenue}{average\ assets} \times \frac{Average\ assets}{Equity}$$

Tax burden = 1 − tax rate = 1 − 0.3 = 0.7

ROE = 0.7 x 0.6 x 0.12 x 2 x 1.5 = 0.1512 = 15%

Ratios used in equity analysis and credit analysis

Equity Analysis: Ratios used in equity analysis include- P/E, P/CF, P/S, P/BV, basic and diluted EPS. These ratios help to determine if a stock is overvalued or undervalued.

Credit analysis: Ratios used in credit analysis include - interest coverage ratios, return on capital, debt-to-assets ratio, cash flow to total debt. High coverage ratios would indicate good credit quality.

Financial Reporting and Analysis

Segment reporting

A business or geographic segment is a portion of a company that has risk and return characteristics distinct from the rest of the company and accounts for more than 10% of the company's sales or assets. Companies are required to report some items for significant segments separately. Ratios can be computed for business segments to evaluate how units within a business are performing.

Forecasting earnings using ratios and common-size statements

Analysts often use common-size analysis and ratio analysis to prepare pro-forma financial statements. They forecast future sales and combine the forecasted sales numbers with expected value for key ratios.

R27 Inventories

Costs included in inventories v/s costs recognized as expenses

Costs included in the inventory are:
- Cost of purchase
- Cost of conversion
- Fixed production overhead under normal operating capacity
- Other costs necessary to bring the inventories to its present location and condition

Costs that are recognized as expenses are:
- Storage costs of finished inventory
- Abnormal costs due to waste
- Administrative costs
- Selling costs

Inventory valuation methods

The four inventory valuation methods are:

FIFO
- The cost of the first item purchased is assumed to be the cost of the first item sold.
- Ending inventory is based on the cost of the most recent purchases.

LIFO
- The cost of the last item purchased is assumed to be the cost of the first item sold.
- Ending inventory is based on the cost of the earliest purchases.

Weighted average cost
- Each item in the inventory is valued using an average cost of all items in the inventory.

- COGS and inventory values are between their FIFO and LIFO values.

Specific identification
- Each unit sold is matched with the unit's actual cost.
- This method is usually used for items that are unique in nature, for example – jewelry.

All four methods are permitted under U.S. GAAP. However, IFRS does not permit LIFO method.

Cost of sales, gross profit, and ending inventory under different inventory valuation methods & using perpetual and periodic inventory systems

Suppose you purchased 10 items for $1 each in January and bought 5 items for $2 each in February. You sold 6 items for $3 each in March. Inventory accounting under various methods is as follows:

Item	FIFO (in $)	LIFO (in $)	WAC (in $)
COGS for period	6 x 1 = 6	(5 x 2) + 1 = 11.5	1.33 x 6 = 7.98
Gross profit for period	(6 x 3) – 6 = 12	(6 x 3) – 11.5 = 6.5	(6 x 3) – 7.98 = 10.02
Inventory at end of period	(5 x 2) + (4 x 1) = 14	9 x 1 = 9	9 x 1.33 = 11.97

In a periodic system, inventory values and COGS are determined at the end of the accounting period. The COGS is calculated as:

Cost of goods sold (COGS) = Beginning Inventory + Purchases – Ending Inventory

In a perpetual system, inventory values and COGS are updated continuously. For specific identification and FIFO - periodic and perpetual systems give the same values for COGS and ending inventory. For LIFO and WAC - periodic and perpetual systems may give different values for COGS and ending inventory.

Effects of inflation and deflation on different inventory valuation methods

The following table compares LIFO and FIFO when prices are rising and inventory levels are stable. (We get the opposite effect during periods of falling prices)

LIFO vs. FIFO with rising prices and stable inventory levels		
	LIFO	FIFO
COGS	Higher	Lower
Taxes	Lower	Higher
Earnings before taxes (EBT)	Lower	Higher
Earnings after taxes (Net Income)	Lower	Higher

Financial Reporting and Analysis

Ending inventory	Lower	Higher
Working capital (CA – CL)	Lower	Higher
Cash flow (after tax)	Higher	Lower

For weighted average costs, all values will be between those for the LIFO and FIFO methods.

LIFO reserve and LIFO liquidation

LIFO reserve is the difference between LIFO inventory reported and the amount that would have been reported in inventory if the FIFO method had been used. Under US GAAP, companies that use the LIFO method must disclose the LIFO reserve in their financial notes. This information can be used to adjust reported ending inventory and COGS in order to compare this company with a company using the FIFO method.

LIFO liquidation occurs when the number of units in ending inventory is less than the number of units in the beginning inventory (i.e. the firms sells more than it purchases during the year). If inventory unit costs have gone up from year to year, this will increase gross profits. However this increase in the gross profit margin is temporary and not sustainable.

Conversion from LIFO to FIFO

FIFO inventory = LIFO inventory + LIFO reserve

FIFO COGS = LIFO COGS – (ending LIFO reserve – beginning LIFO reserve)
(The adjusted COGS is also impacted by inventory write-downs)

FIFO NI = LIFO NI + change in LIFO reserve (1 - T)
FIFO retained earnings = LIFO retained earnings + LIFO reserve (1 – T)

Company A accounts for inventory using the LIFO method. During the current period, it reported a COGS of $40,000 and an ending inventory of $15,000. Its LIFO reserve decreased from $5,000 to $4,000 over the period. If the firm had reported using FIFO, what would its COGS be?

Solution:
FIFO COGS = LIFO COGS – change in LIFO reserve
FIFO COGS = $40,000 – ($4,000 - $5,000) = $41,000

Measurement of inventory at the lower of cost and net realizable value

Net realizable value is calculated as estimated selling price under ordinary business conditions minus estimated costs necessary to get the inventory in condition for sale.
Net realizable value = estimated sales price – estimated selling costs.

Financial Reporting and Analysis

Market value is the current replacement cost subject to lower or upper limits. Market value has upper limit of net realizable value and lower limit of NRV less a normal profit margin. Market value limits = (NRV - normal profit margin, NRV)

Under IFRS, inventories are valued at the lower of cost or net realizable value. Inventory write-ups are allowed but only to the extent a previous write-down to net realizable value was recorded. Under US GAAP, inventories are valued at lower of cost or market. If cost exceeds market, inventory is written down. No subsequent write-ups are allowed.

Implications of valuing inventory at net realizable value

When inventory is written down from cost to net realizable value:
- It decreases inventory, assets and equity.
- It increases asset turnover, debt to equity and the debt to assets ratio.
- It results in a loss on the income statement, which decreases net income, net profit margin, return on assets and return on equity.

Disclosures relating to inventories

IFRS requires the following financial statement disclosures concerning inventory:
- The accounting policies used to measure inventory, including the cost formula
- The total carrying amount of inventories and the carrying amount in classification
- The carrying amount of inventories carried at fair value less costs to sell
- The amount of inventories recognized as an expense in the period (cost of sales)
- The amount of any reversal of any write-down recognized as a reduction in cost of sales in the period
- What led to the reversal of a write-down in the inventories
- Carrying amount of inventories pledged as security for liabilities

Disclosures under U.S. GAAP are similar to IFRS except that it does not permit reversal of write down of inventories. In addition, any income from liquidation of LIFO inventory must be disclosed.

Issues to consider when examining a company's inventory disclosures

- If finished goods inventory is increasing while raw material and work in progress inventory is decreasing, then this may indicate decreasing demand for the product.
- If raw material and work in progress inventory is increasing, then this may indicate increasing demand for the product.
- If finished goods inventory is increasing at a greater rate than increases in sales, then this may indicate decreasing demand for the product.
- If the inventory turnover ratio is too low, then this may indicate slow-moving or obsolete inventory.

- If inventory turnover is high and sales growth is low relative to industry, then this may indicate inadequate inventory levels and lost sales because customer orders could not be fulfilled.
- If inventory turnover is high and sales growth is also high relative to industry, then this may indicate greater efficiency rather than inadequate inventory.

R28 Long-Lived Assets

Capitalized costs v/s expensed costs

If an asset is expected to provide benefits only for the current period, its cost is expensed on the income statement for that period. If an asset is expected to provide benefits over multiple periods, its cost is capitalized on the balance sheet and spread over the life of the asset.

Effects of capitalizing v/s expensing costs

If a cost is capitalized the asset value is put on the balance sheet and the cost is expensed over the asset's useful life through either depreciation or amortization.

The following table compares capitalizing with expensing.

	Capitalizing	Expensing
Total Assets	Higher	Lower
Equity	Higher	Lower
Income variability	Lower	Higher
Net Income (1st year)	Higher	Lower
Net Income (later)	Lower	Higher
Cash flow from operating activities (CFO)	Higher	Lower
Cash flow from investing activities (CFI)	Lower	Higher
Debt/Equity	Lower	Higher
Interest Coverage (1st year)	Higher	Lower
Interest Coverage (later years)	Lower	Higher

Intangible assets

Purchased intangible assets: The cost of a finite-lived intangible asset is amortized over its useful life. Indefinite-lived intangible assets are not amortized; they are tested for impairment at least annually.

Internally developed intangible assets: Under IFRS, research costs are expensed but development costs may be capitalized. Under US GAAP, both research and development costs are expensed. (Except in the case of software created for sale to others).

Intangible assets acquired in a business combination: Acquired intangible assets such

Financial Reporting and Analysis

as patents, copyrights and trademarks are recorded at their fair value; similar to long-lived tangible assets.

Depreciation methods

Depreciation methods are:
- **Straight line** – The cost of an asset is evenly distributed over the asset's useful life.
- **Accelerated** – A higher depreciation expense is recorded in the early years and lower depreciation expense is recorded in the later years of an asset's life. Double declining balance (DDB) is one example of an accelerated depreciation method.
- **Units of production** – Cost allocated is based on the actual use of an asset in a particular period.

Straight line depreciation expense = depreciable cost / estimated useful life

DDB depreciation expense = 2 x straight-line rate x beginning book value

Units of production depreciation expense per unit = depreciable cost / useful life in units

Carrying amount = historical cost – accumulated depreciation

Depreciable cost = historical cost – estimated residual value

An analyst gathered the following information about an equipment's expected production life and use. The equipment was purchased for $10,000 and is expected to have 0 salvage value at the end of its useful life.

	Year 1	Year 2	Year 3	Year 4	Year 5
Units produced	1,000	1,100	900	500	500

Calculate the Year 1 depreciation expense under the units-of-production method and the straight-line method.

Solution:

Straight line method:

$$\text{Depreciation expense} = \frac{\text{original cost} - \text{salvage value}}{\text{depreciable life}}$$

Depreciation expense = $10,000/5 = $2000.

Units of production method:

$$\text{Depreciation expense} = (\text{original cost} - \text{salvage value}) \times \frac{\text{output during period}}{\text{total output}}$$

Depreciation expense = $10,000 x 1,000/4,000 = $2,500

Effects of depreciation method and assumptions

Choice of depreciation method: The effect of depreciation method on financial statements and ratios is summarized in the table below.

	Straight Line (SL)	**Accelerated (DDB)**
Depreciation Expense	Lower	Higher
Net Income	Higher	Lower
Assets	Higher	Lower
Equity	Higher	Lower
Return on Assets (NI/Assets)	Higher	Lower
Return on Equity	Higher	Lower
Asset Turnover	Lower	Higher
Operating Profit Margin	Higher	Lower

Assumptions concerning useful life and residual value: Estimates required for depreciation and amortization calculations include the useful life of the equipment and its expected residual value at the end of that useful life. A longer useful life and higher expected residual value result in a smaller amount of annual depreciation relative to a shorter useful life and lower expected residual value.

Amortization methods

Amortization methods for intangible assets with finite lives are same as those used in depreciation: straight line, accelerated, units of production. The calculation of amortization expense is also similar to that of depreciation expense (covered earlier).

Effect of amortization methods and assumptions

The choice of amortization method affects expenses, assets, equity and financial ratios in exactly the same way as the choice of depreciation method does (covered earlier).

Revaluation model

Under the revaluation model, carrying amounts are the fair values at the date of revaluation less any consequent accumulated depreciation or amortization. IFRS permits the use of either the cost model or the revaluation model for the valuation and reporting of long-lived assets, but the revaluation model is not allowed under US GAAP.

If initial revaluation resulted in a loss

- The initial loss is recognized in the income statement and any subsequent gain is recognized on the income statement only to the extent of the previously reported loss.
- Revaluation gains beyond the initial loss do not flow through the income statement. They are directly recognized in shareholder's equity as a revaluation surplus.

If the initial revaluation resulted in a gain

- The initial gain would bypass the income statement and be reported directly as a revaluation surplus.
- Any subsequent loss would then first reduce the revaluation surplus and later flow into the income statement.

Financial Reporting and Analysis

Impairment

Impairment charges reflect an unexpected decline in the fair value of an asset to an amount lower than its carrying amount. (Whereas depreciation and amortization charges allocate the cost of a long-lived asset over its useful life.)

Under IFRS

- An asset is impaired when its carrying value exceeds the recoverable amount.
- The recoverable amount is the greater of fair value less selling costs and the present value of expected cash flows from the asset (i.e. the value in use).
- If impaired, the asset is written down to the recoverable amount.
- Subsequent loss recoveries are allowed, but they cannot exceed the historical cost.

Under US GAAP,

- An asset is impaired if its carrying value is greater than the asset's undiscounted future cash flows.
- If impaired, the asset is written down to the fair value.
- Subsequent loss recoveries are not allowed.

Impairment of assets results in losses in the income statement. However, they have no impact on the cash flow.

An analyst gathered the following information about a manufacturing equipment of XYZ, Inc.

Fair value	$160,000
Costs to sell	$8,000
Value in use	$140,000
Net carrying amount	$190,000

The amount of impairment loss on XYZ's income statement related to this equipment will be?

Solution:

Impairment = max(Recoverable amount; Value in use) – Net carrying amount
Impairment = max($160,000 - $8,000; $140,000) – 190,000
= -$38,000

Derecognition

The three ways in which an asset can be derecognized (removed from a company's financial statements) are:

- **Selling the asset**: The difference between the sales proceeds and the carrying value of the asset is reported as a gain or loss on the income statement.
- **Abandoning the asset**: The carrying value of the asset is removed from the balance sheet and a loss is recognized in that amount in the income statement.

Financial Reporting and Analysis

- **Exchanging the asset**: The carrying value of the old asset is compared to the fair value of the new asset and a gain or loss is reported.

Effect of impairment, revaluation, and derecognition

Impairment: When an asset is impaired, the impact in that period is:
- The value of the asset is written down.
- Activity ratios such as sales/assets are higher.
- Income is lower due to impairment expense.
- Therefore, profitability ratios are lower.
- Cash flows are not impacted (ignoring taxes)

The impact in subsequent periods is:
- Higher income because of reduced depreciation expense.
- Therefore profitability ratios are higher.
- Activity ratios such as sales/assets are lower.

Revaluation
- An upward revaluation will increase assets and equity.
- Therefore debt to assets and debt to equity ratios are lower.
- A downward revaluation will have the opposite effects.
- The impact on net income and profitability ratios depends on whether the revaluation is to a value above or below cost.

Derecognition
- This can result in either a gain or loss on the income statement.
- A loss will lead to lower net income and assets.
- A gain will lead to higher net income and assets.

Disclosures relating to long lived assets

IFRS presentation guidelines
- For each class of property, plant and equipment, a company must disclose the measurement bases, the depreciation method, the useful lives, the gross carrying amount and the accumulated depreciation at the beginning and end of the period, and a reconciliation of the carrying amount at the beginning and end of the period.
- For each class of intangible assets, a company must disclose whether the useful lives are finite or infinite.
- A company must disclose impairment losses and reversal of impairment losses recognized for every asset during the period.

U.S. GAAP presentation guidelines
- A company must disclose the depreciation expense for the period, the balances of major

classes of depreciable assets, accumulated depreciation by major classes or in total, and a general description of the depreciation method(s) used in computing depreciating expense with respect to the major classes of depreciable assets.

Interpretation of financial statement disclosures regarding long lived assets

Analysts can use the financial statement disclosures to calculate the average age, total useful life and remaining useful life of assets.

Average age = accumulated depreciation / annual depreciation expense.
Total useful life = historical cost / annual depreciation expense.
Remaining useful life = ending PP&E / annual depreciation expense

ABC Inc. reported end-of-year gross PP&E and accumulated depreciation of $200 million and $60 million respectively. Its annual depreciation expense for the current year is $10 million. Calculate the estimated remaining useful life of ABC's PP&E.

Solution:

$$\text{Remaining useful life} = \frac{\text{ending net PP\&E}}{\text{annual depreciation expense}}$$

Remaining useful life = ($200 - $60)/ $10 = 14 years

Investment property

Investment property is defined as property owned for the purpose of capital appreciation or to collect rent. (Allowed only under IFRS not under US GAAP). Investment properties can be valued using either a cost model or a fair value model. Under the fair value model, increases in the value above historical costs are recognized as gains on the income statement (Unlike revaluation model used for PP&E where increases above historical costs are recognized directly in equity as revaluation surplus)

Effect of leasing rather than purchasing assets

- When an asset is purchased through a financing, both an asset and a liability are recorded on the balance sheet.
- When an operating lease is used to acquire an asset, no asset or liability is recorded on the balance sheet. The full lease payment is recorded as a rental expense on the income statement.
- When a finance lease is used to acquire an asset, the accounting treatment is similar to purchasing the asset with debt. The leased asset is recorded on the balance sheet and depreciated over its useful life. The present value of the lease payment is recorded as a liability and amortized over the term of the lease. The interest portion of the lease payment and the depreciation of the asset are recorded as expenses on the income statement. The interest portion of the lease payment is recorded as an operating cash outflow and the principal portion is recorded as a financing cash outflow.

Financial Reporting and Analysis

Finance and operating leases

Lessor (entity lending the asset) perspective

Operating lease

- The asset remains on the balance sheet and is depreciated.
- The lease payments are recorded as rental income.

Finance lease

- The asset is removed from the balance sheet and replaced with a lease receivable.
- The interest portion of the lease payment is recorded as interest income and the principal repayment portion decreases the lease receivable on the balance sheet.

Lessee (entity using the asset) perspective

Operating lease

- No asset or liability is recorded on the balance sheet.
- The entire lease payment is reported as a rental expense on the income statement and as an operating cash flow.

Finance lease

- The leased asset is recorded on the balance sheet and depreciated over its useful life. The present value of the lease payment is recorded as a liability and amortized over the term of the lease.
- The interest portion of the lease payment and the depreciation of the asset are recorded as expenses on the income statement.
- The interest portion of the lease payment is recorded as an operating cash outflow and the principal portion is recorded as a financing cash outflow.

Compared to an operating lease, a finance lease will result in less profit for the lessee in the early years of the lease and greater profits in the later years.

R29 Income Taxes

Deferred tax liabilities and assets

Accounting profit is the pretax income from the income statement. It is based on accounting standards.

Taxable income is income subject to tax. It is based on the tax returns.

The accounting profit and taxable income are different because of differences between the accounting standards and the tax returns. For example,
- Accounting profit is usually calculated using straight line depreciation. While taxable income is usually calculated using accelerated depreciation.
- Accounting profit is usually based on accrual basis of accounting. While taxable income

is usually based on cash-basis accounting.

Deferred tax assets are created when income tax payable is greater than income tax expense. Provided the difference is temporary and expected to reverse in future periods.

Deferred tax liabilities are created when income tax expense is greater than income tax payable. Provided the difference is temporary and expected to reverse in future periods.

Valuation allowance is a contra account to the DTA account. It is used to reduce DTA based on the probability that future tax benefits will not be realized.

Taxes payable is a liability on the balance sheet calculated using taxable income.

Income tax expense is an expense recognized in the income statement that includes taxes payable and changes in deferred tax assets and liabilities.

Income Tax Expense = Income Tax Payable + ΔDTL - ΔDTA

Creation of deferred tax liabilities and assets

Deferred tax liabilities are created when income tax expense is greater than taxes payable. This can occur if revenues are recognized on the income statement before being included on the tax return (e.g. credit sales) or when expenses are tax deductible before they are recognized on the income statement.

Deferred tax assets are created when taxes payable are greater than income tax. This can occur if revenues are taxable before they are recognized on the income statement (unearned revenue) or when expenses are recognized on the income statement before they are tax deductible.

If deferred tax liabilities are expected to reverse in the future they can be classified as liabilities. If they are not expected to reverse in future, they can be classified as equity.

Tax base of a company's assets and liabilities

Tax base of an asset is the value of an asset for tax purposes. For a depreciable fixed asset, the tax base = cost – any depreciation previously taken for tax purposes. If the asset is sold, the taxable gain or loss on the sale = Sales price – Asset's tax base.

Tax base of a liability is the value of a liability for tax purposes. If there is a difference between the book value of a liability and its tax base, the firm will recognize a deferred tax asset or liability to reflect this future tax or tax benefit. DTL = (Carrying amount – Tax base) x Tax rate

Income tax expense v/s income taxes payable

The table below shows the actual tax paid under tax reporting and the income tax expense under financial reporting.

Financial Reporting			Tax Reporting		
	2010	**2011**		**2010**	**2011**
Sales	100	100	Sales	100	100
Cash expenses	40	40	Cash expenses	40	40
Depreciation (SL)	20	20	Depreciation (Acc Dep)	40	10
PBT	40	40	Taxable Income	20	50
Tax expense (@40%)	16	16	Tax payable (@40%)	8	20
PAT	24	24	PAT	12	30

At the end of 2010, tax payable is 8 which is less than the tax expense of 16, so the difference of 8 which is not paid is recorded as a DTL.

At the end of 2011, the tax payable is 20 which is more than the tax expense of 16, so the DTL reduces by 4 to account for the difference between tax payable and the tax expense. The DTL at the end of 2011 is 4.

Impact of tax rate changes

If there is any change in the firm's income tax rates, then existing DTA and DTL must be adjusted to reflect those changes. An increase in the tax rate will increase both a firm's DTA and DTL. A decrease in the tax rate will decrease both a firm's DTA and DTL.

Temporary v/s permanent differences

Temporary difference is a difference between the tax base and carrying amount of assets and liabilities, which is expected to reverse in future. DTA and DTL are created because of temporary differences.

Permanent difference is a difference between taxable income and pre-tax income that will not reverse in the future. Because it will not be reversed, permanent differences do not create a DTA or DTL.

Valuation allowance

- A valuation allowance is a contra account that reduces DTA value on the balance sheet.
- Deferred tax assets must be assessed for their prospective recoverability. If it is probable that they will not be recovered at all or partly, the carrying amount should be reduced. This is done by increasing the valuation allowance.
- Increasing the valuation allowance increases income tax expense and therefore reduces net income.
- If circumstances change, the DTA can be revalued upward. This is done by decreasing the valuation allowance.
- Decreasing the valuation allowance increases net income.

Financial Reporting and Analysis

Recognition and measurement of current and deferred tax items

Current taxes payable or recoverable are based on the applicable tax rates on the balance sheet date of an entity. On the other hand, deferred taxes should be measured at the tax rate that is expected to apply when the asset is realized or the liability is settled.

Disclosures relating to DTA & DTL

Firms report the details of changes in DTA and DTL over a period as well a reconciliation of the differences between their effective tax rate and statutory tax rate. These details can help in understanding past earnings trends and in predicting future effective tax rates.

IFRS v/s US GAAP

Accounting treatment of income taxes under U.S. GAAP and IFRS are similar in most respects. Some notable differences include:

- Upward revaluations are prohibited under U.S. GAAP, however, they are permitted under IFRS and the deferred taxes are recognized in equity.
- Under IFRS, DTA/DTLs are classified as non-current on the balance sheet. Under U.S. GAAP, they are classified as current or non-current based on the classification of the non-tax asset or liability for financial reporting.
- Under IFRS, a DTA is recognized if it is probable that the taxable profit in future will be sufficient enough to use the temporary difference. Whereas under U.S. GAAP, a DTA is recognized in full but reduced by valuation allowance if it is likely that a DTA will not be realized.

R30 Non-Current (Long-Term) Liabilities

Bonds issued at discount/par/premium

- When a bond is issued, both assets (cash) and liabilities (bonds payable) are increased by the bond proceeds. The proceeds are also reported on the cash flow statement as an inflow from financing activities.
- Subsequently, the book value of the bond liability is calculated as the present value of the remaining future cash flows discounted at the market rate of issuance (also called the effective interest rate). The payment of coupons are recorded as a cash outflow from financing activity on the cash flow statement.
- If coupon rate = effective interest rate → Bond is issued at par.
  If coupon rate > effective interest rate → Bond is issued at premium.
  If coupon rate < effective interest rate → Bond is issued at discount.
- The book value of a premium bond decreases over time until it reaches face value at maturity. The book value of a discount bond increases over time until it reaches face

value at maturity.

Effective interest rate method and amortization of bond discounts/premiums

Under the effective interest rate method, interest expense = book value of the bond liability at the beginning of the period x market interest rate at issuance. The interest expense includes amortization of any discount or premium at issuance.

Premium bond:
- The yield < coupon rate, therefore interest expense < coupon payment.
- The difference is subtracted from the bond liability on the balance sheet, which leads to amortization of the premium.

Discount bond:
- The yield > coupon rate, therefore interest expense > coupon payment.
- The difference is added to the bond liability on the balance sheet, which leads to amortization of the discount.

A firm issues $1 million bonds with a 5% coupon rate, 5-year maturity, and annual interest payments when market interest rates are 6%. Calculate the discount amortized in the first year.

Solution:

Since coupon rate < market rate, the bonds will be issued at a discount. Discounting the future payment to their present value indicates that at issuance the company will record an initial book value of $957,876.36.

The interest expense in the first year = Market interest rate at issuance x book value = 957,876.36 x 6% = $57,472.58

Discount amortized in first year = Interest expense − Coupon payment = $57,472.58 − $50,000 = $7,472.58

Derecognition of debt

If a company redeems bonds before maturity, it reports a gain or loss (which is computed as carrying amount of the bonds less amount required to redeem the bonds). Under US GAAP, any remaining unamortized bond issuance costs must also be written off and included in the gain or loss calculation. Under IFRS, write off of issuance cost is not necessary because they are already included in the book value of the bond liability.

Debt covenants

Debt covenants impose restrictions on the borrower that protect the bond holders' interests. The benefit of including debt covenants is that it reduces the default risk for investors and reduces the cost of borrowing for the company. Examples of debt covenants include limitations on future borrowing or requirements to maintain a minimum debt-to-equity ratio.

Financial Reporting and Analysis

Disclosures relating to debt

- The total amount of a company's long-term debt (debt that is due after one year) is combined into a single line item and shown under the non-current liabilities section of the balance sheet.
- The portion of long-term debt that is due within one year is shown as a current liability.
- Additional information on a company's debt is disclosed in the notes to financial statements
- This usually includes nature of liabilities, maturity dates, call and conversion provisions, restrictions, collateral pledged as security and the amount of debt maturing in each of the next five years.

Motivations for leasing assets instead of purchasing them

Compared to purchasing an asset, the advantages of leasing an asset are:
- Off-balance sheet financing.
- Tax reporting advantage.
- Less costly financing.
- Reduced risk of obsolescence.
- Improved leverage ratios.

Finance lease v/s operating lease

Accounting standards require leases to be classified as either operating leases or finance (capital) leases.

Under IFRS, leases are classified as finance leases when substantially all the risks and rewards of legal ownership are transferred to the lessee. Otherwise, the lease is classified as an operating lease.

Under U.S. GAAP, the lessee must classify a lease as a finance lease if any one of the following criteria is met:
- Ownership of the asset is transferred to the lessee at the end of the lease period.
- A bargain purchase option exists.
- The lease term is for 75% or more of the asset's useful life.
- Present value of lease payments is 90% or more of fair value of leased asset.

Recognition and measurement of leases

Operating Lease:
- Initial measurement: No asset or liability reported. The balance sheet is unaffected.
- Subsequent measurement: Lease payments are recognized as expense in lessee's income statement.

Financial Reporting and Analysis

- Cash flow: Lease payments are reported as operating cash outflows.

Finance Lease:
- Initial measurement: The lower of the present value of future lease payments or the fair value of the leased asset is recognized as an asset and a liability on the lessee's balance sheet.
- Subsequent measurement: Finance lease payment consists of depreciation of the asset and interest on the loan.
- Cash flow: The lease payment is split and reported as an operating cash outflow (interest expense) and financing cash outflow (principal reduction).

At the beginning of 2015, XYZ Inc. enters a finance lease that requires four annual payments of $15,000 each beginning on the first day of the lease. The lease interest rate is 6%. Calculate the amount of interest expense that XYZ will report in 2015.

Solution:
The present value of the lease payments at inception is $55,095.18
(BGN mode: N = 4, I = 6, PMT = $15,000, FV = 0. CPT PV = -$55,095.18)
After the first payment is made the book value of the lease liability will reduce to
$55,095.18 - $15,000 = $40,095.18.
Interest expense for the first year = Book value of the lease x lease interest rate = $2,405.71

Disclosures relating to finance and operating leases

Required disclosures about finance leases and operating leases in the financial statements include:
- A general description of the leasing arrangement.
- Restrictions imposed by the lease agreement.
- The nature, timing, and amount of payments to be paid in each of the next five years. Lease payments after five years can be shown together.
- Amount of lease expense reported in income statement for each period.

Disclosure of defined contribution and defined benefit pension plans

Two types of pension plans are:

Defined Contribution Plans
- The amount of contribution into the plan is specified. However, the amount of pension that is ultimately paid by the plan is not defined and it depends on the performance of the plan's assets.
- The cash payment made into the plan is recognized as pension expense on the income statement.

Financial Reporting and Analysis

Defined Benefits Plans
- The amount of pension that is ultimately paid by the plan is defined, usually according to a benefit formula.
- Under both IFRS and US GAAP, companies must report the difference between the defined benefit pension obligations and the pension assets as an asset or liability on the balance sheet.
- Under IFRS, the change in the defined benefit plan net asset or liability is recognized as a cost of the period. Two components of the change (service cost and net interest expense or income) are recognized in the income statement and one component (remeasurements) is recognized in other comprehensive income.
- Under US GAAP, the change in the defined benefit plan net asset or liability is also recognized as a cost of the period. Three components of the change (current service costs, interest expense on the beginning pension obligation, and expected return on plan assets) are recognized in income statement and two components (past service costs and actuarial gains and losses) are recognized in other comprehensive income.

Leverage and coverage ratios

Solvency refers to a company's ability to meet its long-term debt obligations. In evaluating solvency:
- Leverage ratios focus on the balance sheet and measure the amount of debt financing relative to equity financing.

Leverage Ratio	Numerator	Denominator
Debt to assets	Total debt	Total assets
Debt to capital	Total debt	Total debt + shareholder's equity
Debt to equity	Total debt	Total shareholder's equity
Financial leverage	Average total assets	Average total equity

- Coverage ratios focus on the income statement and cash flows and measure the ability of a company to cover its interest payments.

Coverage Ratio	Numerator	Denominator
Interest coverage	EBIT	Interest payments
Fixed charge coverage	EBIT + Lease payments	Interest payments + lease payments

R31 Financial Reporting Quality

Financial reporting quality v/s quality of reported results

Reporting quality refers to the information disclosed in the firm's financial statements. High-quality reporting means that the financial statements are decision useful and represent the economic reality of the company.

Results quality (earnings quality) refers to the earnings and cash generated by the company's actual economic activities. High quality earnings means that the earnings are sustainable and are expected to continue in the future.

Spectrum for assessing financial reporting quality

Spectrum for assessing financial reporting quality considers both reporting quality and earnings quality. It spans from the highest quality to the lowest quality.

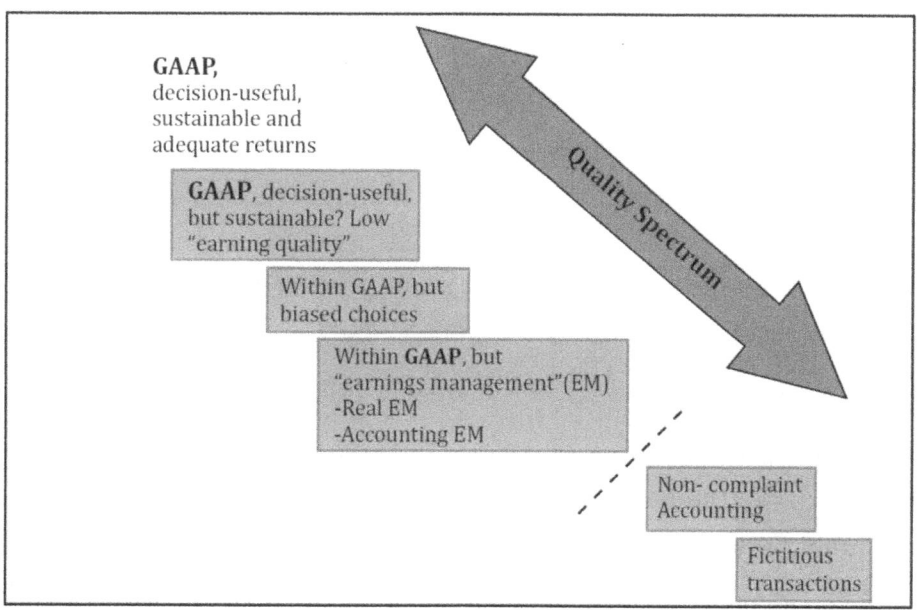

Conservative v/s aggressive accounting

Aggressive accounting refers to biased accounting choices that aim to improve the reported earnings or financial position in the current period.

Conservative accounting refers to biased accounting choices that aim to decrease the reported earnings or financial position for the current period.

Some managers use aggressive accounting when earnings are below targets and conservative accounting when earnings are above targets, to artificially smooth earnings.

Motivations to issue low quality financial reports

Managers may be motivated to issue financial reports that are not high quality in order to:
- mask poor performance.
- boost the stock price.
- increase personal compensation.
- avoid violation of debt covenants.

Financial Reporting and Analysis

Conditions leading to low-quality financial reports

Conditions that are conducive to issuing low-quality financial reports are:

Motivation: Covered above.

Opportunity:
- Weak internal controls.
- Ineffective board of directors.
- Accounting standards that allow a range of choices.

Rationalization: Ability to justify wrong choices to him/herself.

Mechanisms that discipline financial reporting quality

Mechanisms that discipline financial reporting quality include:
- the free market and incentives for companies to minimize cost of capital.
- Auditors.
- contract provisions specifically tailored to penalize misreporting.
- enforcement by regulatory entities.

Non-Standard Measures

Pro-forma earnings (also called non-GAAP or non-IFRS earnings) adjust earnings as reported on the income statement. For example, earnings that exclude certain nonrecurring items. Companies are required to make additional disclosures when presenting any non-GAAP or non-IFRS metric. Firms are required to define and explain the relevance of any non-GAAP measures and reconcile them to the most comparable IFRS measure.

Biased accounting choices and estimates

Examples of accounting choices that affect income statement and balance sheet include:
- inventory cost flow assumptions.
- estimates of uncollectible accounts receivable.
- estimated realizability of deferred tax assets.
- depreciation method.
- estimated salvage value of depreciable assets.
- estimated useful life of depreciable assets.

Accounting warning signs

A company may manipulate earnings by:
- Biased revenue recognition.
- Biased expense recognition.

Financial Reporting and Analysis

The biases may relate to:
- Timing of recognition – e.g. deferring expenses by capitalizing them.
- Location of recognition – e.g. recording a loss in OCI directly by bypassing the income statement.

Warning signs for detection include:
- Revenue recognition policies that make it easier to record revenue prematurely.
- Use of barter transactions.
- Use of rebate programs.
- Revenue growth out of line with its competitors or industry.
- Decreases in turnover ratios like receivables, inventory or total asset over time.
- Net income not supported by operating cash flows.
- Depreciation methods, assumptions of useful lives and salvage values not comparable to peers.
- Fourth-quarter earnings surprises.
- Classification of expenses as non-recurring.
- Use of non-standard measures (pro-forma earnings).

R32 Financial Statement Analysis: Applications

Evaluating past financial performance

Evaluating a company's past financial performance helps understand not only what happened but also the reasons behind the company's performance and how the performance reflects the company's strategy.

Forecasting a company's future net income and cash flow

A company's future income and cash flows are projected by forecasting sales growth. Then the analyst uses estimates of profit margins and level of investment in working and fixed capital required to support projected sales, to calculate net income and cash flows.

Role of financial statement analysis in assessing credit quality

Credit analysis uses financial statement analysis to assess credit quality. Indicators include:
- tolerance for leverage
- operational stability
- margin stability

Use of financial statement analysis in screening for potential equity investments

Potentially attractive equity investments can be identified by screening a universe of stocks, using minimum or maximum values of one or more ratios. When ratios constructed

from financial statement data and market data are used to screen for potential equity investments, fundamental decisions include:
- which metrics to use as screens.
- how many metrics to include.
- what values of those metrics to use as cutoff points.
- what weighting to give to each metric.

Adjustments to a company's financial statements

Sometimes it is necessary to adjust a company's financial statements. For example, when comparing companies that use different accounting methods or assumptions. Adjustments include those related to:
- investments
- inventory
- property, plant and equipment
- goodwill
- off-balance-sheet financing

Corporate Finance

R33 Corporate Governance and ESG: An Introduction

Corporate governance overview

Corporate governance refers to the system of controls and procedures by which individual companies are managed. It outlines the rights and responsibilities of various groups and how conflicts of interest among the various groups are to be resolved.

Stakeholder groups

The primary stakeholders of a company include:
- Shareholders
- Creditors
- Managers and employees
- Board of directors
- Customers
- Suppliers
- Government/Regulators

Stakeholder relationships

The principal-agent relationship refers to owners hiring agents to perform a particular task or service on their behalf. Such relationships can lead to conflicts because the agent's interest may not align with those of the owner's.

Stakeholder management

Stakeholder management includes identifying, prioritizing, and understanding the interests of various stakeholder groups. Based on these inputs the company's relationship with its stakeholders is managed. The management of stakeholder relationships is constructed on the company's legal, contractual, organizational, and governmental infrastructure.

Mechanisms to manage stakeholder relationships

Mechanisms to manage stakeholder relationships include:
- general meetings
- board of directors
- audits
- company reporting and transparency
- related party transactions
- remuneration policies etc.

Company's board of directors & committees

A board of directors is the central pillar of corporate governance. The board of directors is elected by shareholders to act in their interest. **Executive (internal)** directors are typically members of senior management employed by the company. **Non-executive (external)** directors have no other relationship with the company. They are also called independent directors.

A board primarily has these two duties - duty of care and duty of loyalty towards the shareholders. A company's board of directors can have several committees that are responsible for specific functions. For example,

- audit committee
- governance committee
- remuneration committee
- nomination committee
- risk committee
- investment committee

Factors that can affect stakeholder relationships and corporate governance

Factors that can affect stakeholder relationships and corporate governance are:

- Shareholder engagement and communication.
- Shareholder activism - Includes a range of strategies that may be used by shareholders when seeking to force a company to act in a desired manner.
- Company's legal and regulatory environment.
- Threat of hostile takeover and presence of anti-takeover defenses.
- Firms that provide advice on proxy voting and also rate a company's corporate governance.

Risks of poor corporate governance & benefits of good corporate governance

The risks of poor corporate governance include:

- weak control systems
- ineffective decision making
- legal risk
- regulatory risk
- reputational risk
- default risk

The benefits of effective corporate governance include:

- higher operational efficiency, control, operating and financial performance.
- lower default risk which translates into lower cost of capital.

Analyst considerations

Factors relevant to the analysis of corporate governance and stakeholder management

Corporate Finance

include:
- economic ownership and voting structure
- board composition
- management remuneration and company performance
- investor composition
- strength of shareholders' rights
- management of long-term risks

ESG considerations in investment analysis

ESG integration means factoring environmental, social, and governance factors in the investment process. Terms used in relation to ESG integration include:
- sustainable investing
- responsible investing
- socially responsible investing
- impact investing

ESG implementation methods

Methods of integrating ESG concerns into portfolio construction are:
- **Negative screening**: Excludes certain companies or sectors from investment that do not meet ESG criteria.
- **Positive screening**: Focuses on investments with favorable ESG aspects.
- **Thematic investing**: Focuses on a single factor, such as energy efficiency or climate change.

R34 Capital Budgeting

Capital budgeting process

Capital budgeting is the process utilized by companies to decide which projects are profitable and worth implementing. The method analyzes the cash flows generated by long-term projects or decisions. The capital budgeting process includes the following steps:

Idea generation → Analyzing project ideas → Create firm-wide capital budget → Monitoring decisions and conducting a post-audit

The following are the five categories of capital budgeting projects with examples:
1. **Replacement projects:** Analyzing whether the replacement of existing equipment would be profitable.

2. **Expansion projects:** Constructing a new plant or expanding capacity of the existing one.
3. **New products and services:** Diversifying current business operations to maintain competitive edge.
4. **Mandatory projects:** Regulatory, safety and environmental laws mandated by a governmental agency or an insurance company.
5. **Other projects:** Pet projects of senior management or high-uncertainty projects like R&D that are difficult to analyze using the traditional methods.

Basic principles of capital budgeting

1. **Decisions should be based on incremental cash flows (not on accounting income as it is based on accrual basis):**
   - Exclude sunk costs
     For example, already incurred costs like preliminary consulting fees should not be included in the analysis.
   - Include externalities - Both positive/negative externalities should be considered in the analysis.
     For example, negative impact of a new diet soda product launch on the sales of existing soda products.

(Note: In a conventional cash flow, the sign of cash flows changes only once during the life of the project; while an unconventional cash flow has more than one sign change.)

2. **Timing of cash flows is vital:** Due to time value of money, cash flows received earlier are more valuable than cash flows received later.
3. **Cash flows are based on opportunity cost**
   For example, if you plan to use an existing office space rather than renting it out, then rental income from the office space is an opportunity cost.
4. **Cash flows are analyzed on an after-tax basis:** Shareholder value increases only on the cash that they have earned. Hence, any tax expenses must be deducted from the cash flows.
5. **Financial costs are ignored:** Financial costs are already included in the cost of capital (discount rates) used to discount cash flows to arrive at the present value. Hence, to avoid double-counting, they must not be deducted from the project's cash flows.

Mutually exclusive projects, project sequencing, and capital rationing

Independent projects vs. mutually exclusive projects: Independent projects are unrelated projects that can be analyzed separately, while mutually exclusive projects compete with each other. Two independent projects can both be executed if they individually meet the criteria. If two projects are mutually exclusive, then either of the two can be undertaken, not both.

Project sequencing: Certain projects are linked through time, i.e. completion of one project creates an opportunity to invest in another project later based on its profitability.

Unlimited funds vs. capital rationing: A firm can undertake all the profitable projects if it has access to unlimited funds. A company having limited capital must prioritize and allocate funds to projects that maximize shareholder value.

Net present value (NPV), internal rate of return (IRR), payback period, discounted payback period & profitability index (PI)

Net present value (NPV) is the expected impact to shareholder wealth if the project is undertaken. It is the present value of the future after tax cash flows minus the value of investments made in the project.

$$NPV = CF0 + \left[\frac{CF1}{(1+r)^1}\right] + \left[\frac{CF2}{(1+r)^2}\right] + \left[\frac{CF3}{(1+r)^3}\right]$$

Decision rule:
- For independent projects:
    If NPV > 0, accept the project.
    If NPV < 0, reject the project.
- For mutually exclusive projects:
    Accept the project with higher and positive NPV.

Internal rate of return (IRR) is the discount rate that makes net present value of all cash flows from a project equal to 0 (i.e. the discount rate that makes present value of all inflows equal to the outflows).

Decision rule:
- For independent projects:
    If IRR > required rate of return (usually firms cost of capital adjusted for project's riskiness), accept the project.
    If IRR < required rate of return, reject the project.
- For mutually exclusive projects:
    Accept the project with higher IRR (as long as IRR > cost of capital).

Payback period is the time taken in years to recover the initial cost of investment.
- Advantages: Primarily a measure of firm's liquidity.
- Disadvantages: Ignores time value of money and cash flows after the payback period, like salvage value.

Discounted payback period is the time taken in years to recover the initial cost of investment in present value terms.
- Advantages: Primarily a measure of firm's liquidity and uses time value of money.
- Disadvantages: Ignores cash flows after the payback period, like salvage or terminal

Corporate Finance

value.

Profitability index is the present value of a project's future cash flows divided by the initial outlay.

$$PI = \frac{PV \text{ of future cash flows}}{\text{initial investment}} = 1 + \frac{NPV}{\text{initial investment}}$$

Decision rule:
- If PI > 1, accept the project.
- If PI < 1, reject the project.

NPV profile

NPV profile shows the sensitivity of a project's NPV for different discount rates. It is plotted on a graph where NPVs are on the y-axis with the discount rates on the x-axis.

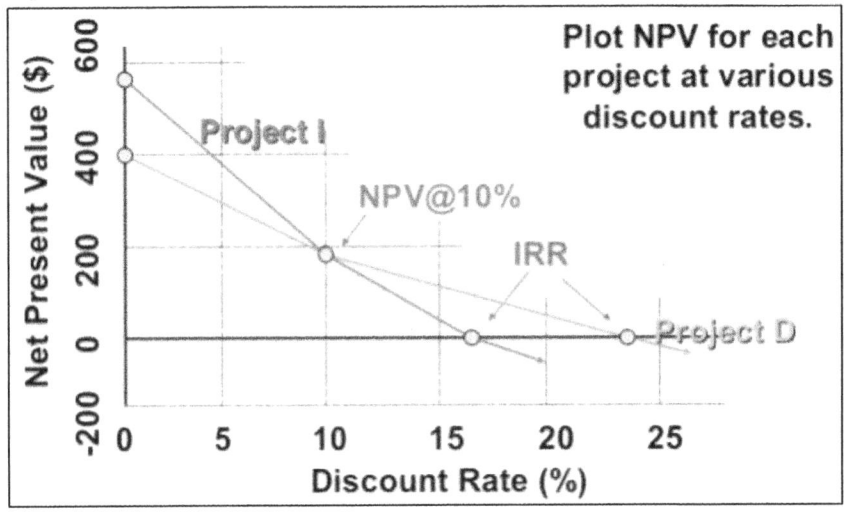

- Crossover rate is the discount rate at which the NPVs of both the projects are equal. The differences in timings of cash flows cause the two profiles to intersect and crossover.
- Both NPV profiles intersect x axis where their NPVs are 0 i.e. at their IRRs.
- In the above NPV profile, if Project I and Project D are mutually exclusive projects, for discount rates greater than 10%, Project D should be selected while for discount rates less than 10%, project I should be selected.

Comparison between NPV and IRR method

NPV method	IRR method
Advantages: <ul><li>Direct measure of expected increase in value of the firm.</li><li>Produces theoretically correct decisions for unconventional cash flows.</li></ul>	Advantages: <ul><li>Gives percentage return on each dollar invested.</li><li>Direct comparison with the cost of capital.</li></ul>

163

Disadvantages:	Disadvantages:
• Ignores project size. (Profitability Index overcomes this drawback.)	• Conflicting rankings that are different from NPV analysis for mutually exclusive projects. (Choose the project with higher NPV.) • Projects with unconventional cash flow pattern can have multiple IRRs or no IRR. • Unrealistically assumes that the money is reinvested at IRR rates.

For mutually exclusive projects, the NPV and IRR methods can have conflicting results due to the differences in project size or timings of cash flows. In such a case, always select project using NPV method. For independent projects, both NPV and IRR analysis yields the same decision.

Relation between net present value (NPV) and share price

A firm's value is a function of its future cash flows. As NPV directly measures the expected change in firm value from a project execution, it is a criterion most closely related to stock prices.

Theoretically, a positive NPV project should cause a proportionate increase in a firm's stock value. However, the street expectations of the NPV of the firm's projects can vary that from the management's and have an impact on the stock prices.

Capital budgeting approaches:
- Public and larger firms: NPV and IRR
- Private and European firms: Payback period

R35 Cost of Capital

Weighted average cost of capital (WACC)

- It is the overall cost of the sources of capital.
- Represents the required return or opportunity costs for the firm as a whole.
- It is the appropriate discount rate for cash flows of projects having similar risk profile as that of the firm.
- Has weights that are derived from target capital structure and market values of each source of capital.
- Is also called the marginal cost of capital (MCC)

$$WACC = w_d r_d (1 - t) + w_p r_p + w_e r_e$$

A firm has the following capital structure: 20% debt (w_d), 10% preferred stock (w_p), and 70% equity (w_e). The before-tax cost of debt is 6% (r_d), cost of preferred stock is 8% (r_p), and cost of equity is 12% (r_e). The firm's marginal tax rate is 30 percent (t). Calculate its WACC.

Solution:

The WACC can be calculated using the formula.

WACC = (0.2) (0.06) (1 - 0.3) + (0.1) (0.08) + (0.7) (0.12) = 10.04%

Impact of taxes

Interest costs on the debt component are tax deductible, while dividends paid to preferred and common stock holders are not tax deductible. To arrive at the after-tax cost of capital, we multiply only the cost of debt by (1 – t).

Alternative methods of calculating the weights used in the WACC

Weights should be based on the market value of each component in the firm's target capital structure. If explicit information about a firm's target capital structure is not available, use:

- Current capital structure based on market values.
- Trend in the firm's capital structure or management statements regarding capital structure policy.
- Industry average capital structure

Marginal cost of capital and the investment opportunity schedule

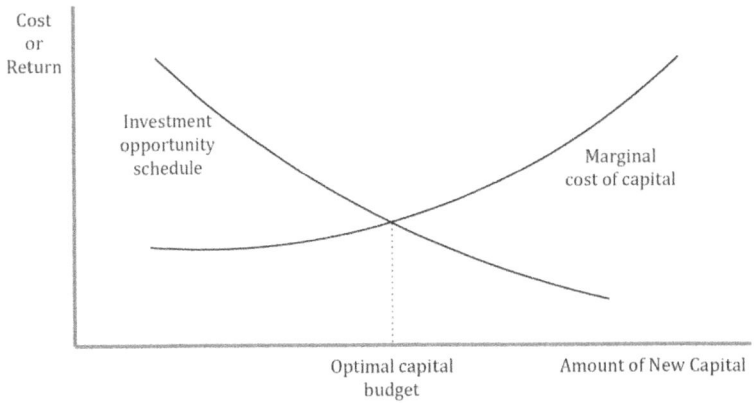

- A company's marginal cost of capital (cost of raising additional capital) may increase as larger amounts of capital are raised (depicted by the rising marginal cost of capital curve).
- On the other hand, the return on investment decreases as a company invests in additional opportunities (depicted by the declining investment opportunity schedule curve).
- The point of intersection gives the optimal capital budget (the point where shareholder value is maximized as all positive NPV projects have been undertaken).

Calculating cost of debt

The **yield to maturity (YTM) approach**: Annualized return an investor earns for holding a bond till maturity.

A company has issued a 5-year, 10% semi-annual coupon bond having a face value of $1000. The bond on issuance sells at $950. If the marginal tax rate for the company is 40%, calculate the after-tax cost of debt.

Solution:
N = 5*2= 10, PV = -950, FV = 1000, PMT = (0.10/2) * 1000 = 50. You will get I/Y = 5.67 %.
To annualize it, multiply the rate by 2. Annual I/Y = 11.34%.
The after-tax cost of debt = 11.34(1 - 0.4) = 6.8%

Debt rating approach: This method is used when the company's debt doesn't have a YTM as it is not publicly traded. In such a case, the approach is as follows:
- Determine the current market rates for comparable bonds with similar ratings and maturities (matrix pricing).
- Analyze the company characteristics like covenants, seniority etc. to get before-tax cost of debt.
- Apply the marginal tax rate to arrive at the after-tax cost of debt.

Cost of noncallable, nonconvertible preferred stock

Cost of preferred stock is the preferred dividend cost that a company pays to preferred stockholders. Cost of preferred stock = preferred dividend/market price of preferred shares

For example, XYZ Company has preferred stock that currently trades $200 per share and has preferred dividend of $10 per share.
Cost of preferred stock = 10/200 = 5.0%

Calculating cost of equity

Capital asset pricing model: Cost of equity can be calculated using the following formula:
$r_e = RFR + \beta [E(R_m) - RFR]$
where:
RFR: risk free rate
β: sensitivity of a stock's return compared to market return
$E(R_m)$: expected market return.

Dividend discount model: Intrinsic value of a stock is the present value of future cash flows to shareholders i.e. dividends. The cost of equity is calculated using the formula:
$r_e = \frac{D_i}{P_0} + g$
where:

Corporate Finance

D_1: next year's dividend
P_0: current stock price
g = (1 − payout rate) * ROE = retention ratio * ROE

Bond yield plus risk premium method: It is an ad hoc method of adding risk premium to bond yield.

r_e = bond yield + risk premium

Beta of a project

Project's beta is a measure of systematic or market risk present in a particular project. It is used to adjust for differences between project's risk and firm's average risk.

Project's beta is estimated using **'Pure play method'**. This method has three steps:

Step 1: Shortlist comparable publicly traded companies.

Step 2: Derive unlevered beta or comparable asset beta for the project using comparable company's D/E and tax rate:

$$\beta_{asset} = \beta_{equity} * \frac{1}{1+\frac{(1-t)D}{E}}$$

Step 3: Get the equity levered beta for the project using project specific D/E and tax rate:

$$\beta_{equity} = \beta_{asset} * \left(1 + \frac{(1-t)D}{E}\right)$$

Drawbacks of **"Pure Play"** method:
- Public companies' betas are dependent on time frequency and indexes used.
- Beta obtained in step 3 may need to be adjusted upwards for small firms.

Country risk premiums

CAPM is modified to adjust for additional risk in a developing market by adding country risk premium (CRP) to market risk premium.

$r_e = RFR + \beta \, [E\,(R_m) - RFR + CRP]$

$CRP = \text{sovereign yield spread} * \frac{\text{annualized standard deviation of equity index}}{\sigma}$

where:

σ = annualized standard deviation of the sovereign bond market in terms of the developed market currency

Sovereign yield spread is the difference between developing country government bond yields and similar maturity treasury bonds.

Marginal cost of capital schedule

Marginal cost of capital schedule is plotted as a graph with the WACC on y-axis and the amount capital raised on the x-axis. It is upward sloping, because the costs of financing increases as the firm raises more capital. It has break points, where cost of capital of a

Corporate Finance

component changes.

$$\text{Break point} = \frac{\text{(amount of capital at which the source's cost of capital changes)}}{\text{(weight of component in capital structure)}}$$

Correct treatment of flotation costs

Floatation costs are the fees charged by investment bankers for raising new capital (typically between 2% - 7%).

Incorrect treatment:

$$r_e = \frac{D_i}{P_0(1-f)} + g$$

where:
f: Flotation costs in percentage

Reason: Flotation expenses are one-time charge and should not be incorporated in the cost of capital for the entire projects duration.

Correct treatment:
Incorporate the dollar amount of flotation costs in the initial investment outlay.

R36 Measures of Leverage

Business risk, sales risk, operating risk, & financial risk

Leverage is the use of fixed costs in a company's cost structure. The two components of leverage are:
- Operating leverage: For example, building rent and equipment leases
- Financial leverage: For example, interest payments

Business risk is the risk associated with operating income. It has two components:
- Sales risk: Uncertainty in firm's sales.
- Operating risk: Uncertainty due to fixed operating costs
  (High for firms having higher proportion of fixed to variable costs).

Financial risk is the risk associated with debt financing.

Calculating degree of operating leverage, financial leverage, and total leverage

Degree of operating leverage (DOL) measures operating risk. It is the ratio of the percentage change in operating income to the percentage change in quantity sold.

$$DOL = \frac{Q(P-V)}{Q(P-V) - F} = \frac{S - TVC}{S - TVC - F}$$

where:
Q: Quantity sold,
P: Unit price,
V: Variable cost per unit,

F: Fixed operating costs
S: Dollar amount of sales,
TVC: total variable costs,

Degree of financial leverage (DFL) measures financial risk. It is the ratio of percentage change in net income to percentage change in operating income.

$$DFL = \frac{Q(P-V)-F}{Q(P-V)-F-I} = \frac{EBIT}{EBIT-interest}$$

where:
Q: Quantity sold,
P: Unit price,
V: Variable cost per unit,
F: Fixed costs
I: Fixed financial costs

Degree of total leverage (DTL) combines DOL and DFL. It is the ratio of percentage change in net income to percentage change in units sold.

$$DTL = \frac{Q(P-V)}{Q(P-V)-F-I} = \frac{S-TVC}{S-TVC-F-I}$$

Effect of financial leverage

Financial leverage has the potential to increase NI and ROE. For example, all else equal for the same level of EBIT, the firm with higher leverage will have higher NI and ROE. However, it also increases the volatility of the NI and ROE. For example, all else equal for the same percentage decline in EBIT, the firm with higher leverage will have a greater decline in its NI and ROE.

Breakeven quantity of sales

Breakeven quantity of sales is the quantity of units sold to earn revenue equal to the fixed and variable costs i.e. for net income to be 0.

$$Q(BE) = \frac{\text{fixed operating costs + fixed financing costs}}{\text{price per unit - variable cost per unit}}$$

Note: (price per unit - variable cost per unit) is also called the contribution margin.

Operating breakeven quantity of sales

Operating breakeven quantity of sales ignores the fixed financing costs i.e. quantity sold for operating income to be 0.

$$Q(OBE) = \frac{\text{fixed operating costs}}{\text{price per unit - variable cost per unit}}$$

Corporate Finance

R37 Working Capital Management

Primary and secondary sources of liquidity

Primary sources:
- Cash sources used in day-to-day operations.
- For example, cash balances, trade credit, lines of credit from bank etc.

Secondary sources:
- Impacts the day-to-day operations and alters the financial structure. May indicate deteriorating financial condition.
- For example, liquidating assets, filing for bankruptcy, negotiating debt agreements etc.

Factors influencing company's liquidity position

Internal factors:
- <u>Company size and growth rate</u>: Liquidity requirements are high for faster and larger organizations.
- <u>Organizational structure</u>: Decentralized companies have higher liquidity requirements.
- <u>Sophistication of working capital management</u>: Liquidity requirements are low for better managed operations.
- <u>Capital market access</u>: Ease of access lowers working capital needs.

External factors:
- <u>Banking services</u>: Countries having developed banking systems will have low liquidity requirements.
- <u>Interest rates</u>: High cost of borrowing will compel more liquidity.
- <u>State of the economy</u>: Downturns make borrowing difficult.
- <u>Competitors</u>: In a highly competitive industry, working capital requirements will be relatively high.

Drags on liquidity reduce cash inflows. For example, bad debts, obsolete inventory, uncollected receivables etc.

Pulls on liquidity accelerate cash outflows. For example, earlier payment of vendor dues etc.

Company's liquidity measures

These ratios should be evaluated in comparison with peer companies from the industry segment.

Liquidity Ratios:
- Current ratio $= \dfrac{\text{current assets}}{\text{current liabilities}}$
- Quick ratio $= \dfrac{\text{cash+short−term marketable securities+receivables}}{\text{current liablities}}$ (also known as acid-test ratio)

Corporate Finance

- Receivables turnover = $\dfrac{\text{credit sales}}{\text{average receivables}}$
- Number of days of receivables = $\dfrac{365}{\text{receivables turnover}} = \dfrac{\text{average receivables}}{\text{average day's credit sales}}$
- Inventory turnover = $\dfrac{\text{cost of goods sold}}{\text{average inventory}}$
- Number of days of inventory = $\dfrac{365}{\text{inventory turnover}} = \dfrac{\text{average inventory}}{\text{average day's COGS}}$
- Payables turnover = $\dfrac{\text{purchases}}{\text{average trade payables}}$
- Number of days of payables = $\dfrac{365}{\text{payables turnover ratio}} = \dfrac{\text{average payables}}{\text{average day's purchases}}$

Operating and cash conversion cycle

Operating cycle is the number of days needed to convert raw materials into cash from sales.

Operating cycle = days of inventory + days of receivables

Cash conversion cycle measures the number of days from paying suppliers of raw materials to collecting cash from sales of finished goods. Shorter cycle implies high cash-generating ability.

Cash conversion cycle = average days of receivables + average days of inventory - average days of payables

Daily cash position

Daily cash position refers to cash balances required for routine expenses. Major sources of cash inflows and outflows should be accurately forecasted to maintain a minimum cash balance. The common sources of cash inflows and outflows are:

Inflows	Outflows
Sales and collection of receivables	Payments to employees
Cash from subsidiaries	Payments to suppliers
Maturing investments	Other expenses
Other income like dividends	Capital expenditures
Tax refunds	Interest expenses
Borrowings	Taxes

Corporate Finance

Calculating and understanding comparable yields

Discount basis yield = $\frac{F-P}{F} * \frac{360}{T}$ (also known as bank discount yield)

Money market yield = $\frac{F-P}{P} * \frac{360}{T}$

Bond equivalent yield = $\frac{F-P}{P} * \frac{365}{T}$

180-day U.S. T-bill with a face value of $1,000 was purchased at a discount rate of 6%. Calculate the money market yield and bond equivalent yield.

Solution:

Solving for P,

Discount basis yield = $\frac{F-P}{F} * \frac{360}{T} = \frac{1000-P}{1000} * \frac{360}{180} = 0.06$

We get P = $970

Solving for,

Money market yield = $\frac{F-P}{P} * \frac{360}{T} = \frac{1000-970}{970} * \frac{360}{180} = 6.19\%$

Bond equivalent yield = $\frac{F-P}{P} * \frac{365}{T} = \frac{1000-970}{970} * \frac{365}{180} = 6.27\%$

The objective of short term investment is to generate a reasonable return without taking excessive credit and liquidity risk (high credit quality and relatively short maturities are preferred). A short-term investment policy statement is written to identify the objective of investment, authorities responsible, limitations on types of securities etc.

Assessing accounts receivables, inventory, and accounts payable

Accounts receivable: A simple method is to compare number of days of receivables with peer group firms or against its own historical performance. A detailed report on accounts receivable is available through the **aging schedule**.

XYZ Inc. has the following aging schedule for the month of March for its accounts receivables. Derive the weighted average collection period.

Given data: Days outstanding, accounts receivables and average collection period for each accounts receivables group.

Aging schedule for March				
Days outstanding	Accounts receivable	Weight	Avg. collection days	Days x weight
< 31 days	4,000	40%	20	8
31 - 60 days	3,000	30%	45	13.5
61 - 90 days	2,000	20%	80	16
> 90 days	1,000	10%	120	12
Weighted average collection period:				**49.5 days**

Corporate Finance

Inventory:
- Ratios to monitor: Inventory turnover ratio and number of days of inventory, compared over time and relative to peer group average.
- Decreasing inventory turnover ratio indicates rise in inventory levels and less products being sold or the company building inventory to avoid stock-outs.

Accounts payable: The **cost of trade credit** tells us whether investing funds in the short term is better than availing the trade credit period to make the payment.

$$\text{Cost of trade credit} = \left[1 + \left(\frac{\%\text{discount}}{1-\%\text{discount}}\right)^{\frac{365}{\text{days past discount period}}}\right] - 1$$

If cost of trade credit > short-term investment rate, then use the trade credit as return is higher.

A company's payment terms are 2/10 Net 80. What does this mean? What is the cost of not taking the discount if the payment is made on the 40th day?

Solution:
"2/10 net 80" means the company gets a 2% discount if the bill is paid within ten days, else the entire bill is due within 80 days.

$$\text{Cost of trade credit} = \left(1 + \frac{0.02}{1-0.02}\right)^{\frac{365}{40-10}} - 1 = 27.9\%$$

The cost of not taking the discount is 27.9%. Compare this cost with the return on the company's short-term investment returns. If cost is greater than the return, the company should avail the discount.

- Ratios to monitor: Payables turnover and number of days of payables.
- Evaluate number of days of payables with the credit terms offered to check if payables are being paid too soon or too late.

Assessing choices of short-term funding

Firms should select the most cost-effective rate given its needs, assets and creditworthiness.

Sources of short-term financing:

Bank sources:
- Line of credit: Uncommitted, Committed or Regular or Overdraft and Revolving (revolving is the most reliable, while uncommitted is the least)
- Banker's Acceptance: Guarantee made by the importing company's bank that payment will be made on receipt of the goods.
- Factoring: Sale of receivables at a discount from their face values. Buyer of the receivables takes on the responsibility of collection.
- Large credit worthy companies use lines of credit. Companies with weaker credit terms

have to use collateral for bank borrowings.

Non-bank sources: Commercial paper, non-bank finance companies, etc.
- Smaller firms with poor credit history may use nonbank finance companies, while large creditworthy companies may issue commercial paper.

R38 Portfolio Management: An overview

Portfolio approach to investing

Portfolio approach to investing evaluates individual investments by their contribution to the risk and return to an investor's total portfolio.

Diversification helps investors reduce portfolio risk without compromising the expected return. Diversification of risk can be measured with **diversification ratio**.

$$\text{Diversification ratio} = \frac{\text{risk of equally weighted portfolio of n securities}}{\text{risk of single security selected at random}}$$

If the average standard deviation of returns of the 3 stocks is 30% and the standard deviation of returns for an equally weighted portfolio of 3 stocks is 16%. Calculate the diversification ratio.

Solution:

Diversification ratio = $\frac{0.16}{0.30}$ = 0.53

Lower ratio indicates better diversification.

Types and distinctive characteristics of investors

The investment needs of different investors are shown in the table below:

	Investment Horizon	Risk Tolerance	Income Needs	Liquidity Needs
Individual Investors	Depends on individual goals.	Depends on the ability and willingness to take risk.	Depends on rationale behind investment.	Depends on individual.
Banks	Short	Low	Pay interest on deposits.	High, to meet the daily withdrawals.
DB pension plans	Long, depends on the employee profile.	High for longer investment horizon.	High for mature funds (payouts are closer), low for growing funds.	Low
Endowments and foundations	Long	High	Meeting spending obligations.	Low

Insurance Companies (P&C)	Short	Low	Low	High
Insurance Companies (Life)	Long	Low (because of high liquidity needs.)	Low	High
Mutual Funds	Varies by fund	Varies by fund	Varies by fund	High to meet redemptions.

Defined contribution and defined benefit pension plans

Defined contribution plan: Each year the firm contributes a sum to the employees' retirement plan. The investment risk lies entirely with the employee as the future value of investments is not pledged by the firm.

Defined benefit plan: Firm promises future benefits to be paid to the employees on retirement and hence takes on the entire investment risk.

Portfolio management process

The three steps in the portfolio management process are:

1. Planning	<ul><li>Analyzing the client's needs: Return, risk, time, tax, liquidity, legal and unique preferences.</li><li>Preparation of investment policy statement. (updated every year or when objectives change)</li></ul>
2. Execution	<ul><li>Risk and return analysis of asset classes.</li><li>Asset allocation proportion among various classes.</li><li>Security analysis to find opportunities within the asset class.</li><li>Portfolio construction with the identified securities.</li></ul>
3. Feedback	<ul><li>Portfolio monitoring and rebalancing.</li><li>Performance measurement, reporting and evaluation.</li></ul>

Pooled investment products

Mutual fund is an investment pool of multiple investors, in which each investor has claim on income and value of the fund in proportion to the investment made by them.

Net asset value = value of assets − liabilities.

Open-end fund: A mutual fund that allows the issuance of new shares or redemption of existing shares, i.e. new investments are allowed. (**No-load funds:** Do not charge fees on redemption and fees for purchasing of shares; while **load funds** can charge either or both the fees). Purchases and sales are made with the fund.

Closed-end fund: No new investment money is accepted after inception. Purchases and sales are made on exchanges or over-the-counter. They can trade at significant discount to NAV due to imbalances in investor supply and demand.

Types of mutual funds:
- Money market funds: Invest in short-term debt securities providing interest income and have very little risk.
- Bond mutual funds: Invest in fixed-income securities and are further classified by maturities, issuers and credit ratings.
- Actively managed stock mutual funds: Investments made with the motive to beat the benchmark index. For example, large cap, small cap, mid-cap etc.
- Passively managed stock mutual funds: Investments made with the motive to track the index performance. For example, index funds.

Exchange traded funds are a pooled investment vehicle that are similar to closed-end funds. They often track an index and are passively managed. ETFs provide joint benefits of closed-end and open-end funds.
- Special redemption process keeps market prices close to NAV, similar to an open-end fund.
- Trade like closed-end funds (continuously traded with other investors).
- Can be bought on margin, sold short and allow intraday positions to be taken.
- Expenses are lower relative to mutual funds, but brokerage commissions need to be paid.
- ETFs have less capital gains taxes as compared to open-ended funds, as securities need not be sold to meet redemptions.
- ETFs pay out dividends in cash, while open-end funds allow reinvesting in additional shares.

Separately managed accounts (SMA)
- Also known as "wrap account", "individually managed account" and "managed account".
- Owned and managed according to the needs of a single investor.
- Requires high initial investment.
- Tax implications have to be considered when buying or selling.

Hedge funds
- Pooled investments that are not regulated to the extent of mutual funds.
- Investments required are quite high.
- Strategies include: Long/short, market neutral, long/short bias, event driven, fixed-income arbitrage, global macro, convertible bond arbitrage etc.

Private equity (buyout funds and venture capital)
- Privately held and play an active role in managing investments.

Portfolio Management

- Leveraged buyout funds buy a public company, make it private, perform a turnaround thereby improving its valuation and later sell it to earn a profit. Typical time frames include three to five years.
- VC funds make initial stage investments in startup companies.

R39 Portfolio Risk and Return: Part I

Major return measures

Holding period return (HPR) is the percentage return earned on an investment over a given period.

HPR single period = capital gain + dividend yield = $\frac{P_T - P_0 + D_T}{P_0}$

where:
P_T = price at the end of the period
P_0 = price at the begining of the period
D_T = dividend paid out over the period

A stock valued at $40 at the start of the period, pays out $2 as dividend and has a value of $44 at the end of the period. Compute the HPR.
Solution:
HPR single period = $\frac{P_T - P_0 + D_T}{P_0} = \frac{44 - 40 + 2}{40} = 15\%$

Arithmetic mean return is a simple arithmetic average of a series of returns.

$AM = \frac{(R_1 + R_2 + R_3 + \ldots + R_T)}{T}$

Geometric mean return is the compounded annual rate of return for a series of returns.

$GM = [(1 + R_1) * (1 + R_2) * \ldots * (1 + R_T)]^{\frac{1}{T}} - 1$

An investor invested $100 in a mutual fund which had the following returns over a three year period: -6%, 8%, 14%. Compute the HPR, arithmetic mean return and geometric mean return.
Solution:
Ending value = (100)*(0.94)*(1.08)*(1.14) = $115.73
HPR = (0.94)*(1.08)*(1.14)-1 = 15.73%
Arithmetic mean return = $\frac{(-6\% + 8\% + 14\%)}{3}$ = 5.33%
Geometric mean return = $\sqrt[3]{(0.94) * (1.08) * (1.14)} - 1 = 4.99\%$

Money-weighted return is the internal rate of return on money invested that considers all the cash inflows and cash outflows. It is similar to the internal rate of return (IRR).

Portfolio Management

An investor purchases XYZ stock at the start of the first year for $20 and ABC stock at the end of the first year for $30. Both the stocks pay year-end dividend of $1 per share. If the investor sold both the shares for $60 at the end of the third year, compute the money-weighted rate of return.

Solution:

Step1:

Determine the cash flows

Time period	Particulars	Cash flow
T = 0	Purchase of XYZ stock	-$20
T = 1	Purchase of ABC stock	-$30
	Dividend from XYZ stock	+$1
T = 2	Sale of both shares	+$60
	Dividend from both stocks	+$2

Step2:

PV $_{inflows}$ = PV $_{outflows}$

$$\frac{62}{(1+r)^2} = \frac{-29}{(1+r)} - 20$$

Alternatively,

Input $CF_0 = -20$, $CF_1 = -29$, $CF_2 = 62$

The money-weighted rate of return is 17.91%.

Annualized return: For periods which are shorter or longer than a year, returns need to be annualized for easy comparison.

$$\text{Annualized return} = (1 + r_{period})^t - 1$$

where: t = number of periods in a year

Portfolio return is simply the weighted average of the individual investment returns.

$$\text{Portfolio return} = \sum_{i=1}^{N} w_i * R_i$$

Other returns:

- **Gross return** is the return earned prior to deducting management and administration fees, while **net return** accounts for all managerial and administrative expenses.
- **Pre-tax nominal return** is the return earned prior to accounting for inflation and taxes (is stated by default), while **after-tax nominal return** accounts for taxes.
- **Real return** is nominal return adjusted for inflation (Real = nominal – inflation; measures the purchasing power of money at the end of the investment period).
- **Leveraged return** is the return on an investor's own cash investment, after accounting for interest paid on the borrowed money.

Characteristics of major asset classes

Asset classes that have the highest returns generally also have the highest standard deviation of returns (risk). While analysing the returns of the asset classes (since it isn't normally distributed); factors like skewness (large negative returns), kurtosis (extreme deviation on both the upside and the downside of returns) and liquidity characteristics (high transaction costs, wide bid-ask spreads) should also be considered.

Listed below are general market observations:

Asset Class	Annual Average Return (Geometric Mean)	Standard Deviation (Risk)
Small-cap stocks	Highest	Highest
Large-cap stocks		
Long term corporate bonds		
Long term treasury bonds	▼	▼
Treasury bills	Lowest	Lowest

Mean, variance, and covariance/correlation of asset returns

Variance is a measure of dispersion of returns about its expected value (variance and standard deviation are both measures of risk).

$$\text{Population } \sigma^2 = \frac{\sum_{t=1}^{T}(R_t - \mu)^2}{T}$$

$$\text{Sample } s^2 = \frac{\sum_{t=1}^{T}(R_t - \overline{R})^2}{T-1}$$

Standard deviation = $\sqrt{\text{Variance}}$

Covariance is a measure of how two variables move together over time with values ranging from $-\infty$ to $+\infty$ and hence is difficult to compare.

$$\text{Cov}_{1,2} = \frac{\sum_{t=1}^{n}\{[R_{t,1} - \overline{R}_1][R_{t,2} - \overline{R}_2]\}}{n-1}$$

where:
$R_{t,1}$ = return on Asset 1 in period t
$R_{t,2}$ = return on Asset 2 in period t
$\overline{R}_1$ = mean return on Asset 1
$\overline{R}_2$ = mean return on Asset 2
n = number of periods

Correlation is a standardized measure of the linear relationship between two variables with values ranging between -1 and +1.

$\rho_{1,2} = \text{Cov}_{1,2}/\sigma_1\sigma_2$

- Correlation of +1 means that both securities will move in the same direction and in the same proportion from their mean (perfectly positively correlated).
- Correlation of -1 means that both securities will move in the opposite direction and in

the same proportion from their mean (perfectly negatively correlated).
- Correlation of 0 means there is no linear relationship between the two securities.

Risk aversion

A **risk-averse** investor prefers less risk to more risk while a **risk-seeking** investor prefers more risk to less risk. A **risk-neutral** investor has no preference regarding risk. If expected returns of two assets are same, a risk-averse investor will prefer asset with lower risk while the risk-seeking investor will prefer the asset with more risk.

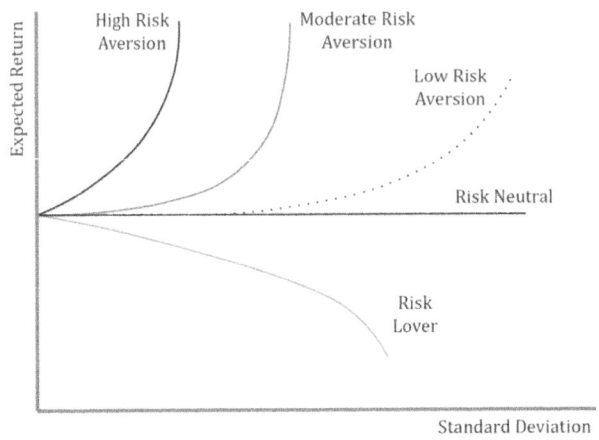

Portfolio standard deviation

The standard deviation of a portfolio of two risky assets:

$$\sigma_p = \sqrt{w_1^2 * \sigma_1^2 + w_2^2 * \sigma_2^2 + 2 * w_1 * w_2 * Cov_{1,2}}$$

$$= \sqrt{w_1^2 * \sigma_1^2 + w_2^2 * \sigma_2^2 + 2 * w_1 * w_2 * \rho_{1,2}\sigma_1\sigma_2}$$

Impact of correlation on portfolio risk

The graph below shows the benefits of diversification. When the correlation of assets in a portfolio decreases, the risk of the portfolio decreases.

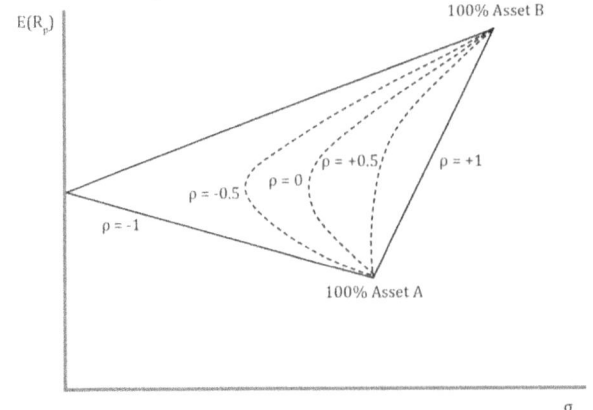

Portfolio Management

Minimum-variance and efficient frontiers

- **Investment opportunity set:** Portfolios with varying weights of all the individual assets (both risky assets and risk free assets) available to the investors are plotted on a graph where return is on the y-axis and standard deviation (risk) is on the x-axis.
- For a given rate of return, there will be a portfolio with minimum variance (risk) available in the opportunity set. The curve connecting such portfolios with minimum variance is called the **minimum-variance frontier**.
- The portfolio having the least risk (variance) among all the portfolios of risky assets is called the **global minimum-variance portfolio.**
- As a risk averse investor will only select the portfolio giving higher return for a given level of risk, the part of minimum-variance frontier above the global minimum-variance portfolio is called the **efficient frontier.**

The graph below shows these points:

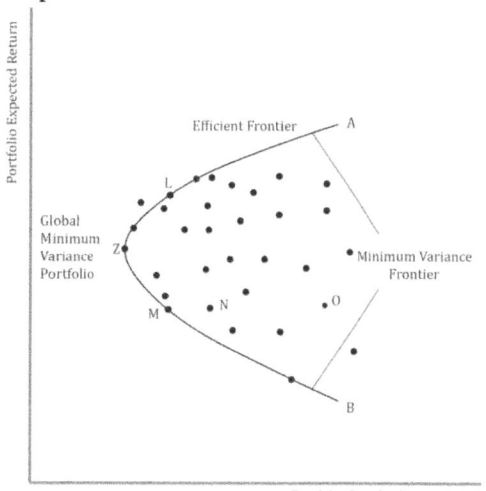

Selection of an optimal portfolio

- If we add a risk free asset to the available investment opportunity set, it will be plotted as a point on the y-axis (since its standard deviation is zero).
- Drawing a line tangent from the risk-free asset to the efficient frontier will give the **capital allocation line (CAL).** The CAL line represents combinations of the optimal risky portfolio and risk-free asset. Along the line, the proportion invested in these two assets varies to produce a return for a desired level of risk.
- The point where this line intersects the efficient frontier is called the **optimal risky portfolio.**
- **Borrowing and lending:** For the part of the CAL line up to the optimal risky portfolio, we invest partly in risk free asset (lending) and partly in optimal risky portfolio to generate the required return. For the part of CAL line, beyond optimal risky portfolio,

we borrow at the risk-free rate to invest in the optimal risky portfolio, to generate the excess return.
- To determine the optimal investor portfolio among the set of possible efficient portfolios i.e. portfolios along the CAL, we must consider the investors risk preferences. The utility of each investor is best represented by his **indifference curves** i.e. a combination of risk and return which the investor finds equally acceptable. For a risk averse investor, the indifference curve will be upward sloping. For a more risk-averse investor, the indifference curve will be steeper (higher risk aversion coefficient). A more risk-averse investor will have less proportion invested in the optimal risky portfolio and more proportion invested in risk-free asset as compared to a less risk-averse investor.
- The **optimal investor portfolio** is the point at which the investor's indifference curve is tangential to the CAL line.

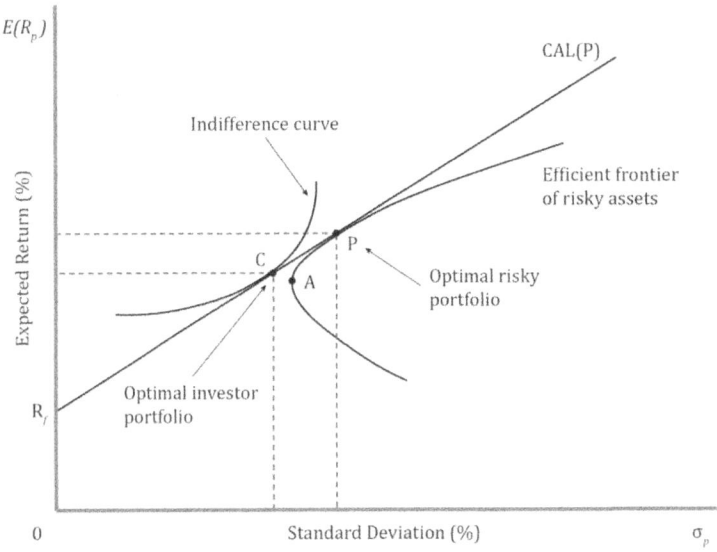

R40 Portfolio Risk and Return Part II

Combining a risk-free asset with a portfolio of risky assets

Since a risk-free asset has zero standard deviation and zero correlation of returns with a risky portfolio, the standard deviation of the portfolio having these two assets is reduced to:

$$\sigma_p = \sqrt{w_1^2 * \sigma_1^2 + w_2^2 * \sigma_2^2 + 2 * w_1 * w_2 * Cov_{1,2}}$$

$$\sigma_p = w_1 * \sigma_1$$

Thus, the risk of the portfolio will be proportional to the weight invested in the risky assets. Portfolio combinations of these two assets in varying weights can be plotted as a straight line extending from the risk-free asset through the portfolio of risky assets.

Portfolio Management

Capital allocation line (CAL) and capital market line (CML)

- Investors having different expectations of market, i.e. different expected returns, standard deviations and correlations, will have different optimal risky asset portfolios and different **CALs**.

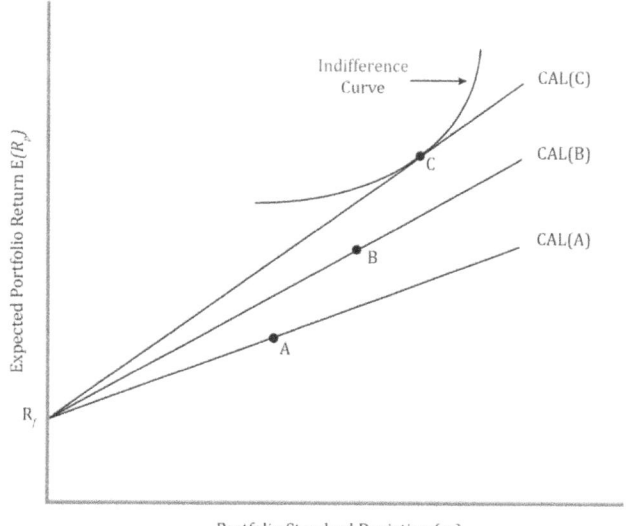

- Under **homogeneity of expectations** (i.e. everyone has same estimates of risk, return and correlations) everyone will have the same efficient frontier. Thus, they will have the same optimal risky portfolio and CAL. This optimal CAL, using homogenous expectations, is termed as the **capital market line**. All the investors in CML will have the same optimal risky portfolio, **market portfolio**.

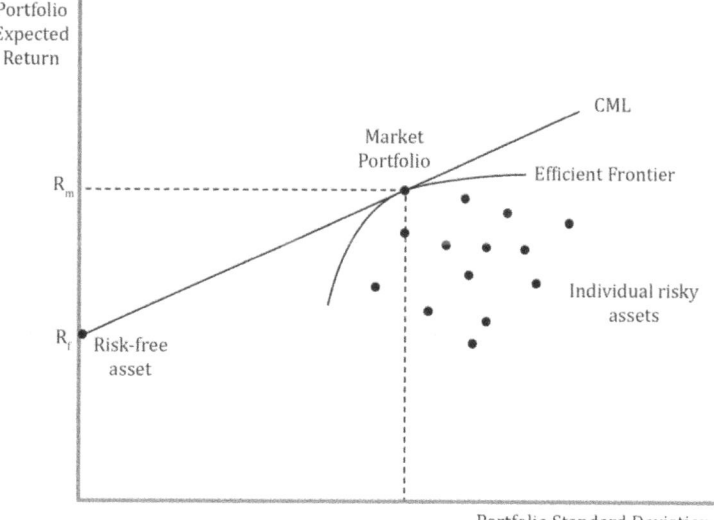

- Y intercept of the CML line is R_f and the slope is $\left(\dfrac{E(R_m) - R_f}{\sigma_m}\right)$. Thus, the equation of the line is:

$$E(R_p) = R_f + (E(R_m) - R_f) * \left(\frac{\sigma_p}{\sigma_m}\right)$$

Intuition: Investor will get one unit of market premium $(E(R_m) - R_f)$ in additional return over the risk-free rate for every unit of market risk (σ_m) the investor takes on.

- **Lending and borrowing portfolios:** The portion of the CML line up to the market portfolio, includes portfolios that invest partly in risk-free assets (lending) and the rest in market portfolio, to get the desired return. Beyond the market portfolio, CML line represents portfolios where money is borrowed at the risk-free rate and invested in market portfolio to achieve a return higher than the market portfolio.

Systematic and nonsystematic risk

Total risk (Standard deviation) = systematic risk + unsystematic risk

Systematic Risk:
- Also called non-diversifiable or market risk.
- Includes risk factors that affect the entire economy and cannot be diversified away. (For example, economic growth rates, interest rates etc.).
- Return earned on a security is only for taking on its systematic risk.

Nonsystematic Risk:
- Also called unique, diversifiable or firm-specific risk.
- Includes risk factors that affect only a particular company or industry (For example, drug approvals, software releases etc.).
- No compensation for nonsystematic risk as it can be diversified away.

Return generating models

Return-generating models estimate the expected return of a security based on certain input factors. Factor types:
- Macroeconomic: for example, GDP growth rates, inflation, interest rates, etc.
- Fundamental: for example, earnings, firm size, growth rates etc.
- Statistical: relations found through data mining.

Multi-factor models: Often use macroeconomic and fundamental factors.
- Fama and French model: uses factors like firm size, firm book value to market value ratio and excess return on market portfolio.
- Carhart model: uses factors of Fama and French model plus the price momentum.

Single-factor model: Uses only one factor.
- Simplest version is CAPM, where the only risk factor is the excess return on market.
- **Market model** is used to determine the security's beta and abnormal returns using the actual market returns.
$R_i = \alpha_i + \beta R_m + e_i$

Portfolio Management

where:

R_i = asset return

α_i = intercept

β = slope coefficient

R_m = market return

e_i = abnormal return (return in excess of the expected return)

Beta interpretation

Beta is a standardized measure of covariance of an asset's returns with the market returns. It measures the systematic or market risk.

$$\beta_i = \frac{Cov(i,M)}{\sigma_M^2} = \frac{\rho_{iM} * \sigma_i * \sigma_M}{\sigma_M^2} = \frac{\rho_{iM} * \sigma_i}{\sigma_M}$$

Stock X has a standard deviation of 20% compared to market indexes' standard deviation of 10%. The correlation of the stock with the market index is 0.7 and its covariance with the market index is 0.014. Compute the Beta.

Solution:

$$\beta_i = \frac{\rho_{iM} * \sigma_i}{\sigma_M} = \frac{0.70 * 0.20}{0.10} = 1.4$$

$$\beta_i = \frac{Cov(i,M)}{\sigma_M^2} = \frac{0.014}{0.10^2} = 1.4$$

Note: In practice, betas are estimated by regressing the returns of the asset with that of the market index.

- **β > 0:** Asset returns move in the same direction as that of the market (positively correlated).
- **β < 0:** Asset returns move in opposite direction to that of the market (negatively correlated).
- **β = 0:** Asset returns have no correlation with the market.
- **β = 1:** Asset returns have the same volatility as that of the market and move in the same direction.
- **β = -1:** Asset returns have the same volatility as that of the market and move in the opposite direction.

Capital asset pricing model (CAPM) and security market line (SML).

Security market line (SML):
- Plots the relationship between asset returns on y-axis and the covariance of the asset returns with the market returns on the x-axis.
- SML plots **systematic risk** with the use of covariance.
- Y-intercept is R_f and slope is $\frac{E(R_m) - R_f}{\sigma_m^2}$. The equation of the line becomes:

$$E(R_i) = R_f + \frac{E(R_m) - R_f}{\sigma_m^2}(Cov(i, M)) = R_f + \beta[E(R_m) - R_f] \ (Using\ beta\ formula)$$

The above relation between systematic or market risk (β) and expected return is known as **capital asset pricing model**.

Assumptions of CAPM are:
- Individuals are **risk-averse, utility-maximizing** (seeking best asset) and **rational investors.**
- **Frictionless markets:** No transaction costs and taxes.
- **Single holding period:** All investors have the same investment horizon.
- **Homogenous expectations:** All investors have same expectations for assets' risk, returns and correlation parameters.
- **Divisible assets:** All the investments are infinitely divisible.
- **Competitive markets:** Investors are price takers and their trades cannot influence market price.

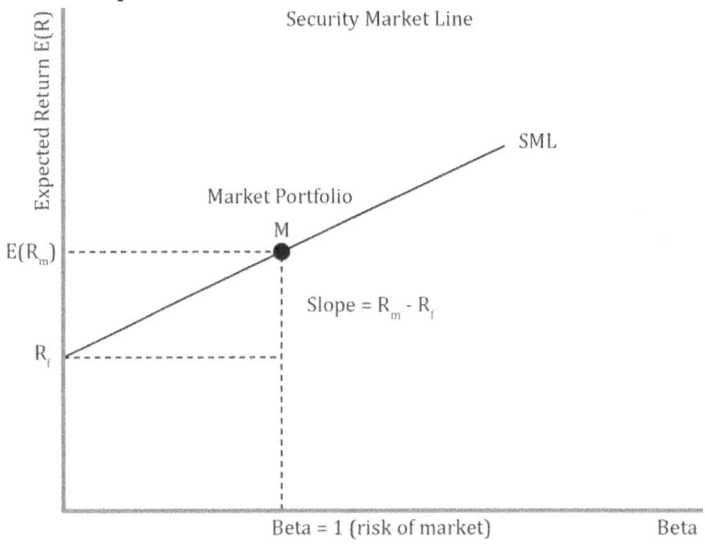

Comparison between CML and SML	
CML	**SML**
Plots returns versus total risk i.e. standard deviation on the x axis.	Plots returns versus systematic risk i.e. beta on the x-axis.
Only efficient portfolios plot on the CML, while not so well diversified portfolios plot inside the efficient frontier.	All fairly priced securities and portfolio of securities, even if not well diversified, will plot on the SML.
Equation of the line: $R_p = R_f + (\frac{R_m - R_f}{\sigma_m}) * \sigma_p$ Where, σ_p is the total risk of the portfolio.	Equation of the line: $R_i = R_f + \beta[E(R_m) - R_f]$ Where, β is the systematic risk. SML is a graphical representation of CAPM.
Both have returns on y-axis and line runs through risk-free asset and market portfolio.	

Portfolio Management

Calculating security returns using CAPM

CAPM

$E(R_i) = R_f + \beta[E(R_m) - R_f]$

The expected market return is 16%, the risk-free rate is 5%, and the beta of the stock is 1.4. Compute the expected (required) return on the stock.

Solution:

$E(R_i) = R_f + \beta[E(R_m) - R_f] = 0.05 + 1.4(0.16 - 0.05) = 20.4\%$

Applications of the CAPM and the SML

- Expected return of an asset will be equal to the required return on the asset for a market in equilibrium.
- SML can be used to find overvalued and undervalued securities.
    - Securities on the SML line → fairly valued,
    - Securities above the SML line → undervalued,
    - Securities below the SML line → overvalued.

The market has an expected return of 16% and a risk-free rate of 5%. Compute the expected and required return on each stock and determine whether they are fairly valued, overvalued or undervalued. The following are the street forecasts for the stocks:

Security	Current price	Expected year-end price	Expected dividend	Beta
X	$10	$10.5	$0.5	0.7
Y	$200	$226.0	$6.0	1.0
Z	$16	$18.0	$2.0	1.3

Solution:

Security	Expected or forecasted return	Required return	Valuation
X	(10.5 − 10 + 0.5)/(10) = 10.0%	0.05 + 0.7 (0.16 − 0.05) = 12.7%	Overvalued
Y	(226 − 200 + 6)/(200) = 16.0%	0.05 + 1.0 (0.16 − 0.05) = 16.0%	Fairly valued
Z	(18 − 16 + 2)/(16) = 25.0%	0.05 + 1.3 (0.16 − 0.0 5) = 19.3%	Undervalued

Appropriate strategy:
- Sell X.
- Ignore Y.
- Buy Z.

Portfolio Management

The four measures commonly used in performance evaluation are:
1. **Sharpe ratio:** is the slope of CML and CAL line.
$$\text{Sharpe ratio} = \frac{\text{portfolio excess returns}}{\text{portolio total risk}} = \frac{R_p - R_f}{\sigma_p}$$

2. **M-Squared** produces same portfolio ranking as that of Sharpe ratio, but is stated in percentage terms.
$$M^2 = \frac{(R_p - R_f)\sigma_m}{\sigma_p} - (R_m - R_f)$$
Intuition: The portfolio excess returns have been levered so that it has the same risk as that of the market (factor used is $(\frac{\sigma_m}{\sigma_p})$). This is then compared with the market risk premium.
Note: Portfolios that lie above the CML line have greater Sharpe ratios than the CML portfolios and positive M^2 values.

3. **Treynor measure** is slope of lines, similar to the Sharpe ratio, but for systematic risk.
$$\text{Treynor measure} = \frac{\text{portfolio risk premium}}{\text{beta risk (systematic risk)}} = \frac{R_p - R_f}{\beta_p}$$

4. **Jenson's alpha** is similar to M^2, but for systematic risk. It gives percentage return in excess of the expected return from SML.
$$\text{Jenson's alpha} = \text{Actual portfolio return} - \text{SML expected return}$$
$$= R_p - [R_f + \beta(R_m - R_f)]$$

Note: Portfolios that lie above the SML line have greater Treynor measures than the SML portfolios and positive Jenson's alpha values.

R41 Basics of portfolio planning and construction

Investment policy statement (IPS)

IPS is the starting point of the portfolio construction and management process. It captures the clients' needs in terms of risk and return, circumstances and constraints.

Major components of an IPS

The major components of an IPS are:
- **Description of client:** Describes the investment objectives, circumstances and state of client.
- **Statement of purpose:** Covers the scope of the IPS.
- **Statement of duties and responsibilities:** Applies to investment manager, client and other parties involved.
- **Procedures:** Methodologies to tackle various circumstances and updating the IPS.
- **Investment objectives:** Desired rate of return and the amount of risk client is willing

to take.
- **Investment constraints:** Liquidity, legal, taxes, time horizon and other unique constraints.
- **Investment guidelines:** Asset classes permitted, selection of asset classes, use of leverage, asset allocation, rebalancing, etc.
- **Evaluation of performance:** The benchmark portfolio to compare investment results with, the frequency of evaluation, and other related information.
- **Appendices:** Contains information on specific guidelines like permitted deviations, strategic asset allocation, rebalancing strategies, etc.

Risk and return objectives

Risk and return objectives can be stated in absolute or relative terms.

Absolute risk objective example: Portfolio should not suffer more than a 5% loss in any 12-month period. Practically, this could be stated as: with 95% probability, portfolio should not lose more than 5% value in any 12-month period.

Relative risk objective example: Return should be within 4% of the S&P 500 index return. The risk objective is expressed relative to a benchmark.

Absolute return objective: For example, an annual return of 7% or 2% excess return over the inflation each year.

Relative return objective: For example, an annual return that exceeds S&P 500 index return by 3%.

Ability and willingness to take risk

Ability to take risk
- Depends on financial situation like assets compared to the outstanding liabilities, time horizon, job security, etc.
- For example, a young employed person belonging to a wealthy family with very few liabilities has a high ability to take risks.

Willingness to take risk
- Depends on the client's psychology and is highly subjective.
- For example, a client who lost a substantial fortune in the credit crisis may not be willing to take risks, even though he has the ability to do so.

Situations:
- Willingness and ability match → no problem selecting a suitable level of risk.
- Willingness is higher than the ability → capacity or ability level is suitable level of risk.
- Willingness is lower than the ability → educate the client → if still reluctant, go with the willingness level of risk.

Investment constraints

The five major investment constraints are:

- **Liquidity:** Ability to convert invested assets into cash without suffering significant price erosion. Cash requirement varies from client to client and some may require a certain portion of assets to be invested in highly liquid investments.

- **Legal and regulatory:** Restrictions on the types of investments and maximum percentage allocation to certain assets for investors like insurance firms, trusts, etc.

- **Time horizon:** Longer the time horizon, higher the ability to take risk and lower are the liquidity needs of the portfolio.

- **Tax concerns:** Investor's tax status, jurisdiction of investments and tax treatment of various types of investment accounts should be considered.

- **Unique circumstances:** Any other unique investing requirement or restriction not mentioned elsewhere in the IPS must be stated here. It may be influenced by religion, personal beliefs, government policies or impact of business activities.

Specification of asset classes

- **Strategic asset allocation** describes the percentage allocation to the different asset classes.
- **Asset classes** should be defined such that the correlation within it should be relatively high and correlation between the different asset classes should be low.
- For example, large cap equity. All securities in this asset class will have relatively high correlation with each other; while their correlation with other asset class like domestic government bonds would be low.
- All assets within an asset class must be homogenous.
- All assets in an asset class must have similar risk and return expectations.
- All asset classes when combined should be collectively exhaustive i.e. they should account for the entire universe of investable assets.

Principles of portfolio construction

1. **Define IPS:** Capture the investor requirements and constraints.

2. **Determine the strategic asset allocation:**
    a. Define the investable asset classes for the portfolio and gather historical data on their risk, return and correlation.
    b. Combine the IPS and the risk/return profile of various asset classes derived from above step, to determine a strategic asset allocation. Up to this step, investment decisions are entirely passive i.e. returns are primarily generated by investing in

asset class indices.

3. **Tactical asset allocation:**
   a. This is the first step of active management.
   b. Determine whether there are any short-term opportunities that warrant a deviation from the strategic asset allocation.
   c. For example, a top-down analysis shows that given the economic cycle, commodities might outperform. Based on this premise, you overweight the commodity asset class.

4. **Security selection:**
   a. This is second step of active management where particular securities are selected.
   b. Identify the relatively strong securities within the favored asset class.
   c. For example, in your analysis you decide to go overweight on the base metals securities.

R42 Risk Management: An Introduction

Risk management definition

Risk management is the process by which an organization or individual defines the level of risk to be taken (i.e. risk tolerance), measures the level of risk being taken (i.e. risk exposure), and modifies the risk exposure to match the risk tolerance. The goal is to maximize the company's or portfolio's value or the individual's overall satisfaction or utility.

Risk management framework

A risk management framework includes:
- risk governance
- risk identification and measurement
- risk infrastructure
- risk policies and processes
- risk mitigation and management
- communication
- strategic risk analysis and integration

Risk governance

Risk governance is the top-level foundation for risk management that provides organization-wide guidance on which risks should be pursued in an efficient manner, which risk should be reduced and which risks should be avoided. The elements of effective risk governance include providing a forum where the management can discuss the risk framework, creating a risk governance committee, and appointing a chief risk officer.

Risk tolerance

Risk tolerance for an organization is the total amount of risk it can take in pursuing its goals. Risk tolerance is set by the top management, where they define which risks are acceptable, which risks are not acceptable, and how much risk the entity can be exposed to.

Risk budgeting

Risk budgeting is the process of allocating the total risk the firm is willing to take i.e. risk tolerance to assets or investments by considering their risk characteristics and how they can be combined to meet the organization's objectives. The goal is to allocate the overall amount of acceptable risk to a mix of assets that have the highest expected returns. The risk budget can be a single risk measure or the sum of various risk factors.

Financial and non-financial sources of risk

Financial risks arise from exposure to financial markets. They include:
- Market risk: Arises from movements in stock prices, interest rates, exchange rates, and commodity prices.
- Credit risk: Risk that the counterparty will not fulfill its contractual obligation.
- Liquidity risk: Risk that, as a result of degradation in market conditions the sales price will be less than the underlying fair value of the asset.

Non-financial risks arise from actions within an entity or from external origins, such as the environment, the community, regulators, politicians, suppliers, and customers. They include:
- Operational risk: Includes human errors and system or process errors.
- Solvency risk: Risk that the entity runs out of cash and will be unable to continue to operate.
- Legal risk: Uncertainty about an organization's exposure to future legal action.
- Accounting risk: Risk that the organization's accounting policies and estimates are judged to be incorrect.
- Regulatory risk: Risk that the regulatory environment will change in an unfavorable manner.
- Model risk: Risk that asset valuations based on the organization's model are incorrect.
- Tail risk: Risk that extreme events are more likely than the organization's analysis indicates.
- Sovereign or political risk: Risk that political actions such as tax rate hikes will be unfavorable to the organization.

Portfolio Management

Individuals also face health risk, mortality or longevity risk, and property and casualty risk.

Many risks arise as a result of other risks therefore risks are not necessarily independent. The interactions between different risks can be non-linear and harmful.

Measuring and modifying risk exposures

Common measures of risk for specific asset types include:
- **Standard deviation**: Measures the volatility of asset prices. It is not suitable for non-normal distributions.
- **Beta**: Measure of sensitivity of a security's returns to the returns on the market portfolio.
- **Duration**: Measure of sensitivity of a debt security's price to changes in interest rates.

Derivatives risk measures include:
- **Delta**: Sensitivity of a derivative's price to changes in price of the underlying.
- **Gamma**: Sensitivity of delta to changes in price of the underlying.
- **Vega**: Measures change in derivative's price to changes in volatility of the underlying.
- **Rho**: Sensitivity of derivative's price to changes in interest rates.

Tail risk (possibility of extreme negative outcomes) measures include:
- **Value at risk (VaR)**: The minimum loss expected over a period with a specific probability.
- **Conditional VaR (CVaR)**: The expected value of a loss, given that loss exceeds the value at risk.

Risk can be modified by:
- Prevention and avoidance.
- Risk transfer – using insurance.
- Risk shifting – using derivatives.
- Risk can be mitigated internally by self-insurance or diversification.

To determine which method is best for modifying risk, the benefits of the method are weighted against the costs of the methods, while considering the overall final risk profile and adhering to the risk governance objectives.

R43 Fintech in Investment Management

Fintech

Fintech = Finance + Technology

Fintech refers to the technological innovation in the design and delivery of financial products and services.

The major drivers of fintech have been:
- Rapid growth in data
- Technological advances

The major applications of fintech are:
- Analysis of large datasets
- Analytical tools
- Automated trading
- Automated advice
- Financial record keeping

Big Data, artificial intelligence, and machine learning

Big Data refers to vast amount of data generated by industry, governments, individuals and electronic devices. Characteristics of big data typically include:
- Volume: The amount of data that we are dealing with has grown exponentially.
- Velocity: We are now increasingly working with real time data.
- Variety: Historically we only dealt with structured data. However, we are now also dealing with unstructured data such as text, audio, video etc.

Artificial intelligence (AI) computer systems perform tasks that have traditionally required human intelligence. They exhibit cognitive and decision making ability comparable or superior to that of human beings.

Machine learning (ML) computer programs:
- learn how to complete tasks or predict outcomes
- improve performance over time with experience.

Machine learning programs rely on training dataset and validation dataset. Training dataset allows the ML algorithm to:
- identify relationships between variables
- detect patterns or trends
- create structure from data.

These relationships are then tested on the validation dataset.

Two main approaches to machine learning are:
1. Supervised learning: Both inputs and outputs are identified or labeled. After learning from labeled data, the trained algorithm is used to predict outcomes for new data sets.
2. Unsupervised learning: The input and output variables are not labeled. Here we want the ML algorithm to seek relationships on its own.

Fintech applications to investment management

Major fintech applications include:
- **Text analytics and natural language processing**: Text analytics refers to the use of computer programs to derive meaning from large, unstructured text or voice based data. Natural language processing is an application of text analytics whereby computers analyze and interpret human language.
- **Robo-advisory services**: Refers to providing investment solutions through online platforms by replacing a human advisor with an online platform. Services provided include: automated asset allocation, rebalancing, tax strategies, trade execution.
- **Risk analysis**: Big Data and ML techniques can provide insight into changing market conditions. This can allow us to predict adverse market conditions and adverse tends, which can result in better risk management.
- **Algorithmic trading**: Algorithmic trading refers to computerized trading based on pre-specified rules and guidelines. It can help us decide – when, where and how to trade. Benefits of algorithmic trading include – speed of execution, anonymity and lower transaction costs.

Financial applications of distributed ledger technology

DLT networks allow us to create, exchange and track ownership of financial assets on a peer-to-peer basis. There is no central authority to validate the transactions.

Major DLT applications include:
- **Cryptocurrencies**: These are electronic currencies that allow near real-time transactions to take place between buyers and sellers without the need for an intermediary like a bank.
- **Tokenization**: It is the process of representing ownership rights to physical assets such as real-estate on a blockchain or distributed ledger. DLT can create a single digital record of ownership and reduce efforts required in ownership verification and examination.
- **Post-trade clearing and settlement**: DLT can streamline the post-trade clearing and settlement process by providing near-real-time trade verification, reconciliation and settlement.
- **Compliance**: DLT can streamline the compliance process and bring down costs. It can allow firms and regulators to get near-real-time access to transaction data, as well as other relevant compliance data and help them quickly uncover fraudulent activities. DLT can also reduce compliance costs associated with know-your-customer and anti-money-laundering regulations which require verification of the identities of clients and business partners.

R44 Market Organization and Structure

Main functions of financial system

Three main functions of the financial system are to:
1. Allow entities to utilize its six main purposes.
   - **Saving:** Entities can earn returns that match the risk of investment.
   - **Borrowing:** Needful entities can borrow money from lenders that require adequate collateral and return for the risk taken.
   - **Issuing equity:** Provides a medium for entities to issue new shares to raise capital.
   - **Managing risks:** Allows trading of hedging instruments that cover risks like interest rates, currency values, default of debts, commodity prices etc.
   - **Exchanging assets:** For example, trading one currency for another currency.
   - **Trading on information:** Investors can earn surplus returns by identifying undervalued and overvalued securities.
2. Determine equilibrium rates of return that equate the total lenders and the total borrowers.
3. Allow for efficient allocation of resources.

Classifications of assets and markets

Classification of assets		
Based on the underlying	**Financial assets** represent a claim on real assets and future income generated by these assets. For e.g. stocks and bonds.	**Real assets** include physical assets like real estate, equipment, commodities, and other assets.
Based on the nature of claim by financial securities	**Debt securities:** Periodic interest payments made on borrowed funds which might be collateralized.	**Equity securities:** Represent ownership positions and claim on the future cash flows of the business.
Based on where the securities are traded	**Publicly traded:** These securities trade in public markets through exchanges or dealers and are subject to regulatory oversight.	**Privately traded:** These securities are not traded in public markets. They are often not subject to regulation.
Classification of markets		
Based on delivery	**Spot market:** Markets for immediate delivery of assets.	**Forward market:** Contracts that call for future delivery of assets and include forwards, futures and options.

Equity

Based on issuance of security	**Primary market**: Issuers sell securities directly to investors.	**Secondary market**: Investors buy and sell securities among themselves.
Based on maturity	**Money market**: Securities with maturities of one year or less.	**Capital market**: Securities that have more than one-year maturity or equities that don't have any maturity.
Based on the type of investment markets	**Traditional investment markets**: Include all publicly traded debts and equities.	**Alternative investment markets**: Include hedge funds, private equity, commodities, real estate etc.

Securities, currencies, contracts, commodities, and real assets

Securities can be broadly classified into:

Fixed income: refers to debt securities where the borrower is obligated to pay interest and principal at pre-determined schedule. They may be collateralized, which means that investors have claim on certain physical assets. The different types are:
- Bonds: Long-term debts.
- Notes: Intermediate-term debts.
- Bank borrowings: Long to short term involving revolving credit lines and other debt instruments.
- Convertible: Debt can be exchanged for a specified number of equity shares.

Equity: refers to ownership claims by investors in companies. The different types are:
- Common shareholders: have a residual claim over any assets and income, after all the senior securities have been paid.
- Preferred shareholders: are paid scheduled dividends before the common shareholders.
- Warrants: give the holder a right to buy the firm's security at a price called the exercise price, within a specified time period (similar to options).

Pooled investments: refer to structures that combine investment from many investors. The different types are:
- Mutual funds: can either be open-end (shares purchased from fund) or close-end (shares purchased from other investors) funds.
- Asset backed securities: represent claim on cash flow earned by the assets in the portfolio like mortgages, car or credit card debt.
- Exchange traded funds (ETFs): combine the advantages of open-end and closed-end funds.
- Hedge funds: utilize different strategies and often rely on leverage.

Equity

Contract is an agreement between traders to perform some action in the future which can either be settled physically or in cash. The types of contracts (also termed as derivatives) are:

Forward contract is an agreement to trade the underlying asset at a future date at a pre-specified price. It is not standardized and not traded on public exchanges.

Futures contract is a standardized contract where the amount, asset characteristics and delivery date are the same for all contracts. It is exchange trade and has higher liquidity because of standardization.

Swap contract is an agreement to swap payments of one asset for the other. The different types are:
- Interest rate swap: Floating rate payments are swapped for fixed-rate payments for a specified period.
- Currency swap: Currency amount swapped for another currency for a specified period.
- Equity swap: Returns earned on one investment are swapped for the other.

Options are contracts that give the holder a right, but not the obligation, to buy/sell an underlying security at a specified price, at or before a specific date. The different types are:
- Call option: Buyer gets the right but not the obligation to buy the underlying security at a predetermined price; seller of the call option gets the premium but has to the sell the security if the buyer exercises his option to buy.
- Put option: Buyer gets the right but not the obligation to sell the underlying security at a predetermined price; seller of the put option gets the premium but has to the buy the security if the buyer exercises his option to sell.

Credit default swaps offer insurance and make payment to the insurance holder if a borrower defaults on its bonds.

Currencies, are legal tenders issued by national monetary authorities, that trade in the spot, forward, or futures markets (also called as the Forex market).

Commodities include energy products, precious metals, industrial metals, agricultural products, and carbon credits. They trade in spot, forward and futures markets.

Real assets are physical assets which are normally used by operating companies as factors of production. (For e.g. real estate, plant and equipment etc.)

Types of financial intermediaries

Financial intermediaries facilitate transaction between buyers and sellers allowing them to exchange asset, capital and risk. The different types are:

1. **Brokers, Exchanges, and Alternative Trading Systems:**
   - Brokers: find counterparties for transactions (other entities willing to take the

opposing side in a transaction) and do not indulge in trade with their clients directly.
- Block brokers: provide similar services as brokers, except that their clients have large trade orders that might potentially impact the security prices if the trade is executed without proper care.
- Investment banks: provide advice for corporate actions like mergers & acquisitions and help firms raise capital by issuing securities such as common stock, bonds, preferred shares etc.
- Exchanges: provide places where traders can meet. They regulate traders' actions to ensure smooth execution of the trades.
- Alternative trading systems (ATS): serve the same trading function as exchanges but have no regulatory oversight. ATS where client orders are not revealed are also called dark pools.
- Dealers: trade directly with their clients by taking the opposite side of their trades. They provide liquidity by buying or selling from their own inventory and earn profits on the bid-ask spreads.

2. **Securitizers:**
   - They pool together large amounts of securities or assets. A special purpose entity (SPE) or special purpose vehicle (SPV) buys these assets and interests in this entity are sold off to investors.
   - Assets that are often securitized include mortgages, car loans, student loans, credit card receivables and bank loans.
   - Investors then earn returns from the cash flows of the underlying assets.
   - Pooling of resources offers economies of scale, creates liquidity for these securities and reduces the total risk for these assets.

3. **Depository institutions:** include commercial banks, savings and loan banks, credit unions and similar institutions that raise funds from depositors and other investors and lend it to borrowers.

4. **Insurance companies:**
   - They help entities offset risks by issuing insurance contracts that payout if a specified event occurs.
   - The insured entity in turn pays an insurance premium for availing this benefit.
   - The event risk is spread over large entities such that the total insurance premium earned is more than the insurance payout.
   - Three key risks inherent in insurance system:
     - Moral hazard: Insured entity is likely to take more risks.
     - Adverse selection: Entities that are at most risk, are likely to buy the assets.

Equity

- o Fraud: Entities claiming factitious losses or purposely indulging in damaging behavior.

5. **Clearinghouses:** act as intermediaries between buyers and sellers, thereby lowering the counterparty risk and increasing the reliability of the trades.

6. **Depositories or custodians:** hold securities for their clients. This helps prevent loss of securities through fraud, oversight or natural disasters.

7. **Arbitrageurs:** indulge in buying and selling of mispriced securities and earn a riskless profit in the process. They provide added liquidity to the market by removing any price inefficiencies.

Positions an investor can take in an asset

An investor's position in a security may either be a long position or a short position.

Long positions
- are created when a trader owns an asset or has a right or obligation under a contract to purchase an asset.
- Investors who are long benefit from increases in price of the security.

Short positions
- are created when traders borrow an asset and sell it, with the obligation to replace the asset in the future.
- Investors who are short benefit from decreases in price of the security.
- The seller must keep the proceeds of the short sell as collateral with the broker.
- The deposit kept with the broker earns an interest rate, termed as the short rebate rate.
- The seller must also pay all payments like interest or dividends the security might have earned to the lender. These payments are called payments-in-lieu of dividends or interest.

Hedgers
- use contradictory positions to their natural risk exposure to eliminate the risk.
- For example, a maize farmer will sell (take a short position) maize future contracts to offset the risk of the price drop of maize when he harvests the produce.

Options
- Buyer of an option is long the contract while seller or writer of an option is short the option.
- For e.g. an investor who buys a put option is long the put option.

Leveraged positions
- Use of loans to make asset purchases is termed as leveraged position.
- The borrowed funds are termed as the margin loan and interest rate paid is called the

Equity

call money rate.
- The initial equity required to make the purchases is termed as the initial margin requirement.
- Financial leverage magnifies both gains and losses.

Leverage ratio and margin call price

Leverage ratio: is used to calculate the amount of borrowed funds in a transaction. The borrowed money is called the margin loan and the interest paid is called the call money rate.

$$\text{Leverage ratio} = \frac{\text{value of position}}{\text{value of equity invetsment in that position}}$$

Calculate the leverage ratio and return earned by an investor over a period of one year. The details of the transaction are as follows:

Shares purchased	500
Price at the start of the year	€200
Dividend on the share for the year	€5
Commission per share	€0.1
Price at the end of the year	€220
Initial margin requirement	50%
Call money rate	3%

Solution:

1. Leverage ratio = $\frac{1}{0.5} = 2$
2. Purchase amount = 500 * 200 = €100,000

Initial margin requirement = purchase amount * initial margin % = 100,000 * 0.5 = €50,000
Borrowed amount = €50,000
Purchase commission = 0.1 * 500 = €50
Dividend earned = 5 * 500 = €2,500
Selling amount = 500 * 220 = €110,000
Call money rate paid = call money % * borrowed amount = 3% * 50,000 = €1,500
Selling commission = 0.1 * 500 = €50
Total gain = 110,000 − 100,000 + 2,500 − 1,500 − 50 − 50 = €10,900
Initial equity investment = Initial investment + purchase commission = 50,000 + 50 = €50,050
The gain on the transaction = 10,900/50,050 = 21.78%

Margin call price:
- An investor must maintain a minimum equity percentage called **maintenance margin requirement**, to ensure that the loan for a transaction is covered by the value of the asset.

Equity

- If the value of the asset drops, then the investor (considering he is long that security) will have to increase his equity in the account to provide more collateral for the loan.

$$\text{Margin call price} = \text{initial purchase price} \times \frac{(1 - \text{initial margin})}{(1 - \text{maintenance margin})}$$

If the share price is €200 with an initial margin requirement of 50% and maintenance margin requirement of 30%, compute the margin call price.

Solution:

Margin call price $= \frac{200(1-0.50)}{1-0.30} = €142.86$

Margin call for this trade will be at a price below €142.86.

Execution, validity and clearing instructions

Orders entered must specify what security to trade, size of the trade and whether to buy or sell. The order can also include additional instructions:

- **Execution instruction:** specifies how the order will be filled.
- **Validity instruction:** specifies when the order may be filled.
- **Clearing instruction:** specifies how the final settlement will be done.

Execution instructions types are:

- Market orders: are immediately executed at the best price available; however, there can be substantial slippages in execution price if a stock is thinly traded.

- Limit orders: set a minimum execution price on sell orders and maximum execution price on buy orders. This ensures that an investor never exceeds his price limit on a transaction. However, there is a possibility that the order may not execute at all if the markets are fast moving or there isn't enough liquidity.

- All or nothing orders: will be executed only if the entire quantity can be traded. They are beneficial when the trading costs depend on the number of executed trades and not on the size of the order.

- Hidden orders: are large orders that are known only to the brokers or exchanges executing them until the trades are executed.

- Iceberg orders: A small visible portion of a large hidden order is executed first, to gauge the market liquidity before the entire order is executed.

Validity instructions types are:

- Day orders: expire if they are unfilled on the trading day on which they were submitted.
- Good-till-cancelled orders: last until the order is executed or the trader cancels the order.
- Immediate or cancel (fill or kill) orders: are to be immediately filled i.e. when they are received by the broker or exchange. If it fails to execute, the order is canceled from the

system.
- <u>Good-on-close (market-on-close)</u>: can only be filled at the close of trading. Mutual funds often rely on this order type.
- <u>Stop orders (also called stop-loss orders):</u> come with a trigger price. Stop-sell order executes only if the price is at or below the stop price or trigger price. Stop-buy order executes only if the price is at or above the stop price or trigger price.

Clearing instructions convey who is responsible for clearing and settling the trade.

Market orders v/s limit orders

	Market order	**Limit order**
Execution	Executed at the best available market price.	Sets a minimum execution price on sell orders and maximum execution price on buy orders.
Advantages	Quick execution when a trader believes that the prices are volatile.	Avoids slippages as the orders are executed at the pre-determined or better prices.
Disadvantages	Quick execution can lead to unfavorable trade prices and has trade price uncertainty.	In a volatile market, the order might be partially filled or not filled at all, making the possibility of missing out on trade.
Additional information	Trader sacrifices price certainty for immediate liquidity.	Types of limit orders: • **Marketable or aggressively priced:** Limit buy order above the best ask or a limit sell order below the best bid. It will be immediately executed. • **Making a new market or inside the market:** Limit price is between best bid and the best ask. • **Behind the market:** Limit buy order with limit price below the best bid and limit sell order with limit price above the best ask. If the limit prices are way behind the market, they are termed as **far from the market limit orders.**

Primary and secondary markets

Primary markets refer to the sale of an issuer's newly issued securities to investors.

Equity

The sale can be either of the two types:
- **IPO (Initial Public Offering):** issuers sell new securities, that aren't publicly traded, to the investors for the first time.
- **Seasoned or secondary offering**: issuers sell additional new units of their securities, which already trade on the public exchanges.

Based on the investors targeted, primary market offerings can be either:

Public offerings:
- The firm seeks capital from retail or individual investors and for this it uses the services of an investment bank.
- The investment bank disseminates information like the financial performance of the firm and the purpose for which the capital is raised.
- The investment bank can use either of the two methods:
  - **Underwritten offering:** Investment bank agrees to buy the unsold portion of the issue at a pre-negotiated price if enough interest is not generated in the issuance. This creates a conflict of interest between the bank and the firm, as the bank would like the price to be low.
  - **Best efforts:** Investment bank is not obligated to purchase the unsold portion.

Private placements: Large blocks of securities are sold directly to qualified investors. The costs and disclosures are low as compared to public offerings.

Secondary markets are where investors buy or sell securities from other investors.
- Companies are not directly involved in the secondary markets i.e. do not gain capital from it.
- However, liquid secondary markets lower the cost of raising capital for the company in primary markets.

Quote-driven, order-driven, and brokered markets

The two categories of securities market **based on when they are traded** are as follows:
1. **Call markets:**
   - Trade takes place only at specific times of the day where all the traders are present and the entire bid-ask quotes are used to arrive at one negotiated price.
   - Markets are highly liquid when the market is in session and illiquid when the market isn't in session.
   - Usually used for smaller markets or to determine the opening and closing prices at stock exchanges.
2. **Continuous markets:**
   - Trades can occur at any time the market is open and the prices are either quote driven or auction driven.

The three categories of the securities market **based on how they are traded** are as follows:
1. **Quote Driven Markets:**
   - Trade takes place at the price quoted by dealers who maintain an inventory of the security.
   - Dealers provide liquidity in these markets and gain from the difference in bid-ask spread.
   - They are also called over-the-counter markets, price-driven or dealer markets.
2. **Order Driven Markets:**
   - Trading rules match buyers to sellers, thus making them supply liquidity to each other.
   - Trading follows two sets of rules:
     - Order matching rules: establishes the order precedence based on price, their arrival time and other factors.
     - Trade pricing rules: determines the price of the transaction.
3. **Brokered Markets:**
   - Brokers arrange trades between counterparties.
   - Used for instruments that are unique or illiquid like real estate or art pieces.

The two categories of the securities market **based on when the information is disclosed** are as follows:
1. **Pre-trade transparent:** trade information on quotes and orders is publicly available prior to the trades.
2. **Post-trade transparent:** trade information on quotes and orders is publicly available after the trade.

Characteristics of a well-functioning financial system

Four characteristics of a well-functioning financial system include:
1. Entities can trade securities that help to solve their financial problems or take advantage of the opportunities available i.e. firms can share or hedge risks, borrow at a reasonable rate and investors can earn adequate rate of returns on their investments.
2. **Operationally efficient markets** where trading costs like commissions, bid-ask spreads and price impacts are low, increases market pricing efficiencies.
3. **Informational efficient markets** allow for absorption of timely financial disclosures making the prices a close reflection of the fundamental values.
4. **Allocationally efficient markets** allow for better utilization of capital by allocating it to the most productive use.

Equity

Objectives of market regulation

The key objectives of market regulation are to:
- control fraud.
- control agency problems.
- promote fairness.
- set mutually beneficial standards.
- prevent undercapitalized financial firms from exploiting their investors by making excessively risky investments.
- ensure that long-term liabilities are funded.

R45 Security Market Indexes

Security market index

An index is an indicator, sign, or measure of something. Since an index is a single measure and reflects the performance of the entire security market, it makes it easy for investors to measure and track performance.

Security market indexes measure the value of different target markets such as security markets, market segments, and asset classes. Index value is calculated on a regular basis using actual or estimated prices of constituent securities. Constituent securities are the individual securities comprising an index.

Value, price return, and total return of an index

Index returns can be calculated using two methods:

Price return index or price index measures only the percentage change in price of the constituent securities within the index.

$PR_I = (V_{PRI1} - V_{PRI0}) / V_{PRI0}$

Total return index reflects the prices of constituent securities and the reinvestment of all income (dividend and/or interest) since inception.

$TR_I = (V_{PRI1} - V_{PRI0} + Inc_1) / V_{PRI0}$

Index returns of consecutive periods are linked geometrically.

Choices and issues in index construction and management

Index construction and management includes making the following decisions:
- Which target market should the index represent? E.g. U.S. equities.
- Which securities should be shortlisted from that market to be included in the index? E.g. banking sector stocks.
- How much weight would each security be allocated in the index?

Equity

- When and how often should the index be rebalanced?
- When should the security selection and weighting decision be re-examined?

Target market can be defined broadly (e.g. U.S. equities) or narrowly (e.g. large cap equities in U.S.). The target market can also be based on asset class (e.g. hedge funds), geographic region (e.g. emerging markets), industries (e.g. healthcare), sizes (e.g. mid-cap securities), and other characteristics.

Different weighting methods used in index construction

Index weighting determines how much weight each constituent security will be assigned in the index, thereby impacting the index value. The different weighting schemes used in construction of an index are:

Price weighted index: weight on each security is determined by dividing its price by the sum of all prices.

Equal weighted index: assigns equal weight to each constituent security at inception.

Market capitalization weighted index: weight of each security is determined by dividing its market capitalization with total market capitalization.

Fundamental weighted index: instead of using a stock's price as a measure, fundamental weighting uses measures such as book value, cash flow, revenue, earnings and dividends to calculate the weight of each security.

Method	Pros	Cons
Price	Simple	
Equal	Simple	High market cap stocks are under-represented. Requires frequent rebalancing.
Market Cap	Securities held in proportion to their value.	Influenced by overpriced securities.
Fundamental	Value tilt	Does not consider market value. Requires rebalancing.

Calculating the value and return of an index

Price weighted index:

$$\text{Price weighted index} = \frac{\text{Sum of Stock Prices}}{\text{No. of stocks in index adjusted for splits}}$$

Consider the performance of three stocks over a period of one-year.

Equity

	No of shares	Start price	End price	Earnings	Div. per share
Stock X	200	10	8	10	1
Stock Y	500	20	20	50	2
Stock Z	200	3	8	20	0

Compute the following:
1. Using price weighting compute the price return and total return if the index is constructed using these three stocks.
2. If stock Z splits 2:1, what would be the impact on the index value and return calculations.

Solution:
1. Price return: (Returns only through capital gains)
The weight of each security is its price divided by the sum of all the prices.
The price-weighted index at the start of the period = (10 + 20 + 3) / 3 = 11
The price-weighted index at the end of the period = (8 + 20 + 8) / 3 = 12
Price return over the year = (12/11) - 1 = 9.09% (capital gain return)

Total return: (Returns earned through both capital gains and dividends)
For total return, we compute the income return by dividing total dividends by the starting value of the index = (1 + 2 + 0)/ 11 = 27.27%
Total return = income return + capital gain return = 27.27% + 9.09% = 36.36%.

2. Divisor adjusts to negate the impact of stock splits, while the ending period index value should remain same at 12.
But the new sum of price at the end of the period is 32 (8 + 20 + 4; as stock Z split in two shares).
The divisor should be adjusted such that we get the same index value of 12 at the end of the period = 32/d = 12.
Therefore, the divisor drops from 3 to 2.67.
Every time a stock splits, the divisor decreases.

Equal weighted index:

$$\text{Equal weighted index} = \text{Initial index value} * \left(1 + \frac{\text{average of percentage change in prices}}{100}\right)$$

Consider the performance of three stocks over a period of one-year.

	No of shares	Start price	End price	Earnings	Div. per share
Stock X	200	10	8	10	1
Stock Y	500	20	20	50	2
Stock Z	200	3	8	20	0

Using equal weighting methodology compute the price return and total return if the index

Equity

is constructed using these three stocks.
Solution:
Price return:
Equal weighted index price return is the arithmetic average of the price return earned on each security.
Price return earned on stock X = (8/10) – 1 = -20.0%.
Price return earned on stock Y = (20/20) – 1 = 0.0%
Price return earned on stock Z = (8/3) – 1 = 166.7%
Equal weighted index price return = (-20.0% + 0.0% + 166.7%)/3 = 48.9%
Total return:
For total return, we compute the income return on each security by dividing dividend by the starting price
Income return earned on stock X = (1/10) = 10.0%.
Income return earned on stock Y = (2/20) = 10.0%
Income return earned on stock Z = (0/3) = 0.0%
Equal weighted index income return = (10.0% + 10.0% + 0.0%)/3 = 6.7%
Total return = income return + capital gain return = 6.7% + 48.9% = 55.6%.

Market capitalization weighted index:

$$\text{Market cap weighted index} = \frac{\text{current total market value of index stocks}}{\text{base year total market value of index stocks}} * \text{base year index value}$$

Consider the performance of three stocks over a period of one-year.

	No of shares	Start price	End price	Earnings	Div. per share
Stock X	200	10	8	10	1
Stock Y	500	20	20	50	2
Stock Z	200	3	8	20	0

1. Using market capitalization weighting methodology compute the price return and total return if the index is constructed using these three stocks. The index value should start at 3,000.
2. Compute the price return if stock Z has market float of 60%. The index value should start at 3,000.

Solution:
1. Price return:
Market capitalization of the three stocks at the start of the period = (200 * 10 + 500 * 20 + 200 * 3) = 12,600
As the index value should start at 3,000; we will be using a divisor of 4.2.
Market capitalization of the three stocks at the end of the period = (200 * 8 + 500 * 20 + 200* 8) = 13,200

Equity

Final index value will be calculated using the same divisor of 4.2.
Final index value would be = 13,200/4.2 = 3,142.9
Market capitalization index price return = (3,142.9/3,000) − 1 = 4.76%

Total return:
For total return, we compute the income return by totaling the dividend earned and dividing it by starting market capitalization.
Total dividend earned = (200 * 1 + 500 * 2 + 200 * 0) = 1,200
Income return = 1,200/12,600 = 9.5%
Total return = income return + capital gain return = 9.5% + 4.76% = 14.26%.

2. **Price return:**
Market capitalization of stock Z will be 360 (200 * 60%*3).
Market capitalization of the three stocks at the start of the period = (200 * 10 + 500 * 20 + 120 * 3) = 12,360
As the index value should start at 3,000; we will be using a divisor of 4.12.
Market capitalization of the three stocks at the start of the period = (200 * 8 + 500 * 20 + 120 * 8) = 12,560
Final index value will be calculated using the same divisor of 4.12.
Final index value would be = 12,200/4.2 = 3,048.5.
Market capitalization index price return = (3,048.5/3,000) − 1 = 1.6%

Fundamental weighted index:
Consider the performance of three stocks over a period of one-year.

	No of shares	Start price	End price	Earnings	Div. per share
Stock X	200	10	8	10	1
Stock Y	500	20	20	50	2
Stock Z	200	3	8	20	0

Using fundamental weighting methodology compute the price return and total return if the index is constructed using these three stocks.

Solution:
Price return:
Fundamental weighted index price return uses the weights of the price return earned on each security. These weights are dependent on a fundamental factor, here earnings.
Price return earned on stock X = (8/10) − 1 = -20.0%
Price return earned on stock Y = (20/20) − 1 = 0.0%
Price return earned on stock Z = (8/3) − 1 = 166.7%
Fundamental weighted index price return = [-20.0% * (10/80) + 0.0%* (50/80) + 166.7%* (20/80)] = 39.2%

Equity

Total return:

For total return, we compute the income return on each security by dividing dividend by the starting price.

Income return earned on stock X = (1/10) = 10.0%.

Income return earned on stock Y = (2/20) = 10.0%

Income return earned on stock Z = (0/3) = 0.0%

Fundamental weighted index income return = [10.0% * (10/80) + 10.0%* (50/80) + 0.0%* (20/80)] = 7.5%

Total return = income return + capital gain return = 7.5% + 39.2% = 46.7%

Rebalancing and reconstitution

Rebalancing means adjusting the weights of an index's constituent securities. The weight of each security in an index should reflect the weighting method used. The weights do not remain constant as the prices of securities change.

Reconstitution is the process of changing the constituent securities in an index. It is part of the rebalancing cycle. The frequency of reconstitution varies from index to index.

Uses of security market indexes

Security market indexes serve the following purpose:
- Index performance serves as a proxy of market sentiment.
- Investment management performance can be better evaluated in comparison with a suitable index that serves as a benchmark.
- Serves as a proxy for measuring and modeling returns, systematic risk and risk-adjusted performance.
- Serves as a proxy for asset class performance in asset allocation models.
- Useful in creation of passive portfolios that track index funds and ETFs.

Types of equity indexes

Equity indexes can be classified into:

Broad market index tries to represent the entire market. Typically, 90% of the securities of the selected market are represented in the index.

Multi-market index includes indexes from different countries as they represent multiple security markets based on national markets, geographic region, development groups etc.

Sector index focuses on a specific economic sector such as consumer goods, finance, energy, health care, technology etc. on a national or global basis.

Style index contains securities based on certain characteristics like market capitalization, value, growth, or a combination of any of these.

Equity

Market capitalization index contains securities based on market capitalization such as large cap, mid cap and small cap.

Value/growth index contains a group of stocks based on value/growth criteria.

Market capitalization and value/growth index combines the three market capitalization groups with value/growth classification resulting in the following six basic index style categories: Large-cap value, large-cap growth, mid-cap value, mid-cap growth, small-cap value, small-cap growth.

Types of fixed-income indexes

Dimensions of fixed income indexes	
Geographic region	Global
	Regional
	Country or currency zone
Type of issue	Corporate (with convertible option)
	Collateralized/securitized/mortgage backed
	Government and government undertakings
	Inflation protected
Maturity	Short term (with maturities less than one year)
	Medium term (with maturities greater than one year but less than 10 years)
	Long term (with maturities that exceed 10 years)
Credit rating	Investment grade (e.g. S&P rating of BBB or above)
	High yield

Issues faced in construction of fixed income indexes:
- Universe of securities is large with each entity issuing several versions and the index needs to be reconstituted when securities mature.
- Prices have to be estimated for some securities as the markets are relatively illiquid.

Indexes representing alternative investments

Commodity indexes consist of futures contracts on one or more commodities such as agricultural products (like wheat, sugar), precious metals like gold, and energy like crude oil.

Real estate indexes represent markets for real estate securities (such as REITs) and the market for actual real estate.

Hedge fund indexes reflect the returns on hedge funds. Research organizations collect data on hedge fund returns and compile this information into indexes. Some issues faced in index construction are:

Equity

- As hedge funds are not regulated, only those hedge funds that perform well disclose results. Hence, index performance is biased upwards.
- Fewer sampling periods as the hedge funds report results performance only periodically (for example quarterly). This can understate the deviations (risk) inherent in the investment.

Types of security market indexes

Security market indexes represent asset classes and target markets that can be classified based on geographic location, sector, industry, economic growth, value stocks, growth stocks etc. Some globally known indexes include Dow Jones Industrial average, S&P, Barclays Capital Global aggregate Bond Index etc.

R46 Market Efficiency

Market efficiency

- An **informationally efficient market** is one in which asset prices reflect new information quickly and rationally.
- Market prices should not react to information that is well anticipated, only unexpected information should move prices.
- In a perfectly efficient market, investors should use a passive investment strategy because active investment strategies will underperform due to transaction costs and management fees.

Market value v/s intrinsic value

- **Market value** of an asset is its current price at which the asset can be bought or sold.
- **Intrinsic value** is the value that would be placed on an asset by investors if they had full knowledge of the asset's characteristics.
- In highly efficient markets, full information is available in the market and is reflected in asset prices. Therefore, market value = intrinsic value.
- However, if markets are not efficient, the two prices can diverge significantly.

Factors that affect a market's efficiency

The following factors affect a market's efficiency:
- **Market participants** – More participants increase efficiency.
- **Information availability and financial disclosure** – More information increases efficiency.
- **Limits to trading** – Limitations on arbitrage and short selling decrease efficiency.
- **Transaction costs** – High costs decrease efficiency.
- **Information-acquisition costs** – High costs decrease efficiency.

Equity

Weak form, semi-strong form, and strong form market efficiency

Forms of Market Efficiency	Past Market Data	Public Information	Private Information
Weak form	Yes	No	No
Semi-strong form	Yes	Yes	No
Strong form	Yes	Yes	Yes

Implications of each form of market efficiency

- If markets are weak-form efficient, then purely technical analysis will not generate abnormal profits consistently.
- If markets are semi-strong form efficient, then neither technical nor fundamental analysis will generate abnormal profits consistently.
- If markets are strong-form efficient, then even inside information will not generate abnormal profits consistently.
- Evidence suggests that most developed markets are semi-strong form efficient. In such markets passive management strategies will outperform active management strategies.

Market anomalies

A market anomaly is something that challenges the idea of market efficiency. Some anomalies observed in the market are:

Time series anomalies:
- Calendar anomalies: The returns in January are higher than in any other month, especially for small firms. This phenomenon is known as the January effect.
- Momentum and overreaction anomalies: Investors overreact to events or release of unexpected public information.

Cross-sectional anomalies:
- Size effect: Small-cap stocks tend to perform better than large-cap stocks.
- Value effect: Value stocks tend to perform better than growth stocks.

Other anomalies:
- Closed-end fund discounts: Closed-End funds sell at a discount to NAV.
- Earnings surprise: Investors can earn abnormal profits by buying stock of companies with positive earnings surprise and selling those with negative earnings surprise.
- IPOs: Prices rise on listing day, but underperform in the long term.
- Predictability of returns based on prior information: Research has found that equity returns are related to prior information such as interest rates, inflation rates, stock volatility and dividend yields.

In practice it is not easy to trade and benefit from anomalies. Most research concludes that anomalies are not violations of market efficiency, but are the result of statistical methods used to detect anomalies.

Behavioral finance view

Behavioral finance uses human psychology to explain investment decisions. Some irrational behavior and biases observed in the market are:
- **Loss aversion:** Investors dislike losses more than they like gains of the same amount.
- **Overconfidence:** Overconfident investors do not process information. They place too much confidence in their ability to process and analyze information and value a security.
- **Representativeness**: Investors with this bias will assess probabilities based on events seen before, or prior experiences instead of calculating the outcomes.
- **Gambler's fallacy**: Recent outcomes affect investors' estimates of future probabilities.
- **Mental accounting**: Investors divide investments into separate mental accounts, they do not view them as a total portfolio.
- **Conservatism**: Investors tend to be slow to react to changes.
- **Narrow framing**: Investors focus on issues in isolation.

Although behavioral finance can help explain some of the market anomalies, a market can still be considered efficient even if market participants act irrationally, as long as they cannot consistently beat the market on a risk-adjusted basis.

R47 Overview of Equity Securities

Types of equity securities

There are two types of equity securities: common shares and preference shares.

Common shares represent an ownership interest in a company, including voting rights. They entitle investors to a share of the company's operating performance, participation in decision making in the form of voting rights and claim on the company's net assets in case of liquidation.

- Common shareholders enjoy voting rights. In **statutory voting,** each share gets one vote. In **Cumulative voting,** each shareholder gets to cast one vote per share times the number of positions to be filled and shareholders can direct their total voting rights to specific candidates.
- Common shares may be callable or putable. **Callable** means that the issuer has the right to buy back shares from investors at a price by a specified date. Similarly, in the case of **putable** shares, investors have an option of selling the shares back to the company at a certain price.

Equity

Preference shares are preferred over common shares while claiming a company's earnings in the form of dividends, and net assets upon liquidation. Preference shares can be cumulative, non-cumulative, participating or non-participating.

- **Cumulative**: Dividends accrue (add up) if the company does not pay dividends in one or more periods. When the dividend is paid in the subsequent years, the unpaid dividends accrue and are paid to preferred shares first before common shares.
- **Non-cumulative:** Dividends do not accumulate if a company decides not to pay dividends in one or more periods. However, whenever a dividend is paid, preferred shares get precedence over common shares. Because of this, a cumulative preferred share is worth more than a non-cumulative preferred share, all else equal.
- **Participating:** The right to receive the standard preferred dividend plus an additional dividend based on some condition like if the company's profits exceed a certain level. In case of liquidation, participating shares are entitled to additional distribution of net assets.
- **Non-participating:** The right to receive only a fixed dividend. No share in the additional profits of a company.

Convertible preference shares are those which can be converted to common stock. The conversion ratio is specified when the shares are issued.

Differences in voting rights and other ownership characteristics

A firm can have different classes of equity shares which may have different voting rights and priority in liquidation. For example: Class A shares would have more votes than Class B shares.

Public v/s private equity securities

Private equity refers to the sale of equity capital to institutional investors via private placement. The key characteristics of private equity are:
- Less liquidity as shares are not publicly traded.
- Price discovery can be biased as the security is not available for valuation by a broad base of public participants.
- Management can focus on long term value creation as it doesn't have to worry about reporting results to the market.
- Lower reporting costs due to lesser regulatory requirements.
- Weaker corporate governance due to lesser regulatory requirements.
- Potential for generating high returns when investment is exited.

The types of private equity are:
- **Venture capital:** refers to capital provided to firms in early stages of development. The three stages of funding include: seed/startup capital, early stage and mezzanine

Equity

financing.

- **Leveraged buyout:** Large amount of debt and small amount of capital are used to buy all the outstanding shares of a large publicly traded company. It is usually done to make large acquisitions.

- **Management buyout**: When investors in a leveraged buyout are primarily the company's existing management, they take a controlling interest. A large part is financed by debt and a small part is held as equity by private investors.

- **Private investment in public equity:** A public company that is in need of additional capital urgently sells a sizeable ownership percentage to private investor(s).

Methods for investing in non-domestic equity securities

There are two ways to invest in equity of companies outside the local market:

1. **Direct investment:** refers to directly buying and selling securities in foreign markets. Potential issues with direct investment are:
   - Along with the stock performance, the returns are exposed to the currency risk as the trade is made in foreign currency.
   - Investor must be aware of the investment environment and laws of the foreign land.
   - The disclosure requirements of the foreign country might be low, impeding the analysis process.

2. **Depository receipt (DR):**
   - A foreign company's shares are deposited in a local bank, which in turn issues receipts representing ownership of specific number of shares.
   - The receipts then trade on a local exchange in local currency price. For e.g. a Japanese firm's shares are held by a UK bank, which then issues DR representing this stock to the UK citizens.
   - The depository bank is responsible for handling dividends, stock splits and other events.
   - Based on the foreign company's involvement, DR can either be:
     o **Sponsored DR:** Foreign company is involved in issuance and holders of DR are given voting rights.
     o **Unsponsored DR:** Foreign company is not involved in issuance and the bank retains the voting rights.
   - Based on the geography of issuance, DRs can either be:
     o **Global depository receipt (GDR):**
       - DRs issued outside the company's home country and outside the U.S.
       - GDRs are issued by a depository bank which is located or has branches in the

Equity

countries on whose exchanges the shares are traded.
- **American depository receipt (ADR):**
  - USD denominated DRs that trade like common share on U.S. exchanges.
  - Some ADRs allow firms to raise capital and use shares to acquire other firms in the US.
  - The table below shows the four types of ADRS:

	Level I	Level II	Level III	Rule 144A
Trading places	Over-the-counter (OTC)	Stock exchanges	Stock exchanges	Private placement
SEC Registration	Required	Required	More registration required	Not required
Listing fees	Low	High	High	Low
Capital raising ability	None	None	High	High
Earnings requirements	None	Size constraint is applicable.	Size constraint is applicable.	None

Risk and return characteristics of different types of equity securities

Risk characteristics of different type of equity securities		
Common shares vs. preference shares. Preference shares are less risky.	**Preference Shares** 1. Dividends on preference shares are fixed as a percentage of the par value. 2. Dividends are paid before common shares. 3. On liquidation, preference shareholders get par value of the shares.	**Common Shares** 1. Returns are unknown as can be from capital gains (price appreciation) and dividends. 2. On liquidation, common shareholders have residual claim .i.e. they get paid after claims of debt and preferred shares have been met; hence it is unknown. 3. Foreign investments are subject to currency exposure risk.

Equity

Callable vs. non-callable shares Non-callable shares are less risky.	1. Callable shares are riskier as firm has an option to redeem at a predetermined price if the prices rise. 2. Callable shares benefits firm. 3. Callable shares pay higher dividend to compensate for higher risk and lower potential payout.
Putable vs. non-putable shares Putable shares are less risky.	1. Putable shares are less risky as they can be sold by investors at a predetermined price. 2. Putable shares benefits investors. 3. Putable shares pay lower dividend to compensate for lower risk.
Cumulative vs. non-cumulative preference shares. Cumulative shares are less risky.	1. Any unpaid dividends are accumulated and paid before common stock dividends are paid.

Role of equity securities in the financing of company's assets

Equity securities serve the following purposes:
- **Raising capital:** Enables companies to raise capital for buying long-term assets, expanding business operations geographically and product offerings, and other activities.
- **Currency for transactions:** Mergers & acquisitions and employee incentive programs can be funded directly through equity securities.

Market value v/s book value of equity securities

Book value of equity: is based on balance sheet value of assets minus the liabilities. It increases when management makes decisions to increase net income and retained earnings.

Market value of equity: is the total outstanding shares of a firm multiplied by the current market price. It is based on investors' expectations of the future cash flows generated by the business and the risk inherent in the business.

Book value and market value of equity are rarely equal because the market expectations of future cash flows may not be reflected in the book value.

Cost of equity, accounting return on equity, and investors' required rates of return

Return on equity (ROE)
- Key ratio to determine whether the management is using the capital effectively.
- ROE_t = Net Income / Average book value of equity = $NI_t / (BVE_t + BE_{t-1})/2$

Equity

- ROE can increase over time because of the following reasons:
  - Rapid increase in net income relative to the increase in book value of equity.
  - Rapid decline in book value i.e. net income declines at a slower rate compared to the decline in book value.
  - Increase in leverage that increases net income and reduces book value of equity, thereby increasing overall risk.
- As only the first case is desirable in the above three cases, a proper analysis of the increase in ROE should be done.
- DuPont formula can yield a better understanding of the sources of growth in the ROE ratio.

$$\frac{\text{Net income}}{\text{Equity}} = \frac{\text{Net income}}{\text{Assets}} \times \frac{\text{Assets}}{\text{Equity}}$$

Investors required return vs. cost of equity

- Cost of equity is the minimum rate of return that stockholders require the company to pay them for investing in its equity.
- Companies try to raise capital at the lowest possible cost; hence, company's cost of equity is often used as a proxy for the investor's minimum required rate of return.

R48 Introduction to Industry and Company Analysis

Uses of industry analysis

Uses of industry analysis:
- To understand a company's business and business environment.
- To identify active equity investment opportunities.
- To create an industry or sector rotation strategy.
- For portfolio performance attribution.

Relation of industry analysis to company analysis
- They are closely interrelated.
- Together they can provide insights about the firm's potential growth, competition and risk.

Industry classification systems

The three main methods for classifying companies are:
- **Products and/or services offered**: For example, firms that produce healthcare related products or provide healthcare related services will constitute the healthcare industry.
- **Business cycle sensitivities**: Companies are classified as 'cyclical' – earnings highly dependent on the stage of the business cycle or 'non–cyclical' – earnings are relatively stable over the business cycle.

- **Statistical similarities**: Firms that historically have had highly correlated returns are grouped together.

Current industry classification systems are:

Commercial industry classification systems include:
- Global Industry Classification Standard.
- Russell Global Sectors.
- Industry Classification Benchmark.

Governmental industry classification systems include:
- International Standard Industrial Classification of All Economic Activities.
- Statistical Classification of Economic Activities in the European Community.
- Australian and New Zealand Standard Industrial Classification.
- North American Industry Classification System.

A limitation of the current classification system is that all firms in the same narrowest industry classification do not necessarily form a peer group.

Sensitivity of a company to business cycle

Depending on the sensitivity to the business cycle, companies can be classified as:
- **Cyclical**: Earnings are highly dependent on the stage of the business cycle
- **Non-cyclical**: Earnings are relatively stable over the business cycle

Non-cyclical industries can be further divided into:
- **Defensive**: Industries that are least affected by the stage of the business cycle, for example, utilities and consumer staples.
- **Growth**: Industries that have a very strong demand due to which they are largely unaffected by the stage of the business cycle.

Limitations
- Cyclical industries often include growth firms.
- Non-cyclical industries can be affected by severe recessions.
- Business cycles can differ across countries, so it is difficult to measure sensitivity for a global firm.

Peer groups

A peer group is a set of comparable companies engaged in similar business activities. They are influenced by the same set of factors.

Steps in constructing a preliminary list of peer companies:
- Use commercial classification systems. They often provide a useful starting point for identifying companies operating in the same industry.

Equity

- Examine the subject company's annual report. Companies frequently mention specific competitors in their annual reports.
- Examine competitors' annual reports to identify other potential comparable companies.
- Examine industry trade publications to identify additional peer companies.
- Confirm that each comparable or peer company has similar sources of sales and earnings.

Thorough industry analysis

The diagram below provides a framework of a through industry analysis.

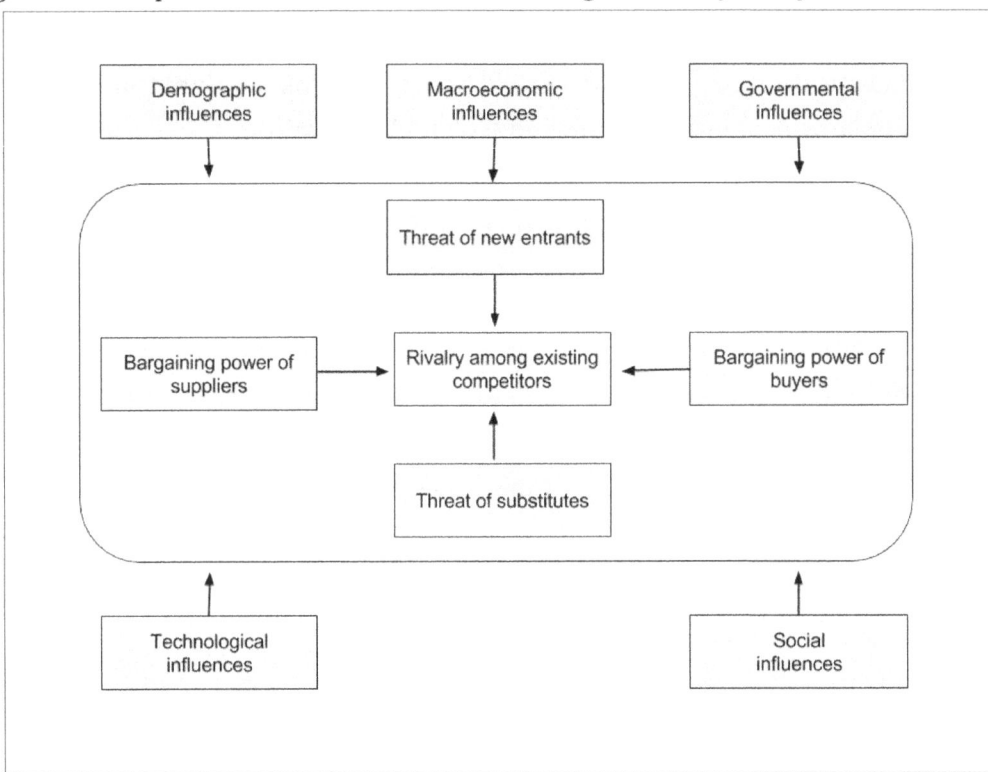

Principles of strategic analysis of an industry

The framework for strategic analysis is known as "Porter's five forces". According to this model the pr28ofitability of companies in an industry is determined by the following five forces:

1. **The threat of new entrants:** Determined by economies of scale, brand loyalty, absolute cost advantages, customer switching costs, and government regulation.
2. **The bargaining power of suppliers:** Determined by product substitution, buyer and supplier groups' concentration, switching costs, entry costs.
3. **The bargaining power of buyers**: Determined by switching costs among customers, ability of customers to produce their own product
4. **The threat of substitutes.**

Equity

5. **The intensity of rivalry among existing competitors**: Determined by industry competitive structure, demand conditions, cost conditions, exit barriers.

Factors affecting pricing power of a company

- If the barriers to entry are high, then it discourages new entrants from entering the industry. However, it does not guarantee a high pricing power. This might happen if price is a large percentage of the customer's purchase decision or the industry has high barriers to exit which can lead to overcapacity.
- In concentrated industries, each player generally has high pricing power. In segmented industries, each player generally has low pricing power and this usually results in strong competition. However, there may be exceptions.
- Under capacity results in high pricing power as demand exceeds supply. Similarly, overcapacity leads to price cuts and a very competitive environment.
- Factors that impact market share stability include: barriers to entry, switching costs, new product introductions, complexity of products and pace of innovation.

Industry life-cycle model

The following diagram shows an industry life cycle model.

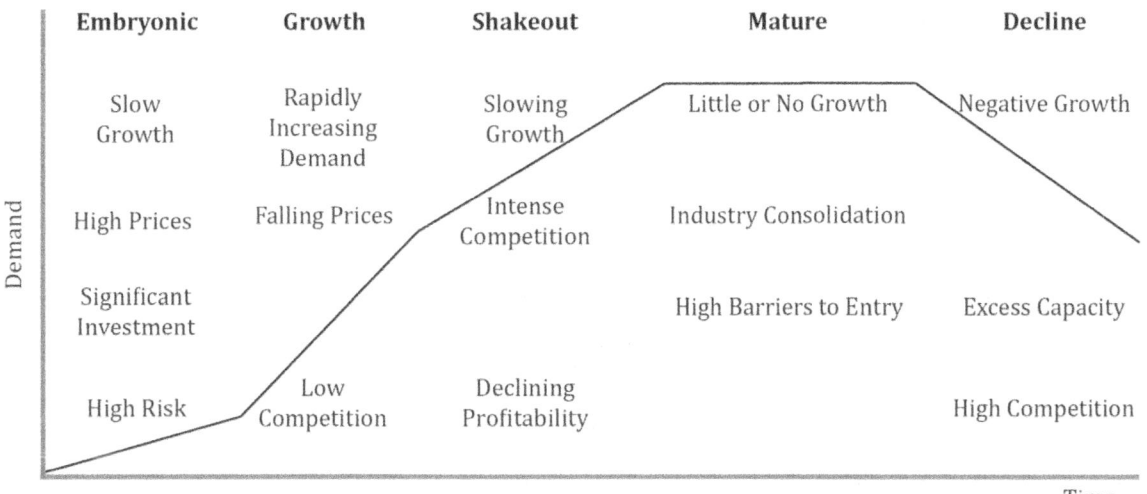

Embryonic
- Slow growth.
- High prices.
- Requires significant investment.
- High risk.

Growth
- Rapidly increasing demand.
- Profitability improves.

Equity

- Prices fall.
- Competition is low.

Shakeout
- Growth starts slowing down.
- Competition is intense.
- Profitability declines.

Mature
- Little or no growth.
- Industry consolidates.
- Barriers to entry are high.

Decline
- Growth is negative.
- Excess capacity.
- High competition.

Limitations of the life cycle model include:
- Some stages may be longer or shorter than expected due to technological changes, government regulations, societal changes or demographics.
- It is less practical for analyzing industries going through rapid changes.

Factors affecting industry growth, profitability and risk

External influences on industry growth, profitability, and risk include:
- **Technology**: Can dramatically change an industry through the introduction of new or improved products.
- **Demographics**: This include changes in population size, age and gender ratio.
- **Government**: This include tax rates, regulations and government purchases of goods and services.
- **Social factors**: Relate to how people work, play and spend their leisure time.
- **Macroeconomic influences**: Include long term trends in factors such as GDP growth, interest rates and inflation.

Thorough company analysis

A through company analysis includes investigation of:
- corporate profile
- industry characteristics
- demand for products/services
- supply of products/services
- pricing

- financial ratios

Porter identified two chief competitive strategies that can be employed by companies:

- **Low-cost strategy (cost leadership)**: Here companies strive to become low-cost producers, offer the lowest prices and generate enough volumes to make a good return.
- **Product/service differentiation strategy:** Here companies strive to offer products and services that are unique either in quality, type, or means of distribution. For this strategy to work, the extra price that customers are willing to pay must be more than the cost of differentiation.

R49 Equity Valuation: Concepts and Basic Tools

Estimated value and market price

- If the estimated value is more than the market price, the security is **undervalued**.
- If the estimated value is equal to the market price, the security is **fairly valued**.
- If the estimated value is less than the market price, the security is **overvalued**.

Securities that are followed by many analysts are more likely to be fairly valued than securities that are neglected by analysts.

Major categories of equity valuation models

Three major categories of equity valuation models are:

Present value models
- They estimate value as present value of expected future benefits.
- Future benefits are defined as either cash distributed to shareholders (dividend discount models) or cash available to shareholders after meeting the necessary capital expenditure and working capital expenses (free cash flow to equity models)

Multiplier models
- They estimate intrinsic value based on a multiple of some fundamental variable.
- For example, stock price / earnings (or sales, book value, cash flow)
- Or Enterprise value / EBITDA (or sales).

Asset-based valuation models
- They estimate the value of equity as the value of assets minus the value of liabilities.
- Book values of assets and liabilities are typically adjusted to their fair values when using these models.

Dividends, stock splits and share repurchases

Cash dividends are payments made to shareholders in cash. The three types of cash dividends are:

Equity

1. Regular cash dividends are paid out on a consistent basis. Stable or increasing dividend is viewed as a sign of financial stability.
2. Special dividends are one-time cash payments when the situations are favorable (also known as extra dividends or irregular dividends; used by cyclical firms).
3. Liquidating dividend is distributed to shareholders when a company goes out of business.

Stock dividends are payments made to shareholders in additional shares instead of cash. Stock splits divide each existing share into multiple shares.

Reverse stock splits are the opposite of stock splits and decreases the total number of outstanding shares.

Share repurchase is when a company buys back its own outstanding shares using cash.

Dividend payment chronology

Dividend payment schedule is as follows:
1. Declaration date: Board of directors approves dividend.
2. Ex-dividend date: Cutoff date on or after which buyers of a stock are not eligible for the dividend. It is also the first date when the stock trades without dividend.
3. Holder-of-record date: A record of shareholders who are eligible to receive the dividend is made (usually two days after the ex-dividend date).
4. Payment date: Dividend payment is made to the shareholders.

Dividend discount and free-cash-flow-to-equity models

Dividend discount model: Value is estimated as the present value of expected future dividends plus the present value of a terminal value.

$$V_0 = \sum_{t=1}^{n} \frac{D^t}{(1+r)^t} + \frac{P^n}{(1+r)^n}$$

A stock paid a $10 dividend last year. The next year's dividend will be 8% higher and the stock will sell at $150 at year-end. Calculate the value of this stock if the required rate of return is 12%.

Solution:
D_1 = D_0 x (1 + dividend growth rate) = $10 x 1.08 = $10.8

$$V_0 = \frac{\$10.8}{1.12} + \frac{\$150}{1.12} = \$143.57$$

Free cash flow to equity model: Value is estimated as the present value of expected future free cash flow to equity. FCFE is the cash available to the firm's equity holders after a firm meets all its other obligations.

FCFE = CFO - FCInv + Net borrowing

Equity

$$V_0 = \sum_{t=1}^{\infty} \frac{FCFE^t}{(1+r)^t}$$

Estimating the required rate of return for equity: CAPM is often used to calculate the required rate of return for a security.

Required rate of return = risk free rate + β [market risk premium]

Preferred Stock Valuation

Preferred stock typically pays a fixed dividend and does not mature. Its value is given as:

$$V = \frac{D}{r}$$

A preferred stock has a par value of $100 and it pays a $6 annual dividend. Calculate the value of this preferred stock if it has a required rate of return of 10%.

Solution:

$$V = \frac{D}{r} = \frac{\$6}{0.1} = \$60$$

Gordon (constant) growth model and Multistage Dividend Discount Models

Gordon growth model (Constant growth dividend discount model): assumes that dividends will grow indefinitely at a constant growth rate. The value of the stock is calculated as:

$$V_0 = \frac{D_1}{r - g}$$

Calculate the value of a stock that paid a $10 dividend last year, if dividends are expected to grow forever at 6% and the required rate of return on equity is 8%.

Solution:

$D_1 = D_0 \times (1 + \text{dividend growth rate}) = \$10 \times 1.06 = \$10.6$

$$V_0 = \frac{\$10.6}{0.08 - 0.06} = \$530$$

g is the sustainable growth rate i.e. rate at which earnings and dividends can continue to grow indefinitely. It is calculated as:

g = retention rate * ROE

Multi-stage dividend discount model: used for companies with high growth rate over an initial few number of periods followed by a constant growth rate of dividends forever.

$$V_0 = \sum_{t=1}^{n} \frac{D_0(1+g_s)^t}{(1+r)^t} + \frac{V_n}{(1+r)^n}$$

$$V_n = \frac{D_{n+1}}{r - g}$$

Dividends of a company are expected to grow at 15% per year for three years, after which they are expected to grow at a constant rate of 5% per year. The last dividend paid was $2.

Equity

Calculate the value of the stock of this company if the required rate of return is 10%.

Solution:

$D_1 = \$2 \times 1.15 = \$2.3$

$D_2 = \$2.3 \times 1.15 = \$2.645$

$D_3 = \$2.645 \times 1.15 = \$3.042$

D_3 will grow at a constant growth rate of 5%. Hence,

$$V_2 = \frac{\$3.042}{0.1 - 0.05} = \$60.84$$

Finally,

$$V_0 = \frac{\$2.3}{1.1} + \frac{\$2.645}{1.1^2} + \frac{\$60.84}{1.1^2} = \$54.55$$

Characteristics of companies for which the constant growth/multistage dividend discount model can be used

- The constant growth model is appropriate for companies that pay dividends that grow at a constant rate. This includes stable and mature firms or non-cyclical firms.
- The two-stage model is used for companies that are transitioning from a growth phase to a mature phase.
- A three-stage model is used for young companies that will go from growth phase to transition phase to maturity phase.

Relationships between price multiples, present value models and fundamentals

Multiples based on comparables

- In a price multiples approach, an analyst compares the stock's price multiple to a benchmark value based on an index or with a peer group.
- It is based on the law of one price. The objective is to identify if a stock is fairly valued, undervalued or overvalued relative to the benchmark or its peers.
- Commonly used price multiples are P/E, P/CF, P/S, P/BV.

Multiples based on fundamentals

- They tell us what a multiple should be based on some valuation models.

$$\text{Forward P/E} = P_0/E_1 = \frac{\frac{D_1}{E_1}}{r-g} = \frac{\text{dividend payout ratio}}{r-g}$$

A company has an expected dividend payout ratio of 70%, and an expected dividend growth rate of 5%. Calculate the firm's fundamental leading P/E ratio if it has a required rate of return of 10%.

Solution:

$$\text{Forward } \frac{P}{E} = \frac{\text{dividend payout ratio}}{r-g} = \frac{0.7}{0.1-0.05} = 14$$

- If a firm has a higher dividend payout ratio, higher growth rate, and lower required return than its peers, then it may be justified having a higher P/E ratio.

Price multiples are widely used by analysts in time series and cross-sectional analysis because they are easy to calculate and are readily available.

The method of comparables

$$\text{Trailing P/E} = \frac{\text{price per share}}{\text{trailing 12 month earnings per share}}$$

$$\text{Forward P/E} = \frac{\text{stock price}}{\text{leading 12 month earnings per share}}$$

$$\text{P/CF} = \frac{\text{price per share}}{\text{cash flow per share}}$$

$$\text{P/S} = \frac{\text{price per share}}{\text{sales per share}}$$

$$\text{P/CF} = \frac{\text{price per share}}{\text{cash flow per share}}$$

Enterprise value multiples

Enterprise value is a measure of the value of the total company. It can be interpreted as what it would cost to acquire the firm.

Enterprise value = market value of debt + market value of equity − cash and short-term investments

The most commonly used enterprise value multiple is EV/EBITDA. It is used for:
- Companies that have negative earnings (that make P/E ratio meaningless)
- Comparing companies with significant differences in capital structure.
- Evaluating the cost of a takeover.

Asset-based valuation models

- Asset based models value equity as the fair or market value of assets minus liabilities.
- Possible approaches to valuing assets are to value them at their depreciated values, inflation-adjusted depreciated values, or estimated replacement values.
- This method is appropriate for companies that have a low proportion of intangible or off-the-book assets.
- It is commonly used for valuing private enterprises.

Advantages and disadvantages of each category of valuation model

Discounted cash flow models

Advantages
- Based on present value of future cash flows which is theoretically sound approach to valuation.
- They are widely used and accepted by analysts.

Disadvantages

- Inputs have to be estimated.
- Calculated values are very sensitive to inputs.

Price multiple models

Advantages

- They are good predictors of stock returns.
- Widely used by analysts.
- Easy to calculate and readily available.
- Allows time series and cross-sectional comparisons.

Disadvantages

- Lagging price multiples reflect the past.
- May not always be comparable across firms. It may be difficult to construct a peer group.
- Price multiples for cyclical firms may be greatly affected by economic conditions.
- Results obtained might conflict with fundamental methods.
- Negative denominator results in meaningless ratios.

Asset-based models

Advantages

- They provide floor values.
- Works well when a company has assets that have easily determinable market values.
- They are increasingly useful for valuing private firms.

Disadvantages

- Market values of assets are usually different from book values and are difficult to determine.
- Does not work well when a firm has a large amount of intangible assets or when future cash flows are not reflected in asset values.
- Asset values are difficult to determine during periods of hyperinflation.

Fixed Income

R50 Fixed-Income Securities - Defining Elements

Basic features of a fixed-income security

The basic features of a fixed income security include:

Issuer: Bonds can be issued by:
- supranational organizations
- sovereign governments
- non-sovereign governments
- quasi-government entities
- corporate issuers

Maturity: Also known as a bond's tenor.
- If original maturity is one year or less; bond is called money market security.
- If original maturity is more than a year; bond is called capital market security.

Par value: The principal amount that is repaid to bond holders at maturity; also known as face value, maturity value or redemption value.
- If market price > par value; bond is trading at a premium.
- If market price < par value; bond is trading at a discount.
- If market price = par value; bond is trading at par.

Coupon rate and frequency:
- Coupon rate is the percentage of par value that the issuer agrees to pay to the bondholder annually as interest.
- This can be a fixed rate or a floating rate.
- The coupon frequency may be annual, semi-annual, quarterly or monthly.

Currency denomination:
- Bonds can be issued in any currency.
- Dual currency bonds pay interest in one currency and principal in another currency.

Bond indenture

The bond indenture or trust deed is a legal contract between the bond holder and the bond issuer. It specifies:
- Bond's features such as the type of the bond, face value, maturity, coupon rate and frequency.
- The source of funds for repayment.
- Assets pledged as collateral. Secured bonds have a claim on specific assets. Unsecured bonds have a claim on overall assets and cash flows of the issuer.
- Credit enhancements.

Fixed Income

- Covenants that the issuer must comply with.

Affirmative v/s negative covenants

Bond covenants are legally enforceable rules that borrowers and lenders agree on at the time of a new bond issue. Two types of bond covenants are:

Affirmative covenants: They specify what a bondholder is required to do. For example: the issuer will make interest and principal payments on time.

Negative covenants: They specify what an issuer is prohibited from doing. For example: the issuer will not sell assets that have been pledged as collateral.

Legal, regulatory, and tax considerations

Legal and regulatory considerations

Places where bonds are issued and traded
- Bonds issued in a particular country in local currency are domestic bonds if they are issued by entities incorporated in the country and foreign bonds if they are issued by entities incorporated in another country.
- Eurobonds are issued internationally, outside the jurisdiction of any single country and are denoted in currency other than that of the countries in which they trade. They are less regulated as compared to bonds issued in the national bond markets.
- Global bonds are issued in the Eurobond market and at least one domestic market simultaneously.

Issuing entity: The issuing entity may be a government, a corporation or a special purpose entity.

Source of repayment
- For sovereign bonds: The country's taxing authority.
- For non-sovereign bonds: The taxing authority or revenues from a project.
- For corporate bonds: The funds from the firm's operations.
- For securitized bonds: The cash flows from a pool of financial assets.

Collateral
- Bonds are secured if they have a claim on specific assets.
- Otherwise, bonds are unsecured if they have a claim on overall assets and cash flows of the issuer.

Credit enhancement
- Credit enhancement can be internal or external.
- Examples of internal credit enhancement include subordination, overcollateralization, and reserve accounts.

Fixed Income

- Examples of external credit enhancement include a bank guarantee, a surety bond, a letter of credit, and a cash collateral account.

Tax considerations

- The income portion of a bond investment is generally taxed at the ordinary income tax rate.
- The gains from selling a bond are generally taxed at the capital gains tax rate.
- However, for discount bonds the increase in value towards par is considered interest income (and not capital gain).

Cash flows of fixed-income securities

Bullet structure: Pays coupon periodically and entire payment of principal occurs at maturity.

Amortizing bond

- An amortizing bond is a bond that repays part of its principal at each payment date.
- For a fully amortized bond, the amortizing bond's outstanding principal amount is reduced to zero by the maturity date.
- However, for a partially amortizing bond, a balloon payment is required at maturity to repay the remaining principal as a lump sum.

Sinking fund agreements: Here the issuer is required to retire a portion of the bond issue at specified times during the bond's life.

Floating rate notes (FRN)

- A bond whose coupon is set based on some reference rate plus a spread.
- FRNs can have floors (minimum interest rate), caps (maximum interest rate), or collars (both a minimum and maximum rate).
- An inverse FRN is a bond whose coupon has a negative relationship with the reference rate.

Other coupon structures

- <u>Step-up coupons</u>: Coupons increase by specified amounts on specified dates.
- <u>Bonds with credit-linked coupons</u>: Coupons change when the issuer's credit rating changes.
- <u>Bonds with payment-in-kind coupons</u>: Issuer can pay coupons with additional amounts of the bond issue instead of cash.
- <u>Bonds with deferred coupons</u>: No coupons paid in the initial years but higher coupons paid later.
- <u>Index linked bonds</u>: Coupon payments and/or principal repayments are linked to a price index.

Fixed Income

Contingency provisions

Callable bond
- Gives the issuer the right to redeem the bond prior to maturity at a specified call price.
- This is a benefit to the issuer; therefore, investors demand a higher yield (lower price) for callable bonds as compared to otherwise similar non-callable bonds.

Putable bond
- Gives the bondholder the right to sell bonds back to the issuer prior to maturity at a specified put price.
- This is a benefit to the investor; therefore, investors are willing to accept a lower yield (higher price) for putable bonds as compared to otherwise similar non-putable bonds.

Convertible bond
- Gives the bondholder the right to convert the bond into common shares of the issuing company.
- This is a benefit to the investor; therefore, investors are willing to accept a lower yield (higher price) for convertible bonds as compared to otherwise similar non-convertible bonds.

R51 Fixed Income Markets - Issuance, Trading and Funding

Classifications of global fixed-income markets

Global fixed income markets can be classified based on:

Type of issuer:
- Government and government related sector
- Corporate sector
- Structured finance sector

Credit quality
- Investment grade bonds
- Non-investment grade or high-yield bonds

Original maturity
- Money market securities: Original maturity is a year or less.
- Capital market securities: Original maturity is longer than a year.

Currency: A majority of the bonds are denominated in either euros or US dollars.

Geography
- Bonds are classified as domestic, foreign, Eurobond or global.
- Bond markets can also be classified as developed or emerging bond markets.

Coupon: Fixed rate or floating rate.

Other classifications: For example, inflation-linked bonds or tax-exempt bonds.

Interbank offered rates

- Interbank offered rates are rates at which banks borrow/lend unsecured funds from/to other banks in the interbank market.
- Interbank lending rates such as LIBOR (London Interbank Offered Rate) are frequently used as reference rates for floating rate debt.
- The appropriate reference rate for a FRN is one that matches the FRN's currency and frequency of rate resets. For example, the appropriate reference rate for an annual FRN issued in US dollar is the 12-month U.S. dollar LIBOR.

Mechanisms available for issuing bonds in primary markets

Primary markets are markets in which bonds are sold for the first time by an issuer to raise capital. Bonds may be issued in the primary market through a public offering or a private placement.

Public offering: Any member of the public may buy the bonds. Four types are:
- Underwritten offerings: The investment bank buys the entire issue and takes the risk of reselling it to investors or dealers.
- Best effort offerings: The investment bank serves only as a broker and sells the bond issue only if it is able to do so. (Underwritten and best effort offerings are frequently used in the issuance of corporate bonds)
- Shelf registrations: The issuer files a single document with regulators that allows for additional future issuances.
- Auction: Price discovery through bidding. (It is frequently used in the issuance of sovereign bonds.)

Private placement: Securities are not sold to the public directly; instead the entire issue is sold to a qualified investor or to a group of investors (typically large institutions).

Secondary markets for bonds

- Secondary markets are markets in which existing bonds are traded among investors.
- Most bonds are traded in over-the-counter (OTC) dealer markets. Some bonds are traded on public exchanges.
- Institutional investors are the major buyers and sellers of bonds in secondary markets.

Securities issued by sovereign governments

Sovereign bonds are bonds issued by national governments. They are usually fixed-rate bonds. However, some national governments also issue floating-rate bonds and inflation-

Fixed Income

linked bonds.

Securities issued by non-sovereign governments, quasi-government entities, and supranational agencies

- **Non-sovereign government bonds** are issued by local governments such as provinces or cities. They may be backed by taxing authority or by revenues from a specific project. They have a higher credit risk than sovereign bonds and therefore demand a higher yield.
- **Quasi government bonds or agency bonds** are issued by government sponsored entities. They may be explicitly or implicitly backed by government.
- **Supranational bonds** are issued by multilateral organizations that operate across national borders such as World Bank, IMF etc.

Types of debt issued by corporations

Companies raise debt via:
- **Bilateral loan**: A loan taken from a single bank.
- **Syndicated loan**: A loan taken from multiple banks.
- **Commercial paper**: A money market instrument issued by companies with high credit quality. Many issuers roll over their commercial paper on a regular basis.
- **Corporate bonds**: Based on maturities, coupon payment, and principal repayment structures, we can have different types of corporate bonds. The principal can be repaid based on serial maturity structure, term maturity structure or a sinking fund arrangement.
- **Medium-term notes**: They are securities that are structured to meet the requirements of investors.

Short-term funding alternatives available to banks

The various short-term funding alternatives available to banks are:
- **Retail Deposits:** One of the primary sources of funds for a bank is the money deposited by retail investors in their accounts. The three types of retail accounts are demand deposits, saving accounts and money market accounts.
- **Central bank funds:** When a bank receives deposits from customers, a certain percentage of this money must be kept as a reserve with the central bank. The funds kept in the central bank by all banks are collectively known as central bank funds market.
- **Interbank Funds:** Banks lend to and borrow from each other in the interbank market. It is an unsecured system of lending and the term may vary from overnight to one year.
- **Certificate of deposit:** A savings instrument with a maturity date, fixed interest rate and can be issued in any denomination. The investor or bearer of the certificate

Fixed Income

receives an interest at the end of the deposit period. There are two forms of CD: negotiable CD and non-negotiable CD.

Repurchase agreements (repos)

- A repurchase agreement is similar to a collateralized loan.
- This involves the sale of a security (collateral) with a simultaneous agreement by the seller (borrower) to buy the same security back from the purchaser (lender) at an agreed-on price in the future.
- The repo rate is the implicit interest rate of a repurchase agreement.
- The repo margin (haircut) is the difference between the amount borrowed and the value of the collateral.
- Repurchase agreements are a common source of funding for bond dealers.
- Instead of borrowing funds if a bond dealer is lending funds, then this agreement is known as a reverse repo.

R52 Introduction to Fixed-Income Valuation

Calculating a bond's price given a market discount rate

- The market discount rate is the rate of return required by investors given the risk of investing in the bond.
- The bond's price is the present value of its future cash flows, discounted at the bond's market discount rate (also called yield-to-maturity).

A 5 year, 6% annual-pay bond has a par value of $100. Calculate the price of the bond if it has a yield to maturity of 7%.

Solution:

Bond price $= \frac{6}{1.07} + \frac{6}{1.07^2} + \frac{6}{1.07^3} + \frac{6}{1.07^4} + \frac{106}{1.07^5} = 95.899$

Note: It is advisable to use the TVM function on the calculator on the exam. The inputs will be: N = 5, I/Y = 7, PMT = 6, FV = 100, CPT PV = 95.899

Relationships among a bond's price, coupon rate, maturity, and market discount rate (yield-to-maturity)

The yield-to-maturity is the implied market discount rate given the price of the bond.

Relationship with bond's price
- A bond's price moves inversely with its YTM. An increase in YTM decreases the price and a decrease in YTM increases the price of a bond.
- The relationship between a bond's price and its YTM is convex. Percentage price change is more when discount rate goes down than when it goes up by the same amount.

Relationship with coupon rate

Fixed Income

- A bond is priced at a premium above par value when the coupon rate is greater than the market discount rate.
- A bond is priced at a discount below par value when the coupon rate is less than the market discount rate.
- All else equal, the price of a lower-coupon bond is more volatile than the price of a higher-coupon bond.

Relationship with maturity
- All else equal, generally, the price of a longer-term bond is more volatile than the price of shorter-term bond.
- Assuming no default, premium and discount bond prices are "pulled to par" as maturity approaches.

Calculating the price of a bond using spot rates

A spot rate is the YTM of a zero-coupon bond. It is the appropriate rate to discount a single cash flow. Using spot rates, we can calculate the no-arbitrage price of the bond as:

$$PV = \frac{PMT}{(1+Z_1)^1} + \frac{PMT}{(1+Z_2)^2} + \cdots + \frac{PMT+FV}{(1+Z_N)^N}$$

where Z_N are the spot rates.

If spot rates are 4% for one year, 4.25% for two years and 4.5% for three years. Calculate the price of a $1,000 face value, 3-year, annual-pay bond with a coupon rate of 5%.

Solution:

$$\text{Bond value} = \frac{50}{1.04} + \frac{50}{1.0425^2} + \frac{1,050}{1.045^3} = \$1,014.19$$

Flat price, accrued interest, and the full price of a bond

- When a bond is between coupon dates, the full price of a bond includes flat price plus accrued interest.
- Prices quoted in the market are flat prices (not full prices) because in between coupon dates, the full price will increase daily as a result of interest accruals and suddenly fall when the next coupon is paid. This will create confusion.
- Accrued interest is calculated as a proportional share of the next coupon payment.

Full price or dirty price = flat price + accrued interest

$$\text{Accrued interest} = \frac{t}{T} * PMT$$

An investor is considering selling a $1,000 face value, semi-annual coupon bond with a quoted price of 103 and accrued interest since the last coupon of $25. Ignoring transaction costs, how much will he receive at the settlement date?

Solution:
The seller will receive the full price, which is equal to the flat price plus the interest accrued

Fixed Income

from the last coupon date.
Flat price = $1,000 x 103% = $1,030
Full price = $1,030 + $25 = $1,055

Matrix pricing

Method used to value illiquid bonds by using prices and yields on comparable securities. To find comparable securities we select securities that have same or similar credit risk, coupon rate, and maturity. The steps involved in matrix pricing are:
- Determine the YTM of comparable bonds.
- Determine the average yields of different comparable bonds.
- Calculate the market discount rate using linear interpolation.
- Using the discount rate, compute the price of the bond.

Yield measures for fixed-rate bonds, floating-rate notes, and money market instruments

Effective yield
- The effective yield of a bond depends on its periodicity.
- Annual-pay bonds have effective yields equal to YTM. Bonds with greater periodicity (paying coupon more than once a year) will have effective yields higher than their YTMs.

Street convention yields v/s True yield
- Street convention yields assume payments are made on scheduled dates. Here we neglect weekends and holidays for simplicity.
- True yield is the yield-to-maturity calculated using an actual calendar. Here we consider weekends and holidays.

Current yield & Simple yield
- The current yield is the annual coupon payment divided by the flat price.
- The simple yield is like the current yield but it adjusts the current yield by using straight-line amortization of the discount or premium.

Bonds with embedded options
- For callable bonds, we can calculate the yield to first call, yield to second call and so on.
- The lowest of these yields is called the yield to worst.

A bond with 5 years remaining until maturity is currently trading for 102 per 100 of par value. The bond offers 8% coupon rate with interest paid semiannually. The bond is callable at 103 in two years. Calculate the bond's yield-to-call.

Solution:
N = 4, FV = 103, PMT = 4, PV = -102; CPT → I/Y = 4.15%

Fixed Income

YTM = 2 x 4.15% = 8.3%

Floating rate notes

- A floating-rate note (FRN) has a quoted margin relative to a reference rate, which is often Libor.
- The required margin on a floater is the spread required by investors. If credit quality has decreased, required margin may be greater than quoted margin. If credit quality has increased, required margin may be less than quoted margin.

Money market instruments

- Money market instruments have a maturity of one year or less. Their yields are quoted on a discount rate or add-on rate basis.
- A bond equivalent yield is an add-on rate based on a 365-day year.

A 365-day year bank certificate of deposit has an initial principal amount of $95 million and a redemption amount at maturity of $100 million. The number of days between settlement and maturity is 300. Calculate the bond equivalent yield.

Solution:
For money market instruments, the BEY is equal to the add-on-yield based on a 365 day year.
AOR = (365/Days) x (FV-PV)/PV = 365/300 x 5/95 = 6.40%

Spot curve, yield curve, par curve, and forward curve

- A **spot curve** is a series of yields-to-maturity on zero-coupon bonds.
- A **yield curve** is a series of yields-to-maturity on coupon bonds. The main difference between a yield curve and a spot rate curve is that the yield curve considers the coupon payments as well.
- A **par curve** is a series of yields-to-maturity assuming the bonds are priced at par value.
- A **forward curve** is a series of forward rates, such as 1-year rates available at each year over a future period.

Forward rates

A forward rate is a lending or borrowing rate for a short term loan to be made in the future. Implied spot rates can be calculated as geometric averages of forward rates. Using the same relationship, we can also calculate the forward rate if we are given the spot rates.

The 3-year spot rate is 9.25%, and the 2-year spot rate is 9%. What is the 1-year forward rate two years from today?

Solution:
$(1.0925)^3 = (1.09)^2 \times (1 + 2y1y)$
$2y1y = (1.0925)^3 / (1.09)^2 - 1 = 9.75\%$

Fixed Income

Alternate method,
2y1y ≈ 3(9.25%) − 2(9%) = 9.75%

To value a bond using forward rates, discount the cash flows of the bond by the product of each forward rate and then sum them.

An analyst wants to value a 3-year, 6% annual pay bond. The bond has par value of $1,000. The current spot rate is 4%, 1-year forward rate 1 year from now is 5% and 1-year forward rate 2 years from now is 6%. Calculate the value of this annual coupon pay bond.

Solution:

Value of the bond = $\frac{60}{1.04} + \frac{60}{(1.04)(1.05)} + \frac{1,060}{(1.04)(1.05)(1.06)}$ = $1,028.39

Yield spread measures

A yield spread is the difference between a bond's yield and a benchmark yield or yield curve. Changes in benchmark rates reflect macroeconomic factors that affect all bonds in the market (for example: inflation, economic growth, foreign exchange rates, and monetary and fiscal policy). Whereas changes in spreads typically reflect microeconomic factors that affect a particular bond (for example: credit risk, liquidity, and tax effects).

Types of spread measures are:

G-spread: If the benchmark is yield-to-maturity on government bonds, then the yield spread is known as G-spread.

I-spread: If the benchmark is a swap rate, then the yield spread is known as I-spread.

Z-spread (zero-volatility spread): It is the constant spread that is added to each spot rate to make the present value of the bond equal to its price.

Option-adjusted spread (OAS): OAS is used for bonds with embedded options. For a callable bond, the OAS is the Z-spread minus the theoretical value of the embedded call option.

R53 Introduction to Asset-Backed Securities

Benefits of securitization

What is securitization?

- Securitization refers to a process in which financial assets such as mortgages, loans or receivables are pooled together. Securities that are backed by this pool are called asset backed securities (ABS).
- The cash flows from these financial assets are used to make interest and principal payments to the ABS holders.

Benefits of securitization

- Lowers the cost of borrowing.
- Provides higher risk-adjusted returns to ABS investors.

Fixed Income

- Increases efficiency and profitability of the banking sector.

Parties involved in the securitization process

The parties involved in the securitization process are:
- **Seller of financial assets**: The seller (e.g. bank) originates loans and sells the portfolio of loans to the special purpose entity (SPE).
- **Special purpose entity (SPE)**: An SPE is a bankruptcy remote entity that is independent of the seller. It buys financial assets from the seller and issues asset backed securities (ABS) supported by these financial assets.
- **Servicer**: The servicer collects payments from the underlying loans. It may or may not be the same entity as the seller.

Credit tranching and time tranching

ABS are often created with different types of tranches. The aim is to redistribute prepayment risk and credit risk efficiently among the different tranches.

Credit tranching
- The focus is on redistribution of credit risk – Losses resulting from default of the borrowers whose loans are in the collateral.
- Any credit losses are first absorbed by the tranche with the lowest priority and after that by any other subordinated tranches, in order.

Time tranching
- The focus is on redistribution of prepayment risk - uncertainty that the actual cash flows will be different from the scheduled cash flows as set forth in the loan agreements because borrowers may choose to repay the principal early to take advantage of interest rate movements.
- With sequential tranching, principal repayments flow first to one tranche until its principal balance is repaid and then to the second sequential tranche until its principal value is paid off, and so forth.

Some structures can have both credit tranching and time tranching.

Characteristics of residential mortgage loans that are typically securitized

The characteristics of residential mortgage include:
- maturity.
- interest rate(i.e. fixed rate versus adjustable or variable rate).
- principal repayment (i.e. whether the loan is amortizing and if it is, whether it is fully amortizing or partially amortizing with a balloon payment).
- Prepayment options and prepayment penalties.
- the rights of the lender in a foreclosure (i.e., whether the loan is a recourse or non-

Fixed Income

recourse loan).

Residential mortgage-backed securities

Types and characteristics of residential mortgage-backed security

In the United States, there are three types of residential mortgage backed securities (RMBS)

1. Securities issued by Ginnie Mae (they are considered to be backed by the full faith and credit of the US government)
2. Securities issued by Fannie Mae and Freddie Mac. (they are backed by a government sponsored entity but not by the US government directly)
3. Securities issued by private entities (they are not backed by a government or a GSE)

The first two types are referred to as agency residential mortgage-backed securities (RMBS), and the third type as non-agency RMBS.

A mortgage loan must meet certain criteria to be included in a pool of loans backing an agency RMBS. Listed below are some of the underwriting standards of an agency they must conform to:

- Maximum loan-to-value ratio: it should be below the maximum LTV to conform.
- Maximum size of the loan
- Loan documentation

If a loan meets the underwriting standards, then it is called a **conforming loan**.

Non-conforming mortgages do not meet the underwriting standards and are privately issued by thrift institutions, commercial banks etc.

Mortgage pass-through securities: The cash flow of a mortgage pass-through security depends on the cash flow of the underlying pool of mortgages. The cash flow consists of two components:

- monthly mortgage payments - include interest and scheduled repayment of principal
- any prepayments (unscheduled repayment of principal)

Pass-through rate: a mortgage pass-through security's coupon rate is called the pass-through rate. For example, if the mortgage rate for a pool of mortgages is 8%, the annualized servicing fee is 0.6%, then the investors receive an average return of around 7.4%.

Weighted average coupon (WAC): each of the mortgage loans in the securitized pool may not have the same mortgage rate. The WAC is found by weighting the rate of each mortgage loan in the pool by the percentage of the mortgage outstanding relative to the outstanding amount of all mortgages in the pool.

Weighted average maturity (WAM): similarly, not all the loans in the pool will have the same maturity. WAM is found by weighting the remaining number of months to maturity for each mortgage loan in the pool by the amount of the outstanding mortgage balance.

Collateralized mortgage obligation

- CMOs are securities that are collateralized by RMBS. Each CMO has multiple tranches that have different exposures to prepayment risk.
- In a sequential-pay CMO, all scheduled principal and prepayments flow first to one tranche until its principal balance is repaid and then to the second sequential tranche until its principal value is paid off, and so forth. Thus, the first tranche has the most contraction risk and the last tranche has the most extension risk.
- In a planned amortization class (PAC) CMO, PAC tranches receive predictable cash flows as long as the prepayment rate is within a specified range. Support tranches have more contraction risk and extension risk than PAC tranches.

Prepayment risk

Prepayment risk has two components:

- **Contraction risk**: Risk that when interest rates fall, homeowners will refinance at the new lower rates and the security will have a shorter maturity than anticipated.
- **Extension risk**: Risk that when interest rates rise, homeowners will make fewer repayments because the loan now looks attractive and the security will have a longer maturity than anticipated.

Commercial mortgage-backed securities

Commercial mortgage-backed securities (CMBS) are securities backed by a pool of commercial mortgages.

Two important ratios used for evaluating credit risk of CMBS are:

- **Debt-service-coverage (DSC) ratio**: The property's annual net operating income divided by the debt service. Higher DSC indicates lower credit risk.
- **Loan-to-value ratio (LTV)**: Indicates the percentage of the value of the real estate collateral that is loaned. Lower LTV indicates less credit risk.

As compared to RMBS, CMBS have considerable call protection. Because of this CMBS behave more like corporate bonds than like RMBS.

The call protection comes in two forms

- **At the structure level:** For example, creation of sequential-pay tranches
- **At the loan level**: For example, prepayment lockouts, prepayment penalty points, yield maintenance charges, defeasance.

Non-mortgage asset-backed securities

Fixed Income

ABS may be backed by a wide range of asset types other than mortgages. The most popular non-mortgage ABS are:

Auto loan ABS
- Collateral is automobile loans, which are fully amortizing and have shorter maturities than residential mortgages.
- Prepayments can occur when,
    - Autos are sold or traded in.
    - Insurance proceeds if autos are stolen or damaged.
    - Loans are refinanced
    - Borrower has excess cash and pays off the loan.

Credit card ABS
- Collateral is credit card receivables, which is a non-amortizing revolving debt.
- They typically have a lock-out period during which only interest is paid to investors and principal payments on the receivables are used to purchase additional receivables.

Collateralized debt obligations

- A collateralized debt obligation (CDO) is a generic term used to describe a security backed by a diversified pool of one or more debt obligations that is managed by a collateral manager.
- The structure of a CDO may include senior, mezzanine, and subordinated/equity bond classes.
- The collateral manager buys and sells debt obligations for and from the CDO's portfolio of assets. The aim is to generate sufficient cash flows to meet the obligations of the CDO bondholders and to generate a fair return for the equity holders.

R54 Understanding Fixed-Income Risk and Return

Sources of return from investing in a fixed-rate bond

For a fixed rate bond purchased at par, there are three sources of return:
1. Receipt of the promised coupon and principal payments.
2. Reinvestment of coupon payments.
3. Potential capital gains (or losses) on the sale of the bond prior to maturity.

If a bond is purchased at a discount or premium, the rate of return also includes the effect of the price being "pulled to par" as we approach maturity. Total return of a bond = reinvested coupon interest payments + sale/redemption of principal at maturity.

Changes in interest rate affect the realized rate of return for any bond investor in two ways:
- **Market price risk**: Bond prices are inversely proportional to interest rate movements.

Fixed Income

Bond price decreases when the interest rate goes up.
- **Coupon reinvestment risk**: Value of coupon payments is directly proportional to interest rate movements. The value of reinvested coupons increases when the interest rate goes up.

Market price risk dominates coupon reinvestment risk when the investor has a short-term horizon. Coupon reinvestment risk dominates market price risk when the investor has a long-term horizon: for instance, a buy-and-hold investor.

Macaulay, modified, and effective durations

Bond duration measures the sensitivity of the bond's price to changes in interest rates. The three common measures of duration are:

Macaulay duration: The weighted average of the time to receipt of coupon interest and principal payments.

Modified duration: A linear estimate of the percentage price change in a bond for a 100 basis points change in its yield-to-maturity.

Modified duration = Macaulay duration / (1 + r)

$$\text{Approximate Modified Duration} = \frac{(PV_-) - (PV_+)}{2 * \Delta \text{yield} * PV_0}$$

A 12% annual-pay bond has 10 years to maturity. The bond is currently trading at par. Assuming a 10 basis-points change in yield-to-maturity, calculate the bond's approximate modified duration.

Solution:
The bond is priced at par which means that the initial YTM = coupon rate = 12% and V_0 = 100.
ΔYTM = 0.001
V_- = 100.57
N = 10, PMT = 12, FV = 100, I/Y = 11.9; CPT → PV = 100.57
V_+ = 99.44
I/Y = 12.1; CPT → PV = 99.44

$$\text{Approximate modified duration} = \frac{V_- - V_+}{2 * V_0 * \Delta YTM} = \frac{100.57 - 99.44}{2 \times 100 \times 0.001} = 5.65$$

Effective duration: The linear estimate of the percentage change in a bond's price that would result from a 100 basis points change in the benchmark yield curve.

$$\text{Effective Duration} = \frac{(PV_-) - (PV_+)}{2 * \Delta \text{curve} * PV_0}$$

Fixed Income

Appropriate measure of interest rate risk for bonds with embedded options

- The difference between modified duration and effective duration is that modified duration measures interest rate risk in terms of a change in the bond's own yield-to-maturity, whereas effective duration measures interest rate risk in terms of changes in the benchmark yield curve.
- Bonds with an embedded option do not have a meaningful internal rate of return (YTM) because future cash flows are contingent on interest rates.
- Therefore, effective duration is a more appropriate measure of interest rate risk for bonds with embedded options.

Key rate duration

Key rate duration is a measure of the price sensitivity of a bond to a change in the spot rate for a specific maturity. Key rate durations can be used to measure a bond's sensitivity to changes in the shape of the yield curve.

Effect of a bond's maturity, coupon, and yield level on its interest rate risk

The interest rate risk of a bond is measured by duration. All else equal:
- Duration increases when maturity increases.
- Duration decreases when coupon rate increases.
- Duration decreases when yield to maturity increases.

Limitations of portfolio duration

The duration of a bond portfolio can be calculated in two ways:

The weighted average of the time to receipt of aggregate cash flows.
- This method is better in theory.
- Its main limitation is that it cannot be used for bonds with embedded options or for floating-rate notes.

The weighted average of the durations of individual bonds that compose the portfolio.
- This method is simpler to use and quite accurate when the yield curve is relatively flat.
- Its main limitation is that it assumes a parallel shift in the yield curve.

Money duration and price value of a basis point (PVBP)

Money duration is a measure of the price change stated in currency units. The price value of a basis point (PVBP) is an estimate of the change in the price of a bond given a 1 basis point change in the yield-to-maturity.

$$\text{PVBP} = \frac{PV_- - PV_+}{2}$$

Fixed Income

A bond with exactly 6 years remaining until maturity offers a 4% coupon rate with annual coupons. The bond, with a yield to maturity of 5% is priced at $94.9243 per 100 of par value. Calculate the price value of a basis point for the bond.

Solution:

PVBP = (PV₋ − PV₊)/2 x par value x 0.01

PV₋ is the full price calculated by lowering the yield-to-maturity by one basis point.

N = 6, I/Y = 4.99, PMT = 4, FV = 100. CPT PV = $94.9735

PV₊ is the full price calculated by raising the yield to maturity by one basis point.

N = 6, I/Y = 5.01, PMT = 4, FV = 100. CPT PV = $94.8752

PVBP = ($94.9735 - $94.8752)/2 = 0.049

Approximate convexity v/s effective convexity

Convexity refers to the curvature of a bond's price-yield relationship. A bond's convexity can be estimated as:

$$\text{Approx. Convexity} = \frac{PV_- + PV_+ - 2*PV_0}{(\Delta \text{yield})^2 * PV_0}$$

Effective convexity, like effective duration, is useful for bonds with embedded options.

$$\text{Effective Convexity} = \frac{PV_- + PV_+ - 2*PV_0}{(\Delta \text{curve})^2 * PV_0}$$

Duration + convexity effect

If we are given the bond's modified duration and convexity, the percentage price change of a bond can be calculated using the following formula.

$$\% \Delta PV^{FULL} = (-\text{AnnModDur} * \Delta \text{yield}) + [\frac{1}{2} * \text{AnnConvexity} * (\Delta \text{yield})^2]$$

A bond has an annual modified duration of 8.010 and annual convexity of 75.270. If the bond's yield-to-maturity decreases by 50 basis points, calculate the expected percentage price change in the bond.

Solution:

Total estimated price change = duration effect + convexity effect.

= - duration x ΔYTM + ½ x convexity x(ΔYTM)²

= - 8.010 x -0.005 + ½ x 75.270 x -0.005² = 0.04099 or 4.099%

Effect of term structure of yield volatility on the interest rate risk of a bond

The change in a bond's price is the product of two factors:
1. The impact per basis-point change in the yield-to-maturity: This factor is estimated by duration and convexity.
2. The number of basis points in the yield change: This factor depends on yield volatility.

In calculating duration and convexity, we assumed a parallel shift in the yield curve.

Fixed Income

However, in practice factors such as changes in monetary policy have a greater impact on short-term interest rates than long-term interest rates. Therefore, short term bonds can have more price volatility than long term bonds because of larger basis points yield change (factor 2).

Relationships among a bond's holding period return, its duration, and the investment horizon

The Macaulay duration can be interpreted as the investment horizon for which coupon reinvestment risk and market price risk offset each other.
- If the investment horizon is greater than the Macaulay duration of the bond, coupon reinvestment risk dominates price risk. The investor's risk is to lower interest rates. The duration gap is negative.
- If the investment horizon is equal to the Macaulay duration of the bond, coupon reinvestment risk offsets price risk. The duration gap is zero.
- If the investment horizon is less than the Macaulay duration of the bond, price risk dominates coupon reinvestment risk. The investor's risk is to higher interest rates. The duration gap is positive.

Duration gap = Macaulay duration – Investment horizon

Changes in credit spread and liquidity

A bond's yield spread over a benchmark includes a premium for credit risk and a premium for liquidity risk.
- **Credit risk** refers to the probability of default and degree of recovery if default occurs.
- **Liquidity risk** refers to the transaction costs associated with selling a bond.

The change in the spread of a bond over its benchmark can result from a change in credit risk or liquidity risk. If we are given the bond's duration and convexity, we can calculate the effect on the value of a bond from a given change in yield spread as:

$$\% \Delta \text{PV}^{\text{FULL}} = (-\text{AnnModDur} * \Delta\text{yield}) + [\frac{1}{2} * \text{AnnConvexity} * (\Delta\text{yield})^2]$$

R55 Fundamentals of Credit Analysis

Credit and credit-related risks

Credit risk is the risk of loss if the borrower fails to make scheduled payments of interest and/or principal. Credit-related risks include:
- **Spread risk**: Corporate bonds are usually quoted as a spread (yield premium) over risk-free bonds such as U.S. treasury bonds. The amount of spread is quoted in basis points. Assume the spread was initially 200 basis points, but has now increased to 250 basis points. This widening may be because of two factors: downgrade risk and an

Fixed Income

increase in market liquidity risk.
- **Downgrade risk**: Refers to a decline in an issuer's creditworthiness.
- **Market liquidity risk**: Refers to a widening of the bid-ask spread on an issuer's bonds.

Components of credit risk

Credit risk has two components:
- Risk of default: The probability that the borrower will default.
- Loss severity: If the borrower does default, how severe is the loss.

Expected Loss = Default probability x Loss severity given default

Seniority rankings of corporate debt

Corporate debt is ranked by seniority or priority of claims; depicted in the following diagram:

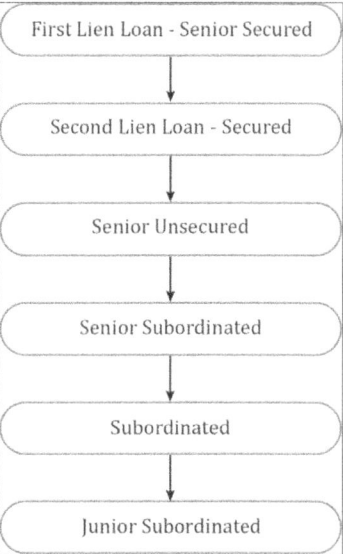

The priority of claims in bankruptcy is not always absolute. In bankruptcy the court may approve a repayment plan that does not follow the priority of claims order.

Issuer credit ratings v/s issue credit ratings

Credit rating agencies, such as Moody's, Standard & Poor's, and Fitch, issue credit ratings for bonds which are opinions about a bond issue's creditworthiness. These ratings help investors compare the credit risk of different debt issues. The rating agencies rate both issuers and issues.
- **Issuer ratings** reflect an issuer's overall creditworthiness—its risk of default.
- **Issue ratings** reflect factors such as their rankings in the capital structure.

Notching refers to the practice of adjusting an issue credit rating upward or downward from the issuer credit rating, to reflect the seniority or other provisions in that specific

Fixed Income

issue.

Risks in relying on ratings from credit rating agencies

The risks in relying on ratings from credit rating agencies are:
- Credit ratings can change over time.
- Market prices of bonds often adjust before ratings change
- Ratings primarily reflect the probability of default but not necessarily the severity of loss given default. Therefore, bonds with the same rating may have significantly different expected losses
- Rating agencies can make mistakes and may not always judge credit risk accurately.

Four Cs (Capacity, Collateral, Covenants, and Character) of traditional credit analysis

The components of traditional credit analysis are known as the 4 Cs:
- **Capacity**: The ability of the borrower to make interest and principal payments on time. Capacity to repay is assessed by examining: Industry structure → industry fundamentals →company fundamentals →competitive position.
- **Collateral**: The quality and value of the assets pledged as collateral against the debt.
- **Covenants**: Provisions in a bond indenture that protect the lenders by requiring the borrower to perform some actions (affirmative covenants) or avoid some actions (negative covenants). Covenant analysis is especially important for high-yield bonds.
- **Character**: Refers to the quality of the management, strategy, quality of earnings and past treatment of bondholders.

Financial ratios used in credit analysis

Key ratios used in credit analysis are:

Profitability ratios:
- Refer to operating income and operating profit margin. Operating income is typically defined as earnings before interest and taxes.
- A higher profitability ratio indicates lower credit risk.

Cash flow measures: Cash flow is measured as,
- Earnings before interest, taxes, depreciation and amortization (EBITDA)
- Funds from operations (FFO)
- Free cash flow before dividends
- Free cash flow after dividends
- A high cash flow indicates lower credit risk.

Leverage ratios: Include,
- Debt-to-capital ratio.
- Debt-to-EBITDA ratio.

Fixed Income

- FFO-to-debt ratio.
- Lower leverage indicates lower credit risk.

Coverage ratios: Include,
- EBIT-to-interest expense ratio.
- EBITDA-to-interest expense ratio.
- Higher coverage ratios indicate lower credit risk.

Factors that influence the level and volatility of yield spreads

- **Credit cycle:** Credit spreads narrow when the credit cycle improves; and they widen when the credit cycle is weakening.
- **Broader economic conditions:** Credit spreads widen in a weak economy and tend to narrow in a strong economy.
- **Market performance:** Credit spreads widen in weak financial markets and tend to narrow under stable market conditions.
- **Broker-dealers' willingness to provide sufficient capital for market listing:** Unlike stocks that primarily trade on exchanges, bonds trade over-the-counter. Brokers and dealers are market makers in the debt market. Credit spreads tend to narrow if the availability of capital from broker/dealers is high.
- **Supply and demand:** If the supply is more and demand is less, credit spreads will widen.

Yield spreads on lower-quality issues will be more volatile than spreads on higher quality issues.

High yield, sovereign, and non-sovereign government debt issuers and issues

High yield bonds
- They are more likely to default than investment grade bonds.
- More emphasis should be placed on an issuer's sources of liquidity, as well as on its debt structure and corporate structure.
- Covenant analysis and using an equity-like approach can be helpful.

Sovereign bonds: Sovereign credit analysis includes assessing both,
- an issuer's ability (ability to pay will be high for debt issued in the country's own currency than for debt issued in foreign currency).
- willingness to pay its debt obligations. (willingness to pay is important because, due to sovereign immunity, a sovereign government cannot be forced to pay its debts).

Non-sovereign government debt
- Non-sovereign debt is usually either general obligation bonds or revenue bonds.
- General obligation (GO) bonds are backed by the taxing authority of the issuing non-

Fixed Income

sovereign government. Therefore, credit analysis of GO bonds is similar to sovereign analysis.
- Revenue-backed bonds support specific projects, such as toll roads, bridges, airports, and other infrastructure. Therefore, credit analysis of revenue bonds depends on the income generating capacity of the project.

Derivatives

R56 Derivative Markets and Instruments

Definition of a derivative

A derivative is a financial instrument that derives its value from the performance of an underlying asset. Two types of derivatives are:
- **Exchange-traded derivatives:** These are standardized, highly regulated, transparent and free from default risk.
- **Over-the-counter derivatives:** These are customized, flexible, less regulated than exchange-traded derivatives, but are not free from default risk.

Forward commitments v/s contingent claims

Derivatives consist of two general classes: forward commitments and contingent claims.
- A **forward commitment** is an obligation to buy or sell an asset or make a payment in the future. Example: forward contracts, futures contracts and swaps.
- A **contingent claim** has a future payoff only if some future event takes place. Example: call option, put option and credit default swap.

Forward contracts, futures contracts, options (calls and puts), swaps, and credit derivatives

Forward contract is an obligation for one party to buy and another party to sell, an underlying asset at a specific price at a specific time in the future. It is an over-the-counter contract.

Futures contract is similar to a forward contract but is a standardized contract and is traded on a futures exchange. Since it is an exchange traded derivative instrument, there is a daily settling of gains and losses.

An **option** is a derivative contract in which the option buyer pays a sum of money to the option seller, and receives the right to either buy or sell an underlying asset at a fixed price at some time in the future. A call is an option that provides the right to buy the underlying. A put is an option that provides the right to sell the underlying.

A **swap** is an over-the-counter derivative contract in which two parties agree to exchange a series of cash flows. Typically one party will pay variable cash flows that depend on an underlying rate and the other party will pay fixed cash flows.

A **credit derivative** is a contract that provides a payment to the credit protection buyer if a specified credit event occurs. The most widely used credit derivative is a credit default swap.

Derivatives

Purposes of and controversies related to derivative markets

Purposes:
- facilitate the transfer of risk
- allows strategies and payoffs not otherwise possible with spot assets
- provide information about the spot market
- offer lower transaction costs
- reduce the amount of capital required
- easier to short derivative than it is to short the underlying
- improve the efficiency of spot markets

Controversies: They are sometimes referred to as a form of legalized gambling that can lead to destabilizing speculation.

Arbitrage

Arbitrage is the condition under which two equivalent assets or derivatives or combination of assets and derivatives sell for different prices. An arbitrageur buys at a low price and sells at a high price, and thus earning a risk-free profit.

Role: The combined actions of arbitrageurs force the prices of similar securities to converge. Hence, arbitrage leads to the law of one price: Securities or derivatives that produce equivalent results must sell at the same prices.

R57 Basics of Derivative Pricing and Valuation

Use of arbitrage, replication, and risk neutrality in pricing derivatives

Arbitrage is the condition under which two equivalent assets or derivatives or combination of assets and derivatives sell for different prices.
- This allows an arbitrageur to buy at a low price and sell at a high price, and earn a risk-free profit from this transaction without committing any capital.
- In well-functioning markets, arbitrage opportunities are quickly exploited. The combined actions of arbitrageurs force the prices of similar securities to converge. Hence, arbitrage leads to the law of one price: securities or derivatives that produce equivalent results must sell for equivalent prices.

Replication is the creation of an asset or a portfolio from another asset, portfolio, and/or derivative. Example: stock + short forward = risk-free asset.

Risk neutrality: The risk aversion of an individual does not impact derivative pricing. The risk-free rate is used for pricing derivatives.

The overall process of pricing derivatives by arbitrage and risk neutrality is called

Derivatives

arbitrage-free pricing. According to this process,
- A derivative must be priced such that no arbitrage opportunities exist, and there can only be one price for the derivative that earns the risk-free return.
- Asset + Derivative = Risk-free asset

Value v/s price of forward and futures contracts

Price: The price of a forward or futures contract is the forward price that is specified in the contract.

Value: The value of a forward or futures contract is zero at initiation. Its value may increase or decrease during its life according to changes in the spot price.
- At initiation the value of forward contract is zero.
- Value at expiration: $S_T - F$
- Value during the life of the contract: $V_t = S_t - \dfrac{F}{(1+r)^{T-t}}$

Monetary and nonmonetary benefits and costs associated with holding the underlying asset

The **forward price** of an asset with benefits and/or costs is the spot price compounded at the risk-free rate over the life of the contract plus the future value of costs minus the future value of benefits.

$$F = S_0(1+r)^t + FV(costs) - FV(benefits)$$
$$F_0(T) = (S_0) \times (1+r)^T - (\gamma - \theta) \times (1+r)^T$$
$$F_0(T) = (S_0 - \gamma + \theta) \times (1+r)^T$$

where:
γ = present value of the benefit. It is subtracted from the spot price because if you own the asset, you receive any benefits associated with the asset, during the life of the contract.
θ = present value of costs incurred on the asset during the life of the contract. These costs make it more expensive to hold the asset and hence increase the forward price.

The following information is provided for an asset.
- spot price of $S_0 = \$100$
- present value of benefits from the asset = $10
- present value of costs associated with holding the asset = $20

Assuming a risk-free rate of 10% and a time period of 3 months, calculate the forward price for this asset.

Solution:
$T = \dfrac{3}{12} = 0.25$
$F_0(T) = (100 - 10 + 20)(1.1)^{0.25} = 112.65$

Derivatives

The **value of a forward contract** is the spot price of the underlying asset minus the present value of the forward price.

$V_t(T) = S_t - \frac{F_0(T)}{(1+r)^{T-t}}$ (without benefits and costs)

$V_t(T) = S_t - (\gamma - \theta)(1+r)^t - \frac{F_0(T)}{(1+r)^{T-t}}$ (with benefits and costs)

In the above example, let's say 1-month later the price of the underlying is $104. Calculate the value of the contract to the long party.

Solution:

t = 1/12 = 0.083; T-t = 2/12 = 0.167

$V_t(T) = 104 - (10 - 20) \, 1.1^{0.083} - \frac{112.65}{(1.1)^{0.167}} = \$3.21$

Forward rate agreement

A forward rate agreement (FRA) is a derivative contract that has an interest rate, rather than an asset price, as its underlying.

Uses

- FRA allows an investor to lock in a certain interest rate for borrowing or lending at some future date.
- One party will pay the other party the difference between the interest rate specified in the FRA and the market interest rate at contract settlement.
- Firms can therefore reduce or eliminate the risk of future borrowing costs using an FRA.

Difference in forward and futures prices

Futures prices can differ from forward prices because of the effect of interest rates on the interim cash flows from the daily settlement.

- If interest rates are constant, or have zero correlation with futures prices, then forwards and futures prices will be the same.
- If futures prices are negatively correlated with interest rates, then it is more desirable to buy forwards than futures.
- If future prices are positively correlated with interest rates, then it is more desirable to buy futures than forwards.

Swap contracts v/s a series of forward contracts

A normal forward contract has a zero value at the start because of no-arbitrage pricing. In a swap, since the fixed price is priced different than the market price, here the forward contract has a non-zero value at the start and is called an off-market forward. Swap is a series of off-market forward contracts where:

Derivatives

- Each forward contract is created at a price and maturity equal to the fixed price of the swap with the same maturity and payment dates respectively.
- This means that the series of FRAs built into a swap are all off-market FRAs: some with positive values and some with negative values.
- The combined value of the off-market FRAs is zero.

Value and price of swaps

Price: The price of a swap is the fixed interest rate specified in the swap contract.

Value
- At initiation, the value of swap is zero.
- The value of a swap during the life of the swap changes according to how expected future floating rates change over time.
- An increase in expected futures rates will result in a positive value for the fixed-rate payer.
- A decrease in expected futures rates will result in negative value for the fixed-rate payer.

Value of a European option at expiration

Call option
- At expiration, the value of a call option is the greater of zero or the value of the underlying asset minus the exercise price.
- $C_T = \max(0, S_T - X)$

Put option
- At expiration, the value of a put option is the greater of zero or the exercise price minus the value of the underlying.
- $P_T = \max(0, X - S_T)$

Exercise value, time value, and moneyness of an option

Moneyness refers to whether an option is in the money or out of the money.
- If immediate exercise of the option would result in positive payoff, then option is in the money.
- If immediate exercise would result in loss, then the option is out of the money.
- If immediate exercise would result in neither a gain nor a loss, then the option is at the money.

	Call Option	Put Option
In-the-money	S > X	S < X
At-the-money	S = X	S = X
Out-of-the-money	S < X	S > X

Derivatives

Exercise value of an option is the maximum of zero or the amount that the option is in the money.

Time value of an option is the amount by which the option premium exceeds the exercise value.
- Prior to expiration an option also has time value in addition to exercise value.
- When an option reaches expiration, the time value is zero.

Factors that determine the value of an option

Increase in	Value of call option will	Value of put option will
value of the underlying	Increase	Decrease
exercise price	Decrease	Increase
risk-free rate	Increase	Decrease
time to expiration	Increase	Increase (exception: a few European puts)
volatility of the underlying	Increase	Increase
costs incurred while holding the underlying	Increase	Decrease
benefits received while holding the underlying	Decrease	Increase

Put-call parity for European options

European put and call prices are related through put–call parity, which specifies that the put price plus the price of the underlying equals the call price plus the present value of the exercise price.

According to put-call parity,
Fiduciary call = Protective put
$$c_0 + \frac{X}{(1+r)^T} = p_0 + S_0$$

Assume call and put options with an exercise price of $100 in which the underlying is at $90 at time t=0. The risk free rate is 10% and the options expire in 3 months. The call price is $2. Calculate the put price.

Solution:
$$p_0 = c_0 + \frac{X}{(1+r)^T} - S_0 = 2 + 100/1.1^{0.25} - 90 = \$9.64$$

Put-call-forward parity for European options

European put and call prices are related through put–call–forward parity, which shows that the put price plus the value of a risk-free bond with face value equal to the forward

Derivatives

price equals the call price plus the value of a risk-free bond with face value equal to the exercise price.

$$c_0 + \frac{X}{(1+r)^T} = p_0 + \frac{F_0(T)}{(1+r)^T}$$

In the put-call parity example covered above, assume a forward contract on the underlying expiring in 3 months. This contract will have a price of $90 \times 1.1^{0.25} = \$92.17$. Using this forward contract instead of the underlying, the put price can be calculated as:

$$p_0 = c_0 + \frac{X}{(1+r)^T} - \frac{F_0(T)}{(1+r)^T} = 2 + 100/1.1^{0.25} - 92.17/1.1^{0.25} = \$9.64$$

Value of an option using a one-period binomial model

- The binomial model is a simple model for valuing options based on only two possible outcomes for a stock's movement: going up and going down.
- π and 1- π are called the synthetic probabilities; they represent the weighted average of producing the next to possible call values.
- By discounting the future expected call values at the risk-free rate, we can get the current call value.

$$\pi = \frac{1+r-d}{u-d}$$

$$c_0 = \frac{\pi c_1^+ + (1-\pi)c_1^-}{1+r}$$

Assume the following data is given:
$S_0 = 40$; $u = 1.2$; $d = 0.75$; $X = 38$; $r = 5\%$; $c_0 = ?$

T = 0
$S_0 = 40$
$X = 38$
$r = 5\%$
$c_0 = \frac{6.67}{1.05} = 6.35$

u = 1.2

T = 1
$S_1^+ = 40 \times 1.2 = 48$
$c_1^+ = \max(0, 48 - 38) = 10$

$\Pi = \frac{1+r-d}{u-d} = \frac{1 + 0.05 - 0.75}{1.2 - 0.75} = 0.667$

$c_1 = 10 \times 0.667 + (1 - 0.667) \times 0 = 6.67$

d = 0.75

T = 1
$S_1^- = 40 \times 0.75 = 30$
$c_1^- = \max(0, 30 - 38) = 0$

The value of the call option at time 0 using the 1-period binomial model is 6.35.

European v/s American options

- If the underlying asset has a cash flow such as dividend or interest, then American call prices will be more than European call prices, because the option can be exercised early to collect this cash flow.
- American put prices will always be higher than European put prices, because the right to exercise early always has value for a put.

Alternative Investments

R58 Introduction to Alternative Investments

Alternative investments v/s traditional investments

Traditional investments include long-only position in stocks, bonds and cash. All other investments are classified as alternative investments.

Alternative investments include investments in:
- real estate
- commodities
- private equity
- hedge funds

Compared to traditional investments, alternative investments typically have:
- lower liquidity.
- less regulation.
- lower transparency.
- higher fees.
- limited and potentially biased historical risk and return data.
- unique legal and tax considerations.

Categories of alternative investments

The main categories of alternative investments are:

Hedge funds are private investment vehicles that manage portfolios of securities and derivative positions using a variety of strategies. They aim for absolute returns independent of market performance.

Private equity funds invest in the equity of private companies or public companies that want to become private. They are further divided into:
- Leveraged buyout funds: Invest in established companies.
- Venture capital funds: Invest in startups.

Real estate: Investments in buildings, farmland, timberland, either directly or indirectly.

Commodities: Investment in physical assets such as grains, metals, crude oil etc. The main vehicles used for investment in commodities are commodity future contracts and funds benchmarked to commodity indices.

Infrastructure: Investments in capital intensive, long-lived, real assets, such as roads, dams, and schools, which are intended for public use and provide essential service.

Others: Investments in any other tangible asset, such as art, wine, stamps, coins or intangible asset such as patents.

Alternative Investments

Potential benefits of alternative investments

- One of the primary drivers for investing in alternative investments is the low correlation of alternative investments with traditional investments.
- This low correlation along with relatively high returns on some alternative investment categories results in a substantial diversification benefit.

Types of alternative investments

Hedge funds

- Uses a partnership structure with a general partner who manages the fund and accepts unlimited liability and limited partners (investors) who own fractional interests in the partnership and have limited liability.
- The general partner typically receives a management fee based on assets under management and an incentive fee based on the performance of the fund.
- Hedge funds are typically classified by strategy into four broad categories:
  - Event-driven: Includes merger arbitrage, distressed/restructuring, activist shareholder and special situation.
  - Relative value: Strategies that seek to profit from pricing discrepancies.
  - Macro: Strategies based on top-down analysis of global economic trends.
  - Equity hedge: Strategies based on bottom-up analysis. Includes market neutral, fundamental growth, fundamental value, quantitative directional, and short bias.
- During financial crisis the correlation of returns between global equities and hedge funds tends to increase, which reduces the hedge funds' usefulness as a diversifying asset class.

Private equity

- Uses a partnership structure with a general partner who manages the fund and accepts unlimited liability and limited partners (investors) who own fractional interests in the partnership and have limited liability
- The general partner typically receives a management fee based on committed capital and an incentive fee based on the performance of the fund.
- Dominant strategies in private equity funds are leveraged buyouts and venture capital. Other strategies include development capital and distressed investing.
- Types of LBOs include
  - Management buyouts: The existing management team is involved in the purchase.
  - Management buy-ins: External management team replaces the current management.
- Stages in venture capital include
  - Formative stage: Consists of angel investing, seed and early stages.
  - Later stage: Company is in expansion phase.

Alternative Investments

- o <u>Mezzanine stage</u>: Company is preparing for an IPO.
- Exit strategies for investments in portfolio companies include
  - o <u>Trade sale</u>: Company is sold to a competitor or another strategic buyer.
  - o <u>IPO</u>: Company is sold to the public.
  - o <u>Recapitalization</u>: Company is re-leveraged when interest rates are low.
  - o <u>Secondary sale</u>: Company is sold to another private equity firm or another investor.
  - o <u>Write off/ liquidation</u>: Assets are sold and liabilities are settled.
- Historically, private equity has provided potential diversification benefits. However, an investor must identify top performing private equity managers to benefit from private equity.

Real estate
- Primary reasons to invest in real estate include:
  - o Potential for competitive long term returns
  - o Rental income
  - o Diversification benefits
  - o Inflation hedge
- Investment characteristics of real estate include:
  - o Indivisibility
  - o Unique characteristics (no two properties are identical)
  - o Fixed location
  - o Operational management
  - o Local markets can be very different from national or global markets
- Basic forms of real estate investments are shown in the following table:

	Debt	**Equity**
Private	Mortgages Construction lending	Direct ownership of real estate Ownership can be through sole ownership, joint ventures, real estate limited partnerships etc.
Public	Mortgage-backed securities (residential and commercial) Collateralized mortgage obligations	Shares in real estate corporations Shares of real estate investment trusts (REITs)

- Historically, real estate returns are highly correlated with global equity returns but less correlated with global bond returns.

Commodities
- Commodity investments can be achieved by investing in actual physical commodities or in companies that produce commodities. However, usually commodity investing is achieved using commodity derivatives.
- The return on a commodity investment includes:

Alternative Investments

- o Collateral yield: Return on collateral posted to satisfy margin requirements.
- o Price return: The gain or loss due to changes in the spot price.
- o Roll yield: Gain or loss resulting from re-establishing future positions. Roll yield is positive if futures market is in backwardation and negative if the market is in contango.
- Commodities are viewed as a good inflation hedge. They also have a low correlation with traditional investments and can provide diversification benefits.

Infrastructure

- Infrastructure assets are real assets that are planned for public use and to provide essential services. They are typically capital intensive and long-lived.
- These assets are expected to generate stable cash flows that should adjust for economic growth and inflation. They may also provide capital appreciation.

Hedge fund fees

- The total fee for a hedge fund consists of a management fee and an incentive fee. Common fee structure is 2 and 20 which means 2% management fee and 20% incentive fee.
- Funds of funds charge an additional 1 and 10 fee (1% management fee and 10% incentive fee).
- Incentive fee is usually calculated on profits net of management fees or on profits before management fee.
- Sometimes, the incentive fee is paid only if the returns exceed a hurdle rate.
- In some cases the incentive fee is paid only if the fund has crossed the high watermark. High watermark is the highest value net of fees (or the highest cumulative return) reported by the fund so far. This is to ensure investors do not pay twice for the same performance.

A hedge fund established a high water mark of $200 million two years ago. The end-of-year value before fees for last year was $180 million. This year's end-of-year value before fees is $210 million. The fund has a '2 and 20' fee structure. Management fees are paid independently of incentive fees and are calculated on end-of-year values. Calculate the total fees of the fund for the current year.

Solution:
Management fee = 2% of $210 million = $4.2 million
Incentive fee = 20% of ($210 million - $200 million) = $2 million.
Total fees = $4.2 + $2 = $6.2 million

Issues in valuing and calculating returns on alternative investments

Hedge funds
- They often invest in securities that are not actively traded. The values of such securities

Alternative Investments

must therefore be estimated.
- They also invest in securities that are illiquid relative to the size of the hedge fund's position. The values of such securities must be adjusted for illiquidity (using trading NAV).

Private equity

Portfolio companies must be valued using one of the following approaches
- <u>Market/comparables approach</u>: Values a company based on multiples.
- <u>Discounted cash flow approach</u>: Present value of expected future cash flows.
- <u>Asset based approach</u>: Value is based on underlying assets minus liabilities.

Real estate

Real estate properties must be valued using one of the following approaches:
- <u>Comparable sales approach</u>: Value is based on recent sales of similar properties.
- <u>Income approach</u>: Present value of expected future cash flows from the property.
- <u>Cost approach</u>: Replacement cost of a property.

REIT (Real Estate Investment Trusts) can be valued using:
- Income based approach
- Asset based approach

Commodities
- A commodity futures price is equal to spot price compounded at the risk free rate + storage costs – convenience yield.
- Convenience yield is the value of having the physical commodity for use over the period of the futures contract.

Risk management of alternative investments

- Alternative investments often have limited and potentially biased historical risk and return data. Because of this managing risks associated with alternative investments can be challenging.
- Traditional risk and return measures such as standard deviation of returns may be misleading as a measure of risk.
- Some key risks to consider are:
  - Operational risk
  - Financial risk
  - Counterparty risk
  - Liquidity risk
- Due diligence is also required to evaluate if:
  - The investment complies with its prospectus.
  - There is a suitable organizational structure and policies in place.

Made in the USA
Middletown, DE
05 April 2019